Composers on Composing for Band

Composers on Composing for Band

edited by **Mark Camphouse**

james **Barnes**
timothy **Broege**
mark **Camphouse**
david **Gillingham**
david r. **Holsinger**
karel **Husa**
timothy **Mahr**
w. francis **McBeth**
robert **Sheldon**
jack **Stamp**
frank **Ticheli**

with a foreword by **Mallory Thompson**

GIA Publications, Inc.
Chicago

G-5745

7404 S. Mason Ave., Chicago, IL 60638
www.giamusic.com
ISBN: 1-57999-195-5
Cover design: Yolanda Duran
Book layout: Robert Sacha

Printed in the United States of America

The future of music may not be with music itself,
but rather...in the way it makes itself a part with the finer
things humanity does and dreams of.

—Charles Ives

To our spouses, partners, and families, whose understanding and tolerance of a composer's schedule and artistic temperament is appreciated beyond measure.

Table of Contents

Foreword

by Mallory Thompson

The most important relationships in a conductor's musical life are with the people they conduct and with the composers whose music they are re-creating. Our university degree programs are filled with numerous methods classes, conducting classes, music theory and history classes, but how do we really learn to create a meaningful connection with a composer? Rather than experiencing what should be a natural relationship between creator and re-creator, composers and conductors often experience a sense of isolation. Composers create something out of nothing, send it out into the world, and hope that their intentions will be understood and valued. Conductors face the daily challenges of interpreting the composer's intentions through a notation system that is inherently inadequate, while at the same time managing the myriad of administrative challenges that exist within each unique situation. How can the conductor and composer be brought together more effectively?

Composers on Composing for Band offers a wonderful opportunity to establish a relationship with the composers whose music we interpret. The insight that can be gained from this book is rooted in the views of the contributing composers themselves, and provides greater understanding and respect for compositional processes. Any time we understand more about one composer, it encourages us to be more inquisitive about others. The chapters are presented in the composers' unique words and clearly communicate thoughts about their creative process, what they expect from us as conductors, and what they envision as the future of the wind band. The ideas they express and how they choose to express them are equally interesting—the composers' personalities, whether serious, humorous, direct, or wry, are clearly expressed through their use of language. The dictum that states that as an artist, you cannot escape who you are is celebrated through the uniqueness in the creators' thoughts as well as the uniqueness of their voices.

As we gain experiences with composers through commissioning, speaking with them, hearing them speak at conventions, or reading their words in this book, conductors will become more fully invested in the collaborative process. I value the opportunities I have had to work with composers on a variety of levels, and many treasured friendships have evolved from these collaborations. As the details of the music are meticulously studied, the process becomes more personal. Whenever I perform the music of Karel Husa, for example, I imagine that he is standing beside me.

The composers' words encourage us to expand our musical world. Each chapter includes discussions of influential figures, mention of composers throughout history whose music has been especially meaningful, a list of ten works every band conductor should study (and not necessarily band music!), and comments about the future of wind music. I have had the pleasure and privilege of performing works by all of the composers included in this book, and from personal experience, I believe it will provide valuable and fascinating reading for musicians at all levels.

— Mallory Thompson, Director of Bands,
Northwestern University, Evanston, Illinois

Introduction

by Mark Camphouse

While valuable for students in the areas of composition, music education, and applied music performance, this book is intended primarily for wind band **conductors** at all levels, who are interested in gaining fresh insights and perspectives from the ultimate source of musical creativity—the **composer.**

The eleven co-authoring composers of this book (many are also highly respected conductors) come from widely varied backgrounds. Their life experiences, professional careers, artistic and educational philosophies, and their approach to the compositional process contrast as vividly as their distinct and unique creative voices. But the reader will also discover some important shared values and principles among the composers, most notably:

- A desire to bring closer the creative and re-creative realms of music and music-making, thereby promoting greater understanding and a more meaningful and mutually beneficial partnership between the composer and the conductor;

- A commitment to leave a legacy of high quality (and in many cases award-winning) wind band literature for future generations to study and perform;

- A passion for teaching and inspiring tomorrow's composers, conductors, and performers.

Each of the ten composers joining me in this volume possesses the highest standards of musical and personal integrity. Each is able to see the "big picture" of our profession, and is influential in shaping its future. And each, I knew, would be faithful in meeting deadlines for this book!

It is hoped the reader will recognize and appreciate the breadth and variety of the composers in this volume, who have a geographical range spanning from Minnesota to Florida, and New Jersey to California. Their music ranges from some of the finest and most enriching repertoire for younger bands, to some of the most challenging and complex works, requiring great musical maturity from our leading college/university and professional military bands.

I am especially pleased to have two particularly distinguished "elder statesmen" composer colleagues join me and fellow baby boom generation composers in this endeavor. They are W. Francis McBeth, Composer Laureate of the State of Arkansas and recipient of the 1963 Eastman School of Music Howard Hanson Prize, and Karel Husa, winner of the 1969 Pulitzer Prize for Music, and 1993 Grawemeyer Award for Music Composition.

The twelve topics addressed by each composer in their respective chapter include:

1. Biographical information
2. The creative process...how a composer works
3. Orchestration
4. Views **from** the composer **to** the conductor, pertaining to what I call "The Four P's"
    - —**preparation** of the score
    - —developing a greater understanding of **proportion** and **pacing**

—how to better convey **passion** in the music

5. Commissioning new works
6. The teaching of composition—mentoring the young composer
7. Influential individuals (former teachers, colleagues, family members, etc.)
8. Ten works all band conductors at all levels should study
9. Ten composers whose music speaks in especially meaningful ways
10. The future of the wind band
11. Other facets of everyday life (family, leisure time, hobbies)
12. Comprehensive list of works for band

There are certainly many fine conducting texts available for the band conductor of today. Most are quite traditional in terms of their content and approach, with major emphasis given to the physical aspects of conducting.

My ten fellow composer colleagues in this volume share my view of there being a need—an important need—for a different kind of book...a book that allows all wind band conductors (middle school through college/university) a rare, unique, and fascinating glimpse into the creative process from the **composer's** perspective.

As I begin my 25th year in our profession, I hope this long overdue book will help foster more stimulating and meaningful interaction and mutual understanding between the composers and conductors of both today **and** tomorrow.

— *Mark Camphouse*
Fall, 2002, Radford, Virginia

chapter 1

james Barnes

A. Biography

James Barnes, the son of a cattleman and grain dealer, was born on September 9, 1949 in Hobart, Oklahoma. His early years were spent working for his father at the family-owned feedlot and participating in 4-H. Carrying on the tradition of his two older sisters and brother, he joined band in the sixth grade, aspiring to become a trombone player, having been duly impressed with the slide going in and out. However, his dreams soon met reality when his older brother told his father that, instead of having to pay $60.00 dollars for a new trombone, Jim could play the "baritone," since the school owned those. After a year and a half of suffering through the muddle of sound in the same octave with all the trombones, saxophones, horns and what not, Jim came to the first turning point of his career when, two weeks before the Christmas concert, the tuba player in the Junior High band moved away and Jim was reassigned to tuba. The difference between the two instruments shocked him: he could hear every note that he played on the tuba—no one was in the way. It took no time at all for Jim to ascertain the importance of establishing the fundamental pitch of the band, and even less time to realize that the tuba player also controlled tempo and, to a certain extent, dynamics. Since that initial revelation, Jim has attempted to take over every band he ever played in.

The next turning point came when, during his eighth grade year, Barnes heard the U.S. Navy Band play a concert at Southwestern State University in Weatherford. "I was astounded," he recalls. "I had no idea that a band could sound like that. I made up my mind on the spot that I wanted to be a musician." That summer, Jim's parents sent him to music camp at The University of Kansas, having no idea what they had triggered. Once thrust into an environment where everyone was as interested in music as he, Jim thrived, and he returned to camp for the next four years. During one of these six-week sessions, Jim was encouraged by a camp counselor to show some of his fledgling compositions to Dr. John Pozdro, a composition professor at KU. Pozdro, an Eastman graduate who had studied with Howard Hanson and Bernard Rogers, spent two summers working with Jim at no charge. When Jim graduated from High School in 1967 he accepted a scholarship to attend the University of Kansas as a composition major.

Shortly after coming to KU, Jim began to write arrangements for the Marching Jayhawks, under the tutelage of Kenneth G. Bloomquist. He studied composition with John Pozdro and, for one year, Allen Irving McHose, who was a Visiting Professor during Jim's senior year. In 1971, Robert Foster became Director of Bands at KU. He hired Jim as Staff Arranger and director of the Men's Basketball Band for $100.00 dollars a month while Jim finished his Master's Degree (which took a while, owing to Jim's negligible skills at mastering the French language.)

Either because of his work with the Basketball Band or because of the immense amount of money that he owed KU for delinquent parking tickets, Jim was hired as Assistant Director of Bands and Staff Arranger in 1975. In 1977, Jim married Carolyn Anne Mingle. They have a son, Billy, who was born in 1994.

Jim became an Associate Professor in 1984 and Full Professor in 1992. In 1998, Barnes left the Division of Bands to enter full-time classroom teaching in the Theory and Musicology Divisions, where he teaches orchestration, composition and history courses. Since that time, he has not moved one music stand, chair or kettledrum.

He has twice received the coveted Ostwald Award, in 1978 and 1983. His many honors include ASCAP Awards to composers of serious music, the Kappa Kappa Psi Distinguished Service to Music Medal and Bohumil Makovsky Award for Outstanding College Band Conductors. He has recorded three CD's of his music with Tokyo Kosei Wind Orchestra, and many other recordings of his music are available with college and professional bands. He has been commissioned to compose works for all five of the major military bands in Washington, DC.

Jim has traveled extensively as a guest composer, conductor and lecturer throughout the United States and in Europe, Australia, Taiwan and Japan. He is a member of ASCAP, the American Bandmasters Association and numerous other professional societies and organizations. Since 1984, his compositions have been published exclusively by Southern Music Company of San Antonio, TX.

B. The Creative Process

When people ask me how I write music, I often tell them "Any way that I can." This seems a tad sarcastic, but there is a grain of truth in this statement, because I don't always use the same method to write music. I know composers who write on a regular schedule, and it usually sounds that way, too. I don't like to waste time sitting at a piano when I'm not ready to write something. I put a lot of thought into several important factors before I ever write a note on paper:

a. **Difficulty**. When writing for wind bands, this *must* be considered. Since perhaps 95 percent of the music we write will be played by amateurs at different levels of playing ability, it is essential to target a particular difficulty level and stay with it. Band repertoire is full of works where 80 percent of a piece is at one ability level and 20 percent is two levels higher. Failure to recognize this consideration can really cut down on performances of a work.
b. The **title**: I can't write music without a title. The right title makes me start thinking about the character of the music, and I go from there.
c. The **form** of the piece. There's not much use in pounding one's head against the piano searching for musical ideas until one has some sort of plan. Simplicity or complexity is not so important as *having a plan* to start with. Form gathers musical ideas into larger statements, and these larger inner structures are what make for clarity in the overall presentation of musical ideas. Form provides the infrastructure, the skeleton, as it were, on which large compositions are built.

Strong form makes great music divine and mediocre music at least bearable.

d. **Tone center relationships**. Even in a time when we don't really write much music in keys anymore, I find it essential to develop a scheme of tonal centers. This allows me to bring logic to the progression of the musical idea(s) (reinforced by the aforementioned framework of strong form) and it aids the listener in more effectively comprehending the composer's larger message.

I love to work on full scores, and I don't even mind editing and extracting parts, now that I am using a computer, but the process of *composing* is incredibly arduous and mentally exhausting. I tell my composition students that you don't write music: *you bleed it*. This is all I will say about composing to the reader, for the rest of how I dream up the sounds that I put on paper is really very private, and it belongs to my other little world of creativity, in which I allow no one to go but me.

People often ask me what I hear when I write music. In the instance of composing for wind band, I hear the whole ensemble playing; it's really just a matter of accurately and effectively writing down what I hear the band in my head playing. Once I start writing a piece, I work on it feverishly because I want to make sure I get all the details on paper before I forget them, and also because I can get the music out of my head so I can sleep.

I think "inspiration" is the most over-rated concept non-composers have about what we do. Once in a while, I do write things very quickly in a moment of inspiration, but usually, the sorts of pieces I write are so large that they cannot be completely written under the "halo" of inspiration.

Single musical ideas often come in inspired moments, but large works are successful because of their *craftsmanship.* I cannot over-emphasize this concept of craftsmanship; it is this quality of technical training that eventually separates professionals from amateurs.

I find that I do my best writing in large clumps of time; at least two or three hours. I can't get a thing done in fifteen minutes at a whack. I always write at the piano. If it was good enough for Stravinsky it is certainly good enough for me. Although I own a synthesizer, I never use it for composing. There's just something "artificial" about it—I keep wanting to play *Wooly Bully.* I never write at the university; there are too many interruptions and distractions. I have my own little "dungeon" in our house, far from the madding crowd, with good morning light. A large portion of my adult life has been spent in this...*cell.*

All my friends were shocked when I finally started using *Sibelius Music Software©,* because I had been such a died-in-the-wool manuscript person. I really enjoy writing manuscript, but it is so time-consuming, and my writing hand is developing such a serious case of chronic tendonitis that I really had very little choice. Also, the costs for paying a copyist and photo-copying were getting so out of hand that I decided to *make* myself learn to set scores on the computer.

C. The Approach To Orchestration

I *love* to teach orchestration. It is the point in the creative process where the architect meets the engineer—the moment when the composer takes his/her abstract musical ideas and puts them down on a score in a practical manner so that this large aggregation of musicians can do their best to help produce the creator's innermost dreams and emotions. As Mel Torme once put it: "To stand out in front of a huge orchestra and hear 85 people play what you've put down on paper is the nearest thing to being God that I can think of."

I regret to say that, in my experience, a lot of pretty good new music that fails in initial performance, eventually ending in the dustbin of time, gets there mainly because it is so poorly orchestrated. This is not only true in the world of wind band music, but *even more so* in today's orchestral music. It doesn't matter how good a musical idea is; it will fail if not well orchestrated. Poor scoring is one of the main reasons why, as it has been during the entire history of music, most contemporary music ultimately becomes only temporary music.

Since I have taught orchestration for the past 25 years, I suppose I should have some sort of magical insight into this area, but I don't. My college orchestration teacher was a nice guy, but he didn't really know much about orchestration, so I learned how to orchestrate by reading books like Cecil Forsyth's *Orchestration,* Rimsky-Korsakov's *Principles of Orchestration,* by studying the great orchestral works of Berlioz, Wagner, Rimsky-Korsakov, Sibelius, Mahler, Debussy, Ravel, Stravinsky, Respighi, and Bartok, and by writing for the bands and orchestra at KU. I looked at some band scores, but back then most of the scoring was so thick, ineffective, and amateurish that I went back to studying orchestral music. When I was an undergraduate, I played a different instrument in the non-music major band almost every semester, just to "get the feel" of them. I took a semester of violin lessons and a semester of percussion lessons, with the understanding that I was more interested in writing for these instruments than I was in playing them, so the teachers and I spent a considerable amount of time talking about how to write for them idiomatically and playing little exercises I had written for the teachers to play. All of this was invaluable experience to prepare me for what I do today.

I have never been able to separate the process of composition from orchestration. When I am writing for wind band, or *any medium* for that matter, these two processes occur simultaneously; the moment I conceive the musical idea, I know who is going to play it. Writing down musical ideas and then trying to find someone who can play them is amateurish; it makes music sound clumsy and forced. I use my skills as an orchestrator to make my musical thoughts crystal clear to the listener; I use it to delight the ear and to set the precise mood for the expression I am striving to make. I don't much believe in special effects or tricky orchestration just for the sake of showing off; I leave that to people who feel they have something to prove. The fact is that effective orchestration can never hurt a well-written piece, but it has saved many a mediocre one.

From time to time, I have heard many otherwise well-informed musicians say that the wind band lacks the color of the orchestra. In fact, the problem with writing for the wind band is that it has *too much* color. The secret to writing for the wind band is not so much knowing how to best write for all these instruments in *tutti* (although that *is* complicated); the true challenge is having the know-how to eliminate all the sounds one *does not wish to hear* so the individual timbres can be more clearly heard. Of course, the other obvious problem in scoring for wind band is *balance,* since the composer never knows how many players will be playing the parts that he/she writes. In orchestral music, if I write three notes for trumpets,

I can be assured that they will be played by three trumpeters. In a wind band it might be three, six, nine, or, in the instance of these monstrosities called "honor" bands, even twelve or sixteen! How does one orchestrate music that will balance any number of players? You tell me; I've never been able to come up with a workable plan.

When composing (and, thus, orchestrating) for the wind band, I think of all the instruments (and more importantly, *the players*) like a large gathering of good friends on a stage. All these old friends have their strengths and weaknesses, and I know them well. (If I don't, then I'm not much of an orchestrator.) All the idiosyncrasies that make these different instruments so delightful are why I so much love composing for wind band. This motley concoction of instruments are to me like permanent characters performing in a very complex drama. I try to emphasize their strengths, and avoid situations in which they might be less well suited. To be a good orchestrator, it is essential that one never composes music for instruments; rather, one should strive to always compose music for the people who *play* those instruments.

I prefer to think of my score as a long, detailed letter to each of these old friends, in which I say: "Dear First Flutes: would you be so kind as to play an eighth note D3 for me on the first beat of measure 10? Not too loud...*mezzo forte* will do, and please tongue the note very lightly (*staccato*)." Or: "Dear Timpanist: would you please play a roll on A for the eight beats of measures 7 and 8, then taper your note on the first eighth note of measure nine? Also, please start the roll *forte*, then diminuendo to *mezzo piano* at the end of the roll. P.S. Please use medium mallets."

Treat instruments and players like any of your other old friends: with reverence and respect. Love them all for what they are, not what you think they should be. Try to never put them in a situation that might embarrass them or make them sound awkward or stupid. In that way, you'll seldom make an enemy in a rehearsal room.

D. Views from the Composer to the Conductor Pertaining to Score Study and Preparation

It seems like every time I attend a conducting clinic, the lecturer invariably prefaces all other remarks with "Know the score." Then they immediately go about their way, talking about gestures, facial expressions, and heaven knows what all. These moments make me think of what my college orchestra conductor, George Lawner, was taught by Rafael Kubelik: that "Bad conductors practice gestures. Good conductors study scores!" I regret to say that a lot of people in the world of wind bands would be more effective conductors if they spent less time in front of a mirror and more time with their head stuck in a score. When it comes to conducting, *nothing* is more important than really knowing the score.

I recently bought a video cassette featuring live performances of several great orchestral conductors. After watching this video two or three times, I was struck by the fact that all these conductors had only *one thing* in common: so far as gestures and technique are concerned, *most of these guys would have made a C in a college band conducting class!* The reason these conductors were so successful went far beyond baton technique. All these men had *ears like a cat* and they knew those scores like the back of their hand. The clearest beat in the world won't do you much good if you don't have a concept of how to shape the music and if you can't hear a door slam.

So, how does one go about learning how to study a score? I suppose everyone has their own *modus operandi,* but I would like to be so bold as to make a few rather harsh but useful suggestions:

1. If you have a recording of the work, *put it away.* You need to *learn* the piece, not just *listen* to it. Listening to a score while you are reading it puts the music in "real time," so, unless you are another Mozart, it might be best to study the score much slower than that. Once you have studied the work thoroughly, then I see no reason why you should not listen to a recording. Another logical argument against using recordings while trying to study a score is: *what will you do if you ever have to premier a new work that has never been recorded?*
2. Carefully read the instrumentation and any performance notes or other suggestions printed on the score. Then look through every page of the score until you grasp all the percussion that is employed. You'll also get a feel for where the thinner sections and the tuttis occur. This will help give you a rough sense of *pacing.*
3. Sit down at the piano and play through individual lines on each page, including not only melody, but bass line, counterpoint, and harmonic progressions. Then make sure you can sing these lines with the correct pitches. If you find this difficult, *then work harder at it until you can do it.* You don't have to play it *a tempo,* but you *do* need to learn to transpose F horn, Bb parts (by reading tenor clef) and Eb parts (by using bass clef.) As you do this, you will begin to recognize

the "groupings" of musical ideas: what instruments are playing the melody, who has the bass line, who has the harmony and counterpoint, etc. Unless you are conducting Ligeti's *Atmospheres*, most music has maybe four or five main things happening at once. What makes full scores look confusing to the eye is the *redundancy of lines*: all the different instruments playing the bass line (hint: *find one in C!*), all the different instruments playing the melody or counterpoint (hint: *try to find one in C!*) and so forth.

4. As you slowly progress through a score in this manner, the form of the work will become revealed to you, because by going slowly, you will more readily recognize the thematic development and transitional passages. I have always used double bars and all sorts of musical hints in scores to help conductors realize the form of the work, but I'm not sure it has helped. Is knowing the form important in the understanding of a work? *Of course it is!* It helps the conductor to better understand the flow and overall message of the work, and aids immensely in a more effective execution of those two terms used by Mark Camphouse in the introduction: *proportion* and *pacing.* These two aspects of performance are almost completely entrusted by the composer to the conductor; it is truly the area where the *great* conductor is defined. The best conductors have an inborn feeling for form and know how to "mold a performance" so that the music glows radiantly and moves both player and audience to its climactic point. Understanding the form of a work gives the conductor a confident feeling of "how this music should go."
5. I've never been much of one for marking up scores with highlighters, etc. If you can't find your way through a score

without color-coding it, then you haven't spent enough time with the music. Also, I think all those marks can be very distracting; I've seen more than one student conductor embarrass themselves on the podium in a rehearsal because he/she panicked when they got up there and couldn't remember whether the melody was supposed to be yellow or green. I often write in larger time signatures, especially with these computer scores, because they are so tiny. However, the other marks in my score usually appear only where I made conducting errors in a rehearsal and I marked the spot just to remind me so I don't make the same mistake twice. Also, I'll occasionally cue section or solo entrances on tricky page turns in the score.

I know this sounds like a lot of work, but unless you are conducting a really advanced band, studying most scores is pretty simple. Let's face it: we're not talking about Berg's *Wozzeck* here. Almost anyone can learn a grade 3 or 4 score fairy intimately in an hour or two.

My students will tell you that I like to teach by parable, and that is how I propose to make my remarks about *passion and the overall interpretation of any given work.* Several years ago, while reading a book about Arturo Toscanini, I came across a wonderful story that I would like to paraphrase here:

Toscanini was a famous conductor by the time he was 25 years old. Not only did he know the venerable Giuseppi Verdi; he conducted the premiere of the Maestro's last masterpiece: the *Four Sacred Pieces.* While preparing this music, Toscanini went to see Verdi in Genoa, to confer with him about the performance. As he played through a portion of the *Te Deum* at the piano, Toscanini said that he came to a spot where, although a *rallentando* was not written, he added one anyway. Verdi said "Bravo!"

When Toscanini stopped playing, Verdi smiled and remarked to him that he had heard him add the *rallentando* at this spot. Toscanini explained that he knew there is no *rallentando* there, but felt that there should be one.

Verdi agreed.

"But, Maestro," asked Toscanini, "If you thought there should be a *rallentando* in that measure, why did you not write one?"

Verdi's answer was, " If I had written it, a bad musician would have exaggerated it; but if one is a good musician, one feels it and plays it, just as you have done, without the necessity of having written it down." (*Toscanini* by Harvey Sachs, Weidenfeld and Nicholson, London 1978.)

I think this little story defines musical interpretation. The moral is: *you have to go by your own musical intuition.* Composers can't write every detail on the page; they expect a certain amount of musicianship from the players *and* the conductor. As I have said many times: *I write music for musicians, and they usually know what to do with it.*

This being said, I would like to make four suggestions about interpretation to you:

1. Be careful with tempos. Composers are more concerned about tempo than almost anything else you do as a conductor, because if you conduct the music at the correct tempo, the music will pretty much play itself.
2. Most composers aren't as dumb as they look, so be sure to get what he/she asks for in the score *first* before you start editing things, changing tempos, etc. Most of the bands I have heard never get to that point in either rehearsal *or*

performance. If you are performing a work by a reputable and experienced composer, you will be *amazed* at how well it will sound if your band actually plays *exactly* what is written on the score.

3. I truly believe in *moderation in all things*. Be careful about playing too fast or too slow, too loud or so soft that your players produce poor sounds. When I go to a concert, I can always tell if the conductor is a poor musician if he/she plays the slow music too slow and the fast music too fast. More performances are ruined by well-meaning conductors because of excessive and exaggerated interpretations than by careful understatement and controlled emotion on the podium. *Let the composer add the passion*; in well-written music it is mostly self-contained. Most bands I hear lose complete control in *fortissimo* sections. Part of the responsibility of being an effective conductor is to not let things get out of hand. Don't let your emotions and adrenaline get the best of you; *listen to what is actually happening* during the performance and, like a good coach, try to keep everybody running in the right direction when they are under pressure.
4. If you feel you have weak musical intuition, then get busy listening to music by the great masters. Most good composers I know have, in one way or another, patterned their style and expressive language after the great masters (*especially* those of the Twentieth Century.) I also suggest that you read biographies of the great composers (and conductors, for that matter.) Doing this gives you much more insight into that all-important question of "Why?" and not just the maudlin "How?" The more you know about great music, the better you will be able to interpret newer works

that have not yet passed that cruel, but usually infallible, test of time.

E. The Relationship Between the Composer and the Commissioning Party

From an historical view, commissions are what have made art prosper in our civilization. Most people do not realize that the majority of the greatest artistic masterpieces of all time were created for a particular reason and on commission. We wouldn't have Michelangelo's Sistine Chapel ceiling or his statue of David, were it not for commissions. The same is true in the world of music: new art is not free—someone has to pay for its creation.

But that's part of the fun, isn't it? Commissioning a new work from a reputable composer is like ordering a "brown bag special" at the sandwich shop: you never quite know what you're going to get until you open it! In the case of younger bands, it is an opportunity for the students to observe the process of creativity before their very eyes. For more mature ensembles, a new work becomes a gift to the whole world of wind band music. Commissioning new works is not so much about *getting* something for the money you pay; it's about *giving* a new piece to the world.

I think I speak for the majority of composers when I say that when we write commissions, we do our very best to please our patrons. I have written a couple of works that failed to please my patrons, and I felt bad about it. However, on both occasions, part of the problem was that the patron had put so many requirements and restraints on what I could and could not do that I probably made a mistake by accepting the commission in the first place.

If you want the composer to give you something really wonderful, *leave the guy alone.* In every case, the most successful commissions I have ever written were pieces where the patrons said "We need an opener—go to it," or "Write whatever you want." Beyond basic factors like difficulty grade (very important in wind band music, as I have already said) and the length of the work, I think it is best to leave the rest up to the composer. Don't tie him/her down with demands like: "write lots of percussion to keep my 'drummers' busy" or "at the end it would be nice to put in the Pachelbel *Canon,* because the band parents are paying for the commission and they like this song."

From time to time, I have had prospective patrons initially complain about my commission fee. I always try to placate them by explaining that if one takes into consideration how much time and effort it will take me to compose a work for their band, by comparison, union plumbers and auto mechanics do much better by the hour! Now that I have turned 50 years of age, it has become even more apparent to me that I only have so much time left in my life to compose music. If someone asks me to dedicate a sizeable portion of that remaining time to writing a work for his or her ensemble, then I should be duly compensated for that, don't you think?

F. Views on the Teaching of Composition and How to Mentor the Young Composer

I'm not sure one can teach students how to compose. Bartok didn't believe in teaching composition; he thought it could not be done. I tend to agree with him, because when you really get down to it, teachers don't make composers; *God does.* Gifted composers are *born* with an artistic sensibility, and they invariably have excellent musical intuition and judgement. A teacher can help them with form, counterpoint, orchestration and so forth, but *no* teacher can teach *creativity*.

The finest composition students I have ever had have always been the most difficult to teach, because they had such strong creative intuition and such a good idea of what they were trying to express artistically that the best I could do was to help steer them along with a few technical and practical suggestions. In fact, if I were to be so bold as to give anyone any advice about teaching gifted composers, it would be this: try to keep them pointed in a positive direction and then *get out of the way*. Whatever you do, don't fool around with their creative process. Tampering with a really talented young composer's creativity would be tantamount to a hitting coach trying to change Ted Williams' swing because he only had a .344 lifetime batting average!

The obvious question now, of course, is: "How does one teach composition students who don't have this born gift?" My answer is that they probably should not be encouraged to be composers in the first place. In the past fifty years, colleges, universities, and conservatories have turned out more people who claim to be composers than at any time in the history of the world. So, where is all the great music that these "highly trained" and "superbly educated" composers should have produced? The sad fact is that in the world of creativity, you've either got it or you don't, and a degree won't fix a lack of talent.

G. Individuals Who Have Been Especially Influential in My Development and Career

This is going to sound a tad predictable, but I really learned a lot from my father, Sid. He was a cattleman and grain dealer.

The things that I learned from him were a lot more important than music. For a man with an eighth grade education, he had more good sense, judgement, and *integrity* than most of the Ph.D's I know.

First and foremost, he taught me how to work. What little I have accomplished in my life can be more attributed to hard work than talent. I know lots of incredibly talented people who never really have had much success in this profession because, to be frank, they're *lazy*.

My Dad once advised me to "take what you do seriously, but never take *yourself* too seriously." His other priceless admonition was that "False modesty is better than none at all." Although I often fail to measure up to these gems of advice, I do strive to live by them.

When I was a senior in high school, I told my Dad I wanted to go out of state to school to become a composer. All he said was "Well—give it a couple of years. If things don't work out, you'll still have plenty of time to do something else." Coming from a man who had absolutely no idea what I was talking about most of the time at the dinner table, this was a pretty magnanimous proclamation, especially since he would be paying the bills!

During my years as a student at KU, I had five great teachers. Dr. Stanley M. Shumway taught my accelerated harmony sequence and suffered through my keyboard harmony exams each Friday. The aforementioned Dr. John Pozdro was not only a fine composition teacher, but also a trustworthy confidant who became like a second father to me after my father died in 1972. Dr. George Lawner, my orchestra conductor, was probably the most brilliant man I have ever known. A Ph.D. graduate of the University of Chicago and a conducting student of Rafael

Kubelik, Dr. Lawner was a walking musical lexicon. I was his librarian for five years, and I *never* had a conversation with Dr. Lawner in which I did not learn something about music. During the one semester that I had the honor of studying with Dr. Allen Irving McHose, I learned *so much* about contemporary styles, form, and the professional aspects of being a composer. My band director, Kenneth G. Bloomquist, was so much fun to play for that, at the time, I didn't realize how much I learned from him about how to run an efficient rehearsal, what a wind band ought to sound like, and how to conduct clearly and concisely. I really missed "Mr. B" when he left Kansas for Michigan State University in 1970.

I would be remiss if I did not mention my publisher, Arthur G. Gurwitz, who allowed me to join the Southern Music Company catalogue on a full-time basis in 1984. Since that time, he has been completely supportive of me and my work to an extent that seldom occurs between composer and publisher. To not have to constantly worry about submitting music to various publishers and not having to deal with different editors all the time has truly been a blessing. Of course, the best thing about being with Southern Music Company is that no one I deal with there has an accent!

H. Ten Works I Believe All Band Conductors At All Levels Should Study

Let me preface my listing by saying that the following ten works are what I would recommend for a conductor; this list would be quite different if I were compiling it for a composer. I regret to say that not much wind band music would appear on a list for composers. There is just too much other more important music that they should study. It is impossible to make a list of works that conductors at *all levels* should study, since the requirements and repertoire in the many facets of what we do differ to such an extreme. I have made a list for those who desire to become advanced wind band conductors. **Please note that these are in no particular order:**

Stravinsky, Igor: *Symphonies of Wind Instruments*
Stravinsky, Igor: *Wind Octet*
Schoenberg, Arnold: *Theme and Variations*, op. 43a
Hindemith, Paul: *Symphony in Bb for Concert Band*
Persichetti, Vincent: *Masquerade*
Grainger, Percy: *Colonial Song*
Mozart, Wolfgang Amadeus: *Serenade No. 10 in Bb* (Gran Partita), K. 361
Dvorak, Antonin: Serenade for Winds, op. 44
Schmitt, Florent: *Dionysiaques*
Messaien, Olivier: *Oiseaux Exotiques*

This is a list of top-drawer music for winds. Unfortunately, there aren't a lot of bands around that can play this music, and that's a shame.

I. Ten Composers Whose Music Overall Speaks to Me in Especially Meaningful Ways

Trying to name only ten composers whose music speaks to me is very difficult. Almost all great composers throughout history speak to me in some manner: from Dufay to Duruflé. Here again, these composers are listed in no particular order:

Johann Sebastian Bach, whose music is so mathematical but *so expressive.* No composer has ever touched Bach as a contrapuntalist. He is truly one of the greatest geniuses of all time. The older I get, the more I appreciate the immensity of this man's contribution to music.

Wolfgang Amadeus Mozart, who makes me angry every time I listen to his music. *No one* should be able to write such exquisite music! His operas and piano concerti are divine.

Ludwig van Beethoven, who was *a man among boys* when it comes to drama, passion, and rhythm. His handling of development and form is unsurpassed. Wagner put it best when he said, "Beethoven was a Titan, wrestling with the Gods."

Richard Wagner, who had it all: imagination, craft, passion, and an unrelenting drive to write his music the way he wanted to no matter what anyone else thought. At age 15 I was smitten with the music of Wagner, and I have never recovered. He was truly an *original* composer.

Giuseppi Verdi, who had the courage to write simple music that touches the soul. Criticized in his own time as being a simpleton and a country bumpkin, his music will live forever because of the unquestionable integrity of his art, which always came directly from *his* soul. Verdi is living proof that music does not have to be difficult or complicated to be wonderful.

Giacomo Puccini, whose music has so much passion and sensitivity. He was truly *the master* of dramatic portrayal. I could listen to *Tosca* every day for the rest of my life and never tire of it.

Jean Sibelius, who spent the large majority of his career in Finland, out of the main stream of the musical world, while he created a lifework of highly original and fascinating music, most of which, unfortunately, is seldom played anymore. But it's amazing stuff. Try: *Luonnotar, Tapiola* or his greatest masterpiece, the *Seventh Symphony.*

Igor Stravinsky, who was my idol when I was a student (he was still alive then!). I really don't know why I love his music so much, but I listen to it all the time. I admire his humor, which, unfortunately, is missing in most other twentieth century music.

Maurice Ravel, whom I believe to be the most underestimated composer of the Twentieth Century.

He was a master craftsman, one of the greatest harmonists of the century, and his orchestration is nothing short of sublime. I admire and love Ravel's music *so much,* especially the music he wrote after World War I: the two piano concerti, his *Sonata for Violin and 'Cello, La Valse* and *L'Enfant et les Sortileges.* It is fascinating music; music almost too good to be true.

Bela Bartók, whom I admire above all other twentieth century composers; even more than Ravel. Hungarian-born and dogmatically trained by excellent German teachers while he was at the Budapest Conservatory, Bartok mixed all that German craftsmanship with the Magyar fire in his belly and mind to create some of the greatest and most original works of the twentieth century. I think his music is *magical.* He was, without any doubt in my mind, the finest contrapuntalist of the Twentieth Century. Bartok didn't need 12-tone rows; he possessed the intuition to *know* what note should come next. That's what composition is all about: *you're supposed to know what note comes next.*

J. The Future of the Wind Band

Throughout the long history of wind bands, some which pre-date the oldest orchestras by hundreds of years, *service* has always been the vital function of these ensembles. This remains true today: most bands are organized and paid for in order to provide services for their sponsors, whether it be the military, schools, universities, or what have you. I really don't see this changing much, because if these perceived needs did not exist, we would have no need for wind bands, and certainly not in the present numbers.

Bands are incredibly mobile. Bands sound good almost anywhere they play. Bands can be heard outside without amplification. Bands can move and play at the same time. Bands are capable of playing a much wider variety of musical styles than any other established ensembles, and at a moment's notice. Bands can quickly subdivide into an incredible number of effective smaller units: jazz ensembles, jazz combos, woodwind quintet, brass quintet, "pep bands," etc. When considered from this perspective, bands seem to be almost *superhuman* in comparison to any other major ensemble.

So, why do so many of us in the band business seem to have an inferiority complex about wind bands and wind band music? Perhaps one answer might be that the average person on the street has heard so many *bad* bands that they think they *all* sound that way.

When discussing this "perception problem" in my band literature course, I use the following analogy: If a person came down from the planet Jupiter, knowing *absolutely nothing* about western art music, and the first two large ensembles he/she/it heard were the United States Marine Band and a high school orchestra from Perspiration, Utah, *what do you think that person's opinion of orchestral music and orchestras would be?* Do you see my point? People cannot help but form their opinions about music and ensembles by what they have heard; *it's human nature.*

I have heard many a wind band aficionado lament the fact that bands are not as respected as orchestras, and, I suppose that's true to an extent. One reason for this might be that excellent recordings of high-quality wind band literature, played by professional musicians, are not readily available to the public, at least not in the US. If most people who appreciate serious music do not know this music exists and they never get to hear it played by a first-rate ensemble, how are we *ever* going to get ourselves out of this "wind band ghetto?"

I don't have any solutions to these problems, but I do have a suggestion: Maybe we ought to stop feeling sorry for ourselves and apologizing so often about *what* we are and concentrate more on *doing a better job at what we do.*

K. Other Facets of My Everyday Life

The best thing that ever happened to me was when my sweet wife, Carolyn, felt pity upon me and married me 25 years ago. We've been through good times and bad, but the best thing that ever happened to the *both* of us was when our son, Billy, was born in 1994. My family always comes first, and it always will. I try to spend as much time with them as I can.

Then comes *fishing*; in the last few years, I have fallen in love with fishing. Having spent most of my young life out of doors, I didn't realize how much I missed being outside until I started fishing again. Standing out there in my bass boat, I watch deer come down to drink at water's edge, bald eagles and ospreys dive for fish, and flocks of ducks and geese swimming around, sounding off and generally being a nuisance. On occasion, I catch a bass, a catfish or a walleye but that is merely secondary to why I go fishing in the first place.

People often ask me in a rather haughty tone, "where does one fish in *Kansas*?" Within a hundred-mile radius of my home, there are about 40 lakes of 200 acres or more (the largest is 15,800 acres—larger than the states some people live in!) Fishing in Kansas is excellent, if you know what you're doing and you know where to go. In the next few years, I am going to make a concerted effort to fish *every one* of these lakes. (My wife doesn't know this yet, so let's just keep this between you and me!) And, of course, we only live a few hundred miles from Wyoming and Montana....

For years, Carolyn encouraged me to acquire a hobby so I wouldn't work so hard. Now that I have found a hobby that I love, *I seldom work at all.* This alarms Carolyn, who now suggests that perhaps a bit of moderation might be in order. I have repeatedly ignored these pleas.

L. Comprehensive List of Works for Band

(**Note:** *Please understand that I wrote some of this music a long time ago, so I can't always remember all the details about every piece. Please forgive me if I have a few "senior moments" when it comes to dates, premiers, commissions, etc.*)

All Pleasant Things

Gr.4 6:00 Southern Music Co.

Commissioned in 1997 by the Northshore Concert Band, Evanston, Illinois, in memory of Barbara Buehlman, long-time Executive Secretary of the Midwest Band and Orchestra Clinic, and a long-time member of the Northshore Concert Band. Premiered in Evanston,

Illinois in October 1997 by the Northshore Concert Band, Stephen Peterson, conducting.

Alvamar Overture

Gr. 4 7:30 Belwin (Warner Bros.)

Commissioned in 1980 by the Wichita Public Schools Jr. High Honor Band. Premiered at Century II Concert Hall with the composer conducting.

Appalachian Overture

Gr. 4 7:30 Wingert and Jones

Commissioned in 1982 by the Alamance County Public Schools in North Carolina. Premiered at a concert there in April of that year with the composer conducting.

Arioso and Presto for Alto Saxophone and Band

Gr. 6-Sx./ 4-Bd. 7:00 Southern Music Co.

Commissioned by saxophone virtuoso Thomas Liley. Premiered by the Joliet, Ill. Community Band at the National Association of Junior Colleges convention in Chicago, Illinois in March 2001. Band parts on rental only.

Autumn Soliloquy for Oboe and Band

Gr. 5-Ob./ 4-Bd. 7:30 Southern Music Co.

Written for Susan Hicks Brashier in 1986. Premiered by Ms. Brashier with the KU University Band, the composer conducting. Also available in flute and clarinet versions, all with piano reduction. Transcribed for Oboe and orchestra by the composer in 1999. (Available on rental.)

Breckenridge Overture

Gr. 4 7:30 Southern Music Co.

Written for the 50th anniversary of Phi Beta Mu. Premiered at the Midwest Band and Orchestra Clinic by the Lake Highlands (TX) High School Band, Malcolm Helm conducting. Published in 1989.

Brookshire Suite

Gr. 3 6:30 Belwin (Warner Bros.)

This is the first piece I ever wrote for younger bands. Originally written in 1974 for Jack Brookshire's Baldwin (KS) High School Band, it was rejected by six publishers before Belwin printed it in 1980. It has been on the Texas UIL Prescribed List for many years.

Caribbean Hideaway (1996)

Gr. 4 3:00 Southern Music Co.

Carnivale in Sáo Paulo

Gr. 4 3:00 Southern Music Co.

An "encore" for symphonic band. Premiered in Kawasaki, Japan in November 2002 by the Senzoku Gakuen Wind Orchestra with the composer conducting.

Centennial Celebration Ov.

Gr. 5 5:00 Southern Music Co.

Written in 1984 on a summer grant from the University of Kansas to celebrate the 100th Anniversary of the Department of Music and Dance. Premiered in spring of 1985 by the University of Kansas Symphonic Band, Robert E. Foster, conducting.

Century Tower

Gr. 4 9:00 Southern Music Co.

Commissioned by the Kappa Kappa Psi and Tau Beta Sigma Chapters at the University of Florida. Premiered in Gainesville in April of 1983 by the University of Florida Band with the composer conducting.

Chorale and Jubiloso (1980)

Gr. 3 5:00 Norman Lee (Barnhouse)

Chorale Prelude On a German Folktune

Gr. 5 9:30 Southern Music Co.

Commissioned by Kappa Kappa Psi/Tau Beta Sigma for the National Intercollegiate Band, this work was premiered in the summer of 1985 at the national KKY/TBS Convention at the University of Kansas in Lawrence, with the composer conducting.

Colours
(with tape) (1970) not available

Commencement Festival Ov.
(1971) not available

Concerto for Tuba
6-Tb/ 5-Bd. 18:00 Southern Music Co. (Rental)
Written for tuba and orchestra in fall of 1995, for Scott Watson, KU's Professor of Tuba. Band version transcribed by Mark Rogers. Wind Band version premiered by Watson with the U.S. Army Band at Ft. Myer, VA in early February 1996, with the composer conducting. Orchestral version premiered in late February 1996 by Watson with the KU Symphony Orchestra, composer conducting.

Crossgate (1983)
Gr. 3 6:00 Southern Music Co.

Dream Journey
Gr. 5 8:30 Southern Music Co.
Commissioned in 1996 to celebrate the 25th Anniversary of the Austin (TX) Independent School District Senior High Honor Band. Premiered by that band in February 1997 with the composer conducting.

Duo Concertante For Tpt., Euph. and Band
Gr. 6/6 11:00 Southern Music Co. (Rental)
Commissioned in 1990 by the United States Air Force Band, Washington, DC to feature the Bowman brothers, Vic and Brian, who were both members of the band at the time. Premiered in March 1991 at the American Bandmaster's Convention in Tallahassee, Florida, with the composer conducting.

Eagle Bend (Ov. for Band)
Gr. 4 7:30 Southern Music Co.
Commissioned in 1999 by Beta Chapter of Phi Beta Mu to honor the career of George Brite, one of the legendary school band directors in Oklahoma. Premiered in Tulsa, OK in January 2000 by the Oklahoma All-State Band with the composer conducting.

Eaglecrest (Ov. for Band)

Gr. 4 7:45 Southern Music Co.

Commissioned in 1982 by Explorer Post 934, Manchester, New Hampshire. Premiered in Manchester in June 1983 by the Explorer Wind Symphony, T.J. Rand conducting.

Early Byrd (1980)

Gr. 1 1:30 Belwin (Warner Bros.)

(Setting of William Byrd's "Earle of Oxford March" for grade school players.)

Eisenhower Centennial March

Gr. 4 3:30 Southern Music Co.

Commissioned in 1989 by the 312th Army Reserve Band (Lawrence, KS) to celebrate the 100th anniversary of Kansas' "Favorite Son." Premiered in Abilene KS at the Eisenhower Library on President Dwight D. Eisenhower's 100th birthday in October 1990, with WO4 Robert Duffer conducting.

Fanfares and Alleluias

Gr. 4 7:30 Southern Music Co.

Commissioned in 1995 by the Fort Walton Beach (FL) High School Band. Premiered in April 1996 in Fort Walton Beach with the composer conducting.

Fanfare and Capriccio

Tp.6/Bd.4 7:00 Southern Music Co.

Written in 1998 for trumpet virtuoso Allen Vizzutti. Premiered in April 1999 by Vizzutti with the KU Concert Band, the composer conducting. (Band parts on rental only.)

Fantasy Variations on a Theme by Niccolo Paganini

Gr. 5 14:00 Southern Music Co.

Commissioned in 1987 by the United States Marine Band. Premiered by the Marine Band at the Music Educators National Conference (MENC) Convention in Indianapolis, IN in April 1988 with Col. John Bourgeois conducting.

Festival Concert March

Gr. 5 5:30 Southern Music Co.

Commissioned in 1981 by the University of Kansas. Premiered by the KU Symphonic Band in August of that year at the ceremony inaugurating Dr. Eugene A. Budig as Chancellor of the University.

Foxfire

Gr. 3 5:30 Southern Music Co.

Commissioned by Texas Region II Small School Band Directors Association. Premiered in January 2001 in Wichita Falls, Texas with the composer conducting.

Golden Brass (Concert March)

Gr. 4 3:30 C.L. Barnhouse

Written in 1972 and published in 1973, this is my first publication for concert band.

Golden Festival Overture

Gr. 5 6:30 Southern Music Co.

Commissioned by the United States Army Field Band to commemorate their 50th anniversary. Premiered in March 1997 by the Army Field Band at the American Bandmasters Convention in San Antonio, Texas with the composer conducting.

Heatherwood Portrait (1984)

Gr. 3 6:00 Southern Music Co.

High Plains Overture

Gr. 2 5:30 Southern Music Co.

Dedicated "to the memory of Gene Clapp, our good friend, teacher and colleague." Gene Clapp was a well-known and highly respected music teacher, who collapsed and died during a rehearsal with his junior high band. Premiered in May 1990 in Hays, Kansas by the combined school bands, with the composer conducting.

Hobart Centennial (March)

Gr. 4+ 3:30 Southern Music Co.

Written for the 100th anniversary of Barnes' home town of Hobart, Oklahoma. Premiered in August 2001 by the 145th Army Reserve Band with the composer conducting.

Hunter Park

Gr. 4 6:00 Southern Music Co.

Written in 1972, this is my first band work published by Southern Music Co.

Impressions of Japan

Gr. 5 10:00 Southern Music Co.

Commissioned by the Saitama Sakae High School Band, Ohmiya, Japan. Premiered in Tokyo in January 1993 by that band with Ohtaki Minori conducting.

Inventions on Marching Songs

Gr. 5 5:30 Southern Music Co.

Commissioned in 1994 by the United States Army Band to commemorate the 50th anniversary of the victory of Allied forces in Europe and the Pacific in 1945. Premiered by the Army Band in January 1995 at the Kennedy Center in Washington, DC with Col. L. Bryan Shelburne, Jr. conducting.

Invocation and Toccata

Gr. 5 7:30 Southern Music Co.

Commissioned by the New Mexico State University Band. Premiered by that band in Las Cruces, New Mexico in April 1981 with the composer conducting.

Legend

Gr. 5 9:30 Southern Music Co.

Since the program notes for *Legend* were accidentally omitted during printing, I am often asked to explain this title. This is a tone poem about the immortal "Phoenix" bird, which, according to Sumerian legend, lives for 500 years, then self-immolates before rising from it's own ashes, each time even more resplendent than before. The conclusion of *Legend* is about as close as I will ever come to writing minimalist music. This work was premiered at Green Bay, Wisconsin during the summer of 1991.

Light in the Wilderness, A

Gr. 5 11:00 Southern Music Co.

Commissioned by the family and friends of Megan Taylor, who was accidentally killed while on a band trip to Europe. Premiered in March 1994 by the Shawnee Mission South High School Band with the composer conducting.

Lonely Beach (Normandy 1944)

Gr. 5 11:00 Southern Music Co.

Written in 1992. Commissioned by the United States Army Band. Premiered on 11 November 1992 at a Veteran's Day concert at George Mason University, Fairfax, VA, Col. L. Bryan Shelburne, Jr. conducting.

The Long Gray Line

Gr. 5 6:15 Southern Music Co.

Commissioned by the West Point Society of New York. Premiered on 4 July 1987 by the United States Military Band at West Point in a concert at the Tanglewood Music Festival with the composer conducting.

Lyric Interlude (1979)

Gr. 3 4:00 Belwin (Warner Bros.)

Maracas from Caracas (2001)

Gr. 2 2:00 Southern Music Co.

Medicine Lodge Overture (1980)

Gr. 3 5:00 Norman Lee (Barnhouse)

Old Guard, The (March)

Gr. 4 3:00 Southern Music Co.

Written in 1993. Dedicated to Col. Eugene Allen, retired Commander/Conductor of the United States Army Band, Ft. Myer, VA.

Overture Energico

Gr. 3 6:00 Belwin (Warner Bros.)

Written in 1981. Premiered in April 1982 by the KU Varsity Concert Band with the composer conducting.

Pershing Rifles, The (1996)

Gr. 2 2:00 Southern Music Co.

Nulli Secundus (March)

Gr. 4 3:00 Southern Music Co.

Written in 1998. Premiered in February 1999 by the University of Kansas Concert Band with the composer conducting. (In Latin: *Second to None.)*

Pagan Dances

Gr. 5 13:40 Southern Music Co.

Commissioned in 1989 by the Kappa Kappa Psi chapter at the University of Central Arkansas. Premiered in February 1990 by the University of Central Arkansas Symphonic Wind Ensemble at a Southwest Region CBDNA convention at Texas Christian University in Fort Worth, Texas with the composer conducting.

Poetic Intermezzo (1984)

Gr. 4 8:30 Southern Music Co.

Quiet Song (1980)

Gr. 1 2:00 Belwin (Warner Bros.)

Rapscallion (Ov.-Scherzo) (1974)

Gr. 4 6:30 Southern Music Co.

Rhapsodic Essay

Gr. 5 9:00 Southern Music Co.

Commissioned in 1996 by the ACC-Heritage of America Band, Langley Air Force Base, VA to commemorate the 50th anniversary of the U.S. Air Force. Premiered in 1998 by that band with Captain Larry Lang conducting. This work was originally entitled *The Gathering of Eagles,* but the composer changed the title before publication in 1999.

Riverfest (1981)
Gr. 4 6:30 Southern Music Co.

Romanza (1989)
Gr. 4 7:35 Southern Music Co.

Silver Gazebo, The (1995)
Gr. 4 2:55 Southern Music Co.

Solemn Prelude, A
Gr. 3 5:00 Southern Music Co.
Commissioned by the Association of Texas Small School Bands for the 2003 ATSSB All-State Band. Premiered in February 2003 by the Concert Band with the composer conducting.

Sorcery Suite, op. 112 (2001)
Gr. 4-5 13:00 Belwin Mills (Warner Bros.)
Commissioned in 2000 by the Northern California Band Directors Association. Premiered in February 2002 by the NCBDA High School Honor Band in Santa Rosa, California with the composer conducting.

Spitfire Overture (1990)
Gr. 3+ 5:30 Southern Music Co.

Sterling Brass (1980)
Gr. 4 4:00 Belwin (Warner Bros.)

Stone Meadows (1986)
Gr. 4 5:10 Southern Music Co.

Sunflower Saga
Gr. 3 6:00 Southern Music Co.
Commissioned in 1993 to celebrate the twentieth anniversary of the Kansas Bandmasters Association. Premiered on July 10, 1994 by the Kansas Intercollegiate Band at the KBA Convention in Wichita with Jerry Junkin conducting.

Symphonic Overture

Gr. 6 9:30 Southern Music Co.

Commissioned in 1990 to celebrate the 50th anniversary of the United States Air Force Band in Washington, DC. Premiered by the USAF Band in March 1991 at the American Bandmasters Association convention in Tempe, Arizona with the composer conducting.

Symphony No. 1, op. 35

Gr. 6 35:00 not currently available

Completed in the spring of 1974, this work is my master's thesis. After its premiere in the spring of 1977 by the University of Kansas Symphonic Band (with Robert E. Foster conducting), it won the Ostwald Award in 1978. At the present time, it is not publicly available because I would like to make some revisions, and the parts are a *mess.*

Symphony No. 2, op. 44

Gr. 6 23:00 Southern Music Co.

Written in the summers of 1980 and 1981 to commemorate the 10th year of Robert E. Foster as Director of Bands at the University of Kansas. Premiered in Lawrence in the spring of 1982 by the KU Symphonic Band (with Foster conducting.) This symphony won the Neil Kjos Memorial Award for Outstanding Contemporary Band Music in 1983. For several years, Kjos carried it in their rental catalogue before I had it transferred to Southern in the late 80's. The work rented so much that Southern decided to publish it in 2000.

Symphony No. 3, op. 89

Gr. 6 40:00 Southern Music Co.

Commissioned in 1992 by the United States Air Force Band, the *Third Symphony* was completed by the composer in June of 1994. Because of delays in production of the parts and other factors, the Air Force Band graciously allowed the work to first be played in June 1996 at Symphony Hall, Osaka, Japan by the Osaka Municipal Symphonic Band, Yoshihiro Kimura conducting. The work was to receive its American premiere at the Virginia Music Educators Association Convention in Roanoke, VA in December 1996, but the Air Force Band was unable to appear at the performance due to budgetary restraints

('96 was the year congress let the government go broke because they couldn't negotiate a budget.) The work was recorded by the USAF Band in January of 1997 and finally played publicly in the U.S. at the VMEA Convention in Roanoke in December 1997 with Col. Lowell Graham conducting.

Symphony No. 4, op. 103 (Yellowstone Portraits)

Gr. 5 23:00 Southern Music Co.

Originally composed for orchestra, the *Fourth Symphony was* commissioned in 1999 by the Youth Symphony of Kansas City to celebrate its 40th anniversary. It was premiered by the Youth Symphony in May 2000 at Yardley Hall in Overland Park, KS with the composer conducting.

In consultation with the composer, it was transcribed by Dr. Mark Rogers in 2001. In February 2002, the wind band version was premiered at the CBDNA Southeast Regional Convention in Atlanta, Georgia by the University of Alabama Wind Symphony with Dr. Gerald Welker, conducting.

Symphony No. 5, op. 110 (Phoenix)

Gr. 6 45:00 Southern Music Co.

Commissioned in 2000 to commemorate the 50th anniversary of the Central Band of the Japanese Ground Self-Defense Force, the *Fifth Symphony* was premiered by that band at Tokyo Metropolitan Hall in Ikebikkurro, Tokyo in June 2001 with Colonel Toyokazu Nonaka conducting.

The Texans (Overture)

Gr. 4 7:30 Southern Music Co.

Commissioned by a High School Band in Garland, Texas to celebrate the 150th anniversary of the State of Texas. Premiered in Garland in February 1986 with the composer conducting.

Three Symphonic Fanfares

Gr. 4+ 5:00 Southern Music Co.

I. *Fanfare for Annapolis* is dedicated to the U.S. Naval Academy Band. Premiered by that band in 1987 with the composer conducting.

II. *Fanfare for West Point* is dedicated to the U.S. Military

Academy Band. It was premiered by the USMA Band with Lt. Col. L. Bryan Shelburne, Jr. conducting. (1986?)

III. *Fanfare for the American Bandmasters Association* was premiered by the University of Kansas Symphonic Band at the March 1988 ABA Convention in Oklahoma City, Oklahoma with Robert E. Foster conducting.

Thunderbolt (Concert March)

Gr. 5 4:00 Medici Music

Commissioned by the Kansas Bandmasters Association for their 1979 summer convention. Premiered by the Kansas Intercollegiate Band in July 1979 in Hutchinson, KS with the composer conducting.

Toccata Fantastica

Gr. 5 8:00 Southern Music Co.

Commissioned by the United States Army Band, Ft. Myer, VA to commemorate the retirement of Col. L. Bryan Shelburne, Jr. Premiered by the Army Band in December 2000 at the Midwest Band and Orchestra Clinic in Chicago, Illinois with the composer conducting.

Torch Dance

Gr. 5+ 9:00 Southern Music Co.

Written in 1984 for the University of Kansas Symphonic Band for a performance at the Southwest Region CBDNA convention at the University of Arkansas in Fayetteville. Premiered in Wichita in February 1984 conducted by Robert E. Foster.

Trail of Tears (1989)

Gr. 3 6:15 Southern Music Co.

Trailridge Saga (1987)

Gr. 3 6:50 Southern Music Co.

Trumpets and Drums (1981)

Gr. 2 2:00 Norman Lee (Barnhouse)

Twin Oaks

Gr. 3+ 5:45 Southern Music Co.

Commissioned by the East Mecklinburg (NC) High School Band.

Premiered by that band in Charlotte, NC in May 2000 with the composer conducting.

Two Preludes (1969-1971)

Gr. 5 8:00/6:00 not available

Valor

Gr. 5 4:00 Southern Music Co.

Written in 2001 to commemorate the 200th anniversary of the United States Military Academy at West Point. Premiered by the USMA Band in January 2002 at West Point, New York with Lt. Col. David Dietrick conducting.

Variants on a Moravian Hymn

Gr. 4+ 9:00 Southern Music Co.

Commissioned in 1990 by the Freedom High School Band to commemorate the 250th anniversary of Bethlehem, Pennsylvania. Premiered by that band in the spring of 1992 with Ronald J. Demkee conducting.

Very American Overture, A

Gr. 4 7:30 Southern Music Co.

Commissioned by the Nebraska Wesleyan University Concert Band for their tour of Japan in 1996. Premiered in Lincoln, Nebraska by that band in March 1996 with the composer conducting.

Visions Macabre

Gr. 6 11:00 Southern Music Co. (rental)

Written in the summer of 1979. Premiered March 1980 in Lawrence, Kansas by the University of Kansas Symphonic Band with the composer conducting. National premiere by KU that April at the MENC Convention in Miami, Florida. Winner of the 1981 ABA Ostwald Award.

We the People

Gr. 4 2:30 Southern Music Co.

Commissioned in 1989 by the Kansas Commission for the Celebration of the Bi-Centennial of the United States Constitution.

Premiered in a ceremony on the capitol steps in Topeka, Kansas in September 1989 by the Washburn University Band, Kurt Seville conducting.

Westport Overture (1987)

Gr. 3 6:00 Southern Music Co.

Westridge Overture (1982)

Gr. 3 4:30 Southern Music Co.

Originally published in 1983 by Norman Lee (Barnhouse). Copyright transferred to Southern Music Co. in 1991.

Wildwood Overture (1996)

Gr. 3 5:00 Southern Music Co.

Yama Midori (Green Mountains)

Gr. 4 5:00 Southern Music Co.

Commissioned by Zushi High School, Kanagawa, Japan to celebrate the school's 80th anniversary. Premiered in Kamakura, November 2002 with the composing conductor.

Yorkshire Ballad (Band)

Gr. 3 4:00 Southern Music Co.

Written in early June 1984. Premiered at the Kansas Bandmasters Association convention in Hutchinson, Kansas in July 1984 by the Kansas Intercollegiate Band, Claude T. Smith conducting.

Yorkshire Ballad (Solo Tuba and Wind Ensemble)

Tb-6/ Bd-4 4:00 Southern Music Co.

Revised version (2000) for tuba virtuoso Patrick Sheridan. Score and parts available on rental.

Arrangements for Wind Band

Home On the Range (Kansas' State Song) by Dan Kelly

Gr. 3	2:00	Norman Lee (Barnhouse)

Joyce's 71st New York Regiment March

by Thornton Barnes Boyer

Gr. 4	3:30	Southern Music Co.

(Modernized wind band version of the *original version* of this march, which was published by J.W. Pepper in 1881.)

Music from *Girl Crazy* by George and Ira Gershwin

Gr. 5	9:30	Warner Brothers/Chappell

My Old Kentucky Home by Stephen Foster

Gr. 3	3:00	Southern Music Co.

Old American Songs

by Aaron Copland (four selections for baritone voice and band)

Gr. 4	6:00	Boosey and Hawkes (rental)

Music from *Porgy and Bess* by George and Ira Gershwin

Gr. 5	9:00	Warner Brothers/Chappell

Star-Spangled Salute to the Music of George M. Cohan

Gr. 5	6:00	Southern Music Co.

Tchaikovsky Suite (from *Album for the Young*), op. 39

I. Folk Song II. Morning Prayer III. Mazurka

IV. Polka V. Waltz

Gr. 3+	6:30	Southern Music Co.

Two Chorales by Johannes Brahms

(from his *Organ Preludes*, op. 122)

Gr. 3	6:00	Southern Music Co.

Whistler and His Dog, The by Arthur Pryor

Gr. 3 2:00 Southern Music Co.

One of Sousa's favorite encores, this humorous "whistle-along" piece has been permanently out of print for many years. Additional parts for the modern symphonic band have been added.

Music from *The Wizard of Oz*

by Harold Arlen and E.Y. Harburg

Gr. 5 9:30 Warner Brothers/Chappell

chapter 2

timothy Broege

A. Biography

The process of becoming a composer is full of mysteries. Who can say why a twelve-year-old boy became fascinated with the inner workings of classical music and jazz? Environment, family, teachers, friends, concert experiences, singing, playing—all of these played a part, to be sure, but it is hard for me to say how, when and why I chose to try and become a composer. It seemed a road I had to travel.

My earliest musical experiences growing up in Belmar, New Jersey were those of many American youngsters in the 1950's: singing in the church choir and in school music classes, and listening to recordings and broadcasts of concerts on radio and television. We were lucky to have a piano in the house up until I was five years old (the piano was sold in 1952 so that a television/entertainment center could be purchased in time for the inauguration of President Eisenhower). My father, though not an accomplished pianist, played frequently and with much enjoyment a repertoire of hymns and college songs (he had briefly attended the University of Pennsylvania). My mother had a lovely singing voice, and I was happy to hear her sing unaccompanied lullabies to my younger brother, Peter. Sometimes I joined in.

I began to take instrumental music lessons at Belmar Grammar School when I was in the fourth grade. Mr. Jack Schwartz, the school orchestra director, was a fine jazz woodwind and sax man, with plenty of experience in the real musical world. Trumpet was my instrument, and though I never had a decent embouchure or tone, I could read music well and very much enjoyed participating in a large instrumental ensemble.

When I entered the sixth grade, I began piano lessons with Mrs. Helen Antonides, who was our church organist and choir director (yes, my parents had to purchase another piano). Not only did she teach me piano, but also theory and elementary composition techniques, using the fine materials written by the composer Paul Hindemith. She also encouraged me to improvise, and to learn about jazz techniques. To receive such extensive early training was invaluable. Although the trumpet long ago fell silent, I remain an active keyboard performer on harpsichord, clavichord, organ, and piano. I cannot imagine a life without keyboard music.

My high school years were disappointing in terms of the musical experiences I encountered. The high school band was second-rate and there was no orchestra. Participating in marching band during football season was a waste of time. I began to realize I was not spending enough time practicing the piano, and I begrudged time spent in less important activities.

Luckily for me, I was able to attend summer music camp programs in 1963 and 1964. These were the first opportunities for me to be surrounded by people who really cared about music. The program took place on the campus of Glassboro State College (now known as Rowan University) in southern New Jersey. With daily rehearsals of orchestra, band, and chorus, as well as private lessons and classes in theory and composition, the camp was easily the best musical thing that happened to me during my high school years.

And then off to college. I was fortunate to attend Northwestern University where I studied piano with Frances Larimer; harpsichord with Dorothy Lane; composition with M. William Karlins, Alan Stout, and Anthony Donato; poetry with E.B. Hungerford and Margaret Walker Alexander; and conducting with John Paynter. I became the pianist for the university orchestra and chamber orchestra during my senior year, and also did plenty of accompanying in the instrumental studios. Whenever possible, I attended the weekly concerts of the Chicago Symphony and the concerts of the Contemporary Chamber Players at the University of Chicago. In my university days Jean Martinon was the music director of the Chicago Symphony and Ralph Shapey led the CCP. Both musicians made an enormous impression on me.

At Northwestern there was a good deal of interest in new music, and there were many performances of recent pieces on recitals and concerts at the university. I was fortunate to have many of my student works performed—there is nothing more valuable for a young composer than hearing her music performed by capable players—and eventually some of my fellow students began asking me to compose pieces for them. Composing "on commission" has been a very comfortable process for me ever since.

Upon graduation from Northwestern, I was faced with being drafted into the military—these were the years of the Vietnam War—and it seemed a good idea to find an alternative. Since there was a serious shortage of teachers in the Chicago Public School System, I was able to go to work as a sixth grade teacher. Training in elementary education was not required, although I did have to undergo a year of night school to acquire the necessary education credits.

It was hard work. Except for playing piano for the school chorus, which was quite an enthusiastic bunch of students, there was not much music going on. I completed only a small number of compositions during this time, although I did receive my first orchestral commission,

Sinfonia No. 1, for jazz ensemble and orchestra. Commissioned by the Evanston Symphony Orchestra, the piece was premiered in June of 1971, launching my series of *sinfonias* for large ensembles. Later that year, I moved back to New Jersey and took a job as an instrumental music teacher in the elementary school in Manasquan, across the street from the high school I had attended years earlier. The instrumental program had been allowed to wither away, so it was my responsibility to build it up and put some students on concert display so that parents and administrators would be proud. My band students were never very accomplished, but I did begin composing music for them, and thus my activities in the area of school band music commenced. Some of my more successful school band pieces, such as *The Headless Horseman, Sinfonias IV* and *VI,* and *Rhythm Machine,* were written during these years especially for my Manasquan Elementary School musicians. By the time I gave up teaching in 1980, there were two bands, a jazz ensemble, and an early music ensemble, along with woodwind and brass ensembles, all functioning reasonably well.

In 1972 I became Organist and Director of Music at the First Presbyterian Church in Belmar. In 2001 I took on the additional position of Organist and Director of Music at the historic Elberon Memorial Church, also in New Jersey. This is a summer-only church, so I am in Belmar September through June and in Elberon for July and August.

Both churches have wonderful tracker-action organs, and both instruments are a joy to play. At home I have a clavichord and two harpsichords, so the majority of my keyboard playing time is spent at "old-style" instruments.

My keyboard performance experiences over the years most certainly have been the greatest influence upon my development as a composer. Although I do not usually compose at the keyboard, I draw upon the riches of the western keyboard tradition—from the renaissance to today, including jazz and blues—continually in my work.

B. The Creative Process

I begin work on a piece by planning the structure, usually in the form of a detailed outline. Description of most of the important events and processes in the piece is essential for me. Knowing where the piece will end up and how it will get there allows me to "dream" the sounds of the piece that will be the bricks and mortar of the structure. Some of my outlines are little more than a paragraph; others require several legal pad pages of careful description. I am free to change my mind, of course, but I find that my initial plan usually survives without major change.

Composition is a combination of craft and imagination as far as I am concerned. I trust my musical language enough to let the notes, rhythms, scoring, etc. take care of themselves. I have never had much interest in consistent pitch organization or harmonic language. What pleases me most is music that is full of contrast and made from both strong gestures and subtle effects. To my ears, some of the most perfect music was composed by Anton Webern, and I keep his pieces always in my ears as I work.

Years ago I did most of my composing at night, but during the last two decades I find myself happily working at almost any time of day. I do not care for the early morning hours, and the late evening hours are best reserved for clavichord playing. The remaining waking hours all are congenial for writing. If fatigue sets in, I take a break and spend some time at one of my keyboard instruments. In fine weather, I take walks on the beach or go for a bicycle ride. I usually work for two or three hours at a time.

Although I sometimes find it helpful to compose at the piano, usually I work at a drafting table, occasionally sounding pitches on an electronic keyboard to keep my ear accurate. I hear the music in its entirety in my head as I work: for me, composition is essentially the process of transcribing the piece I hear in my head. After the piece is initially "transcribed," I edit and correct it as ruthlessly as I can. Except for the simplest keyboard or vocal pieces, I write out all of my music on 11 x 17 inch score paper, using ball-point pen. After all corrections and improvements have been made, I set the piece up on the computer using *Finale* music software, which I find enormously helpful for score preparation and extraction of parts. The playback capabilities of music software are also useful in the proofreading process. I do not use the music software as part of the initial composition process. No doubt this comes from my years of working without a computer.

C. The Approach to Orchestration

As mentioned above, I hear the music in my head complete with instrumental and vocal sounds. On most commissioned projects, the instrumentation is specified and agreed upon prior to my beginning work on the score. I very much prefer this. Like the composers of the Baroque era, I believe my music can easily adapt to different instrumental situations. When one of my harpsichord pieces is played on the piano, I am not bothered in the least and, in fact, I enjoy the different aspects of the music that emerge. Since structure, gesture, and musical rhetoric are most important to me, the actual sounds are necessarily secondary. I try to score the music in an effective manner, but I almost never feel that the music must sound one way and no other.

Except in full ensemble *tutti* passages, doubling should be used very sparingly as far as I am concerned. I love the transparency one hears in Ravel and Webern, and in the jazz scores of Gil Evans. Unless the texture is clear and effective the listener will not "get" what the music is doing. It follows that much of the scoring I hear in symphonic band or wind ensemble music is not to my taste: too much brass, too much percussion, too much doubling, too loud, too clumsy, too vulgar. Composers such as Olivier Messiaen, Joseph Schwantner, Vincent Persichetti, and Warren Benson have shown us how wonderful an ensemble of winds and percussion can sound when the scoring is not influenced by the circus or Hollywood film music.

When composing for less experienced performers—school bands and orchestras, children's choruses, amateur groups of any kind—one is forced to take into consideration the technical limitations of the players. I find that I need not abandon my usual structural or expressive procedures, but I do make large allowances for the needs of such performers. It is cruel to compose exposed lines for solo players or to write passages at the upper limits of an instrument's range under such circumstances. I often refer to the difference between writing for the harpsichord and the piano. Masterpieces have been composed for both instruments, but the limits of the harpsichord, mainly in terms of range and dynamics, must always be considered. When scoring a work for less experienced players or singers, the technical limitations determine most of the orchestration. I try to imagine the music as it might be played by the performers for whom it is intended. When accepting a commission, I ask for as much information as possible about the strengths and weaknesses of the performers who will present the work.

In general, I prefer smaller ensembles over larger. The string quartet seems to me the ideal instrumental ensemble: it is no wonder so much great music has been written for it. In orchestral scoring, I like woodwinds in pairs; the standard four horns, two or three trumpets, three trombones, and tuba are plenty as far as I am concerned. The tendency of modern orchestras to skimp on the string basses is deplorable, I think. At least eight basses (ten is better) are essential.

With regard to the wind band, I don't much care for such oddball instruments as contrabass clarinets or euphoniums, but they seem to have established themselves and I must live with them. One player on a part sounds best to my ears, although I have heard many ensembles in which the clarinet parts were doubled that sounded quite fine. Gigantic "festival" bands are problematic, to put it mildly. Adding the four traditional saxophone parts to the winds of the standard orchestra along with string basses, piano, and (not too much) percussion creates a very satisfying ensemble that suits my music well.

As I look through my wind band scores, I see that much of my orchestration resembles pipe organ registration. Instrument choirs are deployed like the various stops of a cathedral organ. In pieces for less experienced players there is more mixing of instruments, while in the more difficult pieces the instrumental colors are often unblended.

There is too much percussion in contemporary wind band music. If, as I believe, the greatest wind ensemble piece of all time is the Mozart *Serenade* in B-flat major, K.361, then we would do well to keep the methods and sounds of that masterwork in mind as we prepare our scores. I am an advocate for less thumping, crashing, smacking, and chiming. The vocal models that have driven instrumental music for centuries are still valid. Orchestration is the means by which the composer enables the instruments to sing.

D. Views from the Composer to the Conductor Pertaining to Score Study and Preparation

Conductors, as well as performers, are frequently puzzled by my music on initial encounter. The polystylistic or eclectic overall language that I employ can seem unfocused and confusing. Since I regard my music as abstract rather than programmatic, it follows that conductors can enter the sound world of my music most easily by concentrating on those abstract elements—often called parameters—which mean the most to me.

Study and preparation of the score should begin with tempo. Sometimes I indicate tempo with metronome markings, sometimes not, but I like to think the music more times than not suggests the proper tempo. By reading through the score beginning to end the conductor can see what the primary pulse speeds of the music are, and where they occur. I try to avoid gratuitous changes of tempo in my works, so that any tempo indications are important and should be observed fully.

The traditional practice of sitting down to the piano and playing through a score is still the best way for initiating study of a new composition. For conductors without keyboard skills, the hiring of an accomplished pianist (or making use of musical colleagues) is a good idea for large works. I do not believe it is necessary to play every note in the score, but isolating and emphasizing the principal materials is essential.

After some familiarity with the materials of the piece has been gained, the conductor should analyze the structure of the work. I often employ rondo, variation, and/or ground bass forms (i.e., chaconne, passacaglia, or blues) which are easy to spot, but I also like to create arbitrary abstract forms. For instance, a form described as **A-B-C-A-D-E-F-A** might contain aspects of rondo form or traditional sonata form (exposition, development, recapitulation) or it might not. The repetition of material is what provides the structure, needless to say; the conductor should identify the principal repeated passages in the music and be able to justify the repetitions. For each contrasting passage, the conductor should determine whether the material is derived from previous material, or is something new. Like Sibelius or Bruckner, I usually build most of the music from material presented initially. Like Beethoven, I work mostly with short motives rather than extended melodies. Like most composers of the previous hundred years, I believe any pitch can be combined with any other pitch. A three-step process of analysis for each of the main passages in the music would be: first, determine any connection to the principal initial material of the piece; second, identify motives or pitch patterns and determine their derivation, if any; and, third, sound out the vertical pitch combinations and determine tonal centers, if any, along with harmonic relationships to previous material.

Next comes the identification of what I call structural narrative. I use this term as a label for what is happening in the music, on the most basic level. An example of a structural narrative for a movement might read as follows:

> First, a slow chromatic chorale is played in the low brass. Next, xylophone and piccolo disrupt the chorale with rude bird songs. From the pitches of the opening chorale comes a new melodic pattern in the woodwinds accompanied by variants of the piccolo/xylophone material. The new melodic material is developed and passed around the ensemble while the piccolo/xylophone material gradually becomes more diatonic and conventionally tuneful. The opening chorale returns re-harmonized to support both groups of melodic material, and the movement ends with a gradual thinning of the ensemble until only the xylophone is left playing variants of both its original material and the diatonic derivative.

Since this is something like the procedure I follow when planning a new composition, it follows that the conductor can replicate the procedure by creating a structural narrative of his or her own. It needs to be emphasized that the conductor's structural narrative can be quite different from mine. For me, this is the wonderful thing about analysis and interpretation. I trust conductors to have insights into the music that are illuminating for me, as well as for performers and listeners. The best conductors and performers take the music so deeply inside themselves that they supercede the composer. I have encountered this time and time again with regard to my own music and I rejoice in it.

After the creation of the structural narrative, along with identification of the main pitch and rhythm building blocks of the piece, the conductor of my music usually has a good idea of the overall flow. Pacing is a critical issue for performance and is affected by many factors. The acoustics of the concert space and the technical abilities of the players are the most important influences. To obtain clarity in a resonant space requires a slower pace and longer silences. Dry acoustics need a tightening up of the musical flow, since the lack of resonance makes it more difficult for the audience to establish good pitch and pattern memory. Players challenged by the musical requirements of a composition need to be supported with generous tempos and plenty of space between movements or sections. The finest players may need to be pushed to produce tension or excitement, if such is required by the music.

A constantly ebbing and flowing tempo suits much of my music. The exceptions are those pieces or movements using jazz or popular music idioms in which a steady pulse is important. My music relies on the communication of musical gesture and rhetoric. Since this is the nature of so much music from the seventeenth and eighteenth centuries, it follows that the conductor who is comfortable with the structural and expressive flow in the music of Rameau, C.P.E. Bach and Haydn will most likely be comfortable with my work. In other words, a conductor who is comfortable with all of Stravinsky, from the early to the late works, should find my music quite easy to present effectively.

But the conveyance of expression, or passion, is a difficult subject. The child's reaction to a musical passage—"it sounds happy," "it sounds sad,"—is unhelpful to conductors and players, I believe. If my music succeeds, it creates an emotional response in listeners that is beyond words. I am pleased when people say to me they were moved by my music, but find it hard to explain. Achieving the expression that lies beyond conventional language is one of my main goals. Beware of adjectives—*triumphant, martial, regretful, mournful, cheerful, frolicsome,* etc. —and treat the heart and mind as equals. The conductor who lets both heart and mind serve as compass will surely make the musical journey successfully.

E. The Relationship Between the Composer and the Commissioning Party

To be commissioned to create a new musical work is a great honor. I have been fortunate to be commissioned many times by many different musical organizations, including symphony orchestras, choruses, school bands, wind ensembles, recorder ensembles, and harpsichordists. In almost all cases, the relationship between the commissioning party and myself has been a comfortable one.

I think I can account for this happy state of affairs by listing my personal guidelines for commissioned projects:

1. Try to secure as much input from the commissioning party as possible, including details of instrumentation, technical

strengths or weaknesses of the performers, the type of audience that will hear the premiere, and the hopes and dreams of the commissioning party for the piece itself;
2. Keep the commissioning party informed of the progress of the work, notifying the party when actual composition begins, when individual movements are completed, when the score is completed, when the parts will be ready, etc.;
3. Always deliver the finished composition on time, or ahead of time.

With regard to financial matters, my preference is for the commissioning party to tell me how much money is available for the project. I can then decide whether I want to undertake the work for the offered amount. Of course, some commissioning groups or individuals prefer to have the composer quote a commission fee for a given work, and I am willing to do that, if necessary. Ideally, the commissioning party combines a financial offer with a detailed description of what the music might be. I am most comfortable working in that situation. In my non-commissioned works, I feel free to write whatever I want, so I do not mind accepting limits and guidelines from those who are willing to pay me to write a new work for them.

My normal procedure is to request one-third of the commission fee to be paid within thirty days of the signing of a commission agreement, with the balance of the fee to be paid within thirty days of receipt of the finished musical performance materials. When prospective commissioning parties ask me for further guidelines regarding commissions, I suggest that they obtain the pertinent publications from such groups as Meet the Composer and The American Music Center, which are very helpful. My commission agreements seldom run to more than two pages. I have also done a number of commissions for musicians whom I consider my friends. In such cases, a handshake was all that was needed to launch the project.

Perhaps I have been unusually fortunate, but I have been paid in full for all of my commissioned works, and only once in over thirty years did I experience a delay before receipt of payment. Whether professional or amateur, big-time or local, performer or patron, anyone who helps to bring new music into existence is on the side of the angels. I believe the best results come from a genuine partnership between the commissioning party and the composer.

F. Views on the Teaching of Composition and How to Mentor the Young Composer

I do not believe composition can be taught as an academic subject. What can be taught are such disciplines as analysis, counterpoint, orchestration, music history, world music, performance practice, and style. The best training consists of listening to as much music as possible, including one's own work, and studying scores and musical texts of all historical periods and cultures. One learns by doing, and the young composer with an original voice will do best by "doing music" as much as possible.

For the beginning composer, nothing is more helpful than interacting with performers during the rehearsal process, and then interacting with serious listeners after the music is played. Recordings of performances are also essential, so that repeated close listening can occur. Student composers lucky enough to find themselves at a university or conservatory where there are opportunities for performances of new student works have a real advantage. I was extremely fortunate to attend Northwestern University in the second half of the 1960's when the interest in new music, including student works, was very high. Many of my fellow students were happy to play and sing my music, and this was the best way for me to learn.

Regular attendance at professional concert events is also an essential part of a young composer's training. The compositional mentor, whether professor, colleague, or friend, should routinely point the student toward important concerts and recordings. In addition, the mentoring process should include plentiful discussion and conversation. The impossible task for composers, as well as poets, novelists, and painters—all creative artists— is to know everything. To the extent that the mentoring process helps even a little bit in making progress toward that goal—including the sharing of information about the "nuts and bolts" of score preparation, computer software, performing rights, copyright, and self-publishing—the young composer will benefit.

G. Individuals Who Have Been Especially Influential on My Development and Career

As mentioned previously, my childhood music teachers, Helen Antonides, with whom I studied piano and theory, and Jack Schwartz, who was my elementary school instrumental music teacher, launched me on the musical pathway. Both of them enjoyed the company of children, and both of them had professional credentials. They knew what they were doing, and helped me to learn the value of musical knowledge.

At Northwestern University, I was fortunate to study composition with M. William Karlins and Alan Stout. Bill

Karlins was from New York, and had a background of jazz saxophone playing and study with the great composer Stefan Wolpe. The composers of the so-called "New York" school—Bill Karlins, Rolv Yttrehus (the founding president of the Composers Guild of New Jersey), Ralph Shapey, Morton Feldman, and Miriam Gideon, among others—constitute a special group in American art music. I consider their works to be among the best produced in America during the second half of the twentieth century. The sound of their music is always with me.

Alan Stout knew everything about music. Through him I became aware of the new Polish music being created by Lutoslawski and Penderecki in the 1950's and 1960's. Because of Alan Stout I learned about period instrument practice and the new performance styles for seventeenth and eighteenth century music being developed by Nicholas Harnoncourt and the Concentus Musicus of Vienna.

Bill Karlins seemed to know everything about American Music, and Alan Stout seemed to know everything about European Music. What better tandem team could a student composer have in his corner?

Also at Northwestern I studied with two wonderful keyboard teachers: Dorothy Lane, professor of harpsichord, and Frances Larimer, professor of piano. Both of them were enthusiastic about new music, as well as the music of past centuries. Through them my love for keyboard music deepened.

Two of my Northwestern classmates have been valuable musical friends and colleagues ever since our first encounters in 1965. John Forbes, organist, master engraver, and editor, has had a hand in the preparation of many of my scores for publication. His beautiful engraving of a number of my works has given me great pleasure. Currently an editor at Boosey & Hawkes, John has provided enthusiastic support and a wealth of information for which I shall always be grateful. A wonderful pianist and harpsichordist, Paul Rey Klecka, became my roommate for two years at college, and was an eager performer of much of my student music. Paul has been living in Germany since the early 1970's, but he has remained a faithful supporter of my music, having played many performances of my keyboard music in recital and on German radio broadcasts. A beautiful compact disc recorded by Paul featuring the harpsichord music of Bill Karlins and myself was released in 1999.

In the summer of 1981 I spent several weeks studying the recorder with the late Bernard Krainis. The recorder is the only wind instrument I have continued to play (no embouchure—hooray!), and Bernie Krainis imparted many of the "secrets of the trade."

One of the founders of the Composers Guild of New Jersey, Robert Pollock—a fine composer and pianist—became a friend and valued colleague in the 1980's and 1990's. Robert studied with Roger Sessions and carried that tradition well. His and Sessions' music is far more rigorously organized than my own, and it sets standards for which I am always aiming. Robert's uncompromising devotion to serious concert music has been a great inspiration to me.

Since 1983 I have been rehearsing and performing in concert with a wonderful lutenist and guitarist, Francis Perry. Francis has inspired me to compose a number of works for or with guitar, and has taught me much about plucked string performance practice, including lute tablature. Since early harpsichord style grew directly from renaissance lute technique, Francis' playing has been an invaluable guide for authentic performance practice. Most importantly, he makes beautiful sounds whenever he plays.

For twenty-seven years I had the great fortune to work with the Rev. Donald Knight at the First Presbyterian Church in Belmar, New Jersey. Although Don had no formal music training, he loved music and was capable of powerful responses to pieces, both old and new. He and his wife Kathy were valuable members of the church choir and the inspiration for several works I composed to honor them. My experiences with church music have helped me keep in touch with the "real world"; Don and Kathy were my guides and enthusiastic supporters in many church music endeavors.

The makers of fine musical instruments are very special to me. I have been fortunate to encounter many of them, but the maker who has meant the most to me is the man who made my favorite instrument, a clavichord in late 18th century style (after the Schiedmayer clavichord in the Boston Museum of Fine Arts). His name is Carl Fudge. I took delivery of one of his beautiful instruments in 1985, and my life has never been the same.

Almost as important is the organ builder Gilbert Adams, who made the wonderful tracker-action organ at the Belmar Presbyterian Church. I had a small part in the design of this instrument, which was dedicated in 1979. Some organs are little more than machines, but the Belmar organ is as responsive as the best harpsichords. Gil Adam's organ has made me a better player, and for that I will always be grateful.

I have three brothers—two older (Carl and Bob), and one younger (Peter). They are all attorneys. It was Carl, during his later high school and college years, who introduced me to serious jazz, largely through his record collection, which included plenty of Miles Davis, Charles Mingus, Thelonious Monk, and Dave Brubeck. I learned that a vast world of recorded music was available to the avid listener. At the same time Carl provided access to great literature: the poets (Blake, Whitman, Yeats, Ginsburg) and novelists (Mann, Gide, Faulkner, Burroughs) who comprised so much of my student reading.

Almost all composers are at the mercy of a conductor, at least some of the time. Two wonderful instrumental ensemble conductors, Jack Stamp, of Indiana University of Pennsylvania, conductor of the Keystone Wind Ensemble, and Jack Delaney, of Southern Methodist University, conductor of the Meadows Wind Ensemble, have consistently given performances of my wind band works that please me in every way. They understand the stylistic worlds my music inhabits, and they are able to elicit wonderful playing from the musicians with which they work. Under their batons my music is presented in authentic fashion.

Music is a serious undertaking for me. How fortunate I have been in my career to receive so much guidance and support in my struggle to be a worthy practitioner of the art.

H. Ten Works I Believe All Band Conductors at All Levels Should Study

1. **J.S. Bach: *The Goldberg Variations* for solo keyboard instrument**

   I start the list with the greatest music ever composed. Whether played on harpsichord or piano, or arranged for instrumental ensemble, the *Goldberg Variations* operate at a level of structural and expressive invention that has never been surpassed. A simple formal procedure—variations over a ground bass—creates a melodic, rhythmic, and expressive universe. From small things grows a map of the human heart. All musicians—all people who love music—should know this work.

2. **Mozart: *Serenade in B flat major for 13 Wind Instruments, K. 361***

   As mentioned previously, the *Gran Partita* is both a superb example of the classical style and one of Mozart's finest works. The seven movements encompass most of the common forms of the later eighteenth century, and contain a wealth of superb melodies. Mastery of Mozartean style and understanding of *Harmoniemusik* are essentials for conductors.

3. **Stravinsky: *Symphonies of Wind Instruments***

   Just as Bach and Mozart are among the greatest eighteenth century composers, so Igor Stravinsky is one of the titans of twentieth century music. The *Symphonies,* a brief one-movement work cast as an elegy, is among the handful of genuine masterpieces for the wind ensemble.

4. **Stravinsky: *Le Sacre du Printemps (The Rite of Spring)***

   Most of twentieth century music comes out of this piece. Conductors who master this score should find much that comes after it easy to prepare.

5. **Debussy: *Jeux***

   The second fountainhead of modern music, Debussy reinvented form and rhythm in different ways than Stravinsky. *Jeux* is a brilliant and complex score, which repays endless study and frequent listening.

6. **Sibelius: *Symphony No. 6 in D minor, Op. 104***
   One of the first "polystylistic" works, this beautiful and enigmatic symphony is perhaps the most emotionally complex of the seven symphonies of Jean Sibelius. Beginning with somber renaissance counterpoint, the work moves through passages of great joy and great sorrow. Sibelius, like Stravinsky and Debussy, opened the door to modern music.
7. **Olivier Messiaen: *Chronochromie***
   This masterpiece for large orchestra is Messiaen's most tightly structured piece. Containing a wealth of rhythmic and textural complexities, it is nonetheless a highly communicative work. Absent are the annoying bird songs and perfumed harmonies that disfigure some of his works. Study of this score will aid the wind ensemble conductor when it is time to prepare Messiaen's masterpiece for winds and percussion, *Et Expecto Resurrectionem Mortuorum.*
8. **Benjamin Britten: *War Requiem***
   This large-scale oratorio is one of the greatest works of the second half of the twentieth century. Among its many treasures are brilliant text selection and setting, along with remarkably effective orchestration. The use of brass, in particular, is unforgettable. Britten was the greatest composer of vocal music with English texts since Henry Purcell.
9. **Edgar Varese: *Integrales***
   Varese was a composer for whom winds and percussion best served his purposes. *Integrales* is one of his most successful scores, and a truly original approach to the wind and percussion ensemble. It is music reduced to essential elements.

10. **Elliott Carter:** ***A Symphony of Three Orchestras***
    So much of twentieth century music comes together in this wonderful piece. For the conductor this work is one of the great challenges (it is performed with one conductor, not three). For the performer and listener, this is some of the most vibrant and fascinating music ever composed. To echo the above comments regarding Bach's *Goldberg Variations,* everyone with a serious interest in music should know the works of Elliott Carter.

I. Ten Composers Whose Music Overall Speaks to Me in Especially Meaningful Ways

Not necessarily the composers I consider the greatest who ever lived (although some of them are), these ten composers have created works which have become a special part of my life. I have not included the name of Johann Sebastian Bach, since he is beyond category, and unquestionably my favorite composer.

1. **Johann-Jakob Froberger**
   This cosmopolitan seventeenth century keyboard composer—born in Austria, widely traveled in Italy, Germany, France and England—united both the Italian tradition (*toccatas, canzonas, fantasias, ricercares*) and the French (*suites* and unmeasured *preludes*). I find his music very rewarding to play. His contrapuntal mastery and harmonic invention work well on harpsichord, clavichord, or organ.
2. **Jean-Philippe Rameau**
   The greatest French composer of the eighteenth century, Rameau excelled as a composer of operas, chamber music, and keyboard music. I love his mastery of the traditional

French forms, his innovative harmonies, and his beautiful vocal writing.

3. **Carl Philipp Emanuel Bach**

   One of the composer sons of Sebastian Bach, Carl Emanuel is perhaps the greatest composer of clavichord music. He is a fascinating transitional figure who bridges the late baroque and the early classical periods. In addition, he is a delightful and inventive composer of chamber music, symphonies, and concertos. His simple yet eloquent (and enigmatic) late style has been a major influence on my work.

4. **Joseph Haydn**

   Haydn, Mozart, or Beethoven? How to choose from the three greatest masters of the classical era? For me, Haydn's endless invention and emotional directness win out. I rejoice in the string quartets, the symphonies, the piano trios, and, of course, the wonderful keyboard divertimenti and sonatas.

5. **Anton Bruckner**

   I am utterly transported by the symphonies and motets of Bruckner. While not much of a fan of German romanticism, I find Bruckner incomparable. I love all the symphonies, but Number Eight is my favorite. His scherzos are a music unlike any other.

6. **Charles Ives**

   The transcendental fire that burns through so much of Ives' output may be the best thing about his music, but I am also deeply affected by his stylistic diversity, his incredible emotional range, and his brilliant experiments in texture and rhythm. My favorite pieces: *The Concord Sonata for piano, Symphony No. 4, Three Places in New England,* and *The Robert Browning Overture.*

7. **Duke Ellington**
   I love how the Duke treated his band and his music as one and the same, and how he created a body of work along with his brilliant sidekick Billy Strayhorn that has become a part of the American musical vernacular. The songs are "bread and butter" for jazz improvisers, and the larger pieces, especially the suites, demonstrate a kind of formal organization—never far from the blues—that is delightfully liberated from the European tradition.
8. **Benjamin Britten**
   When I was at university, Britten was rather out of fashion with American academic composers. But I had already fallen in love with his music in my early teen years. (See my previous comments about his *War Requiem.*) I consider Britten the finest opera composer of the twentieth century, and the finest composer of song cycles since Schubert. His *String Quartet No. 3* is one of my favorite pieces. The mastery of *passacaglia* form demonstrated in it, and in many of his scores, is unique and wondrous.
9. **Dmitri Shostakovich**
   Fifteen symphonies, fifteen string quartets, preludes and fugues for piano, concertos, operas, song cycles, even film scores—what a prodigious output, and what extraordinary quality for so much music. One of the things that has brought joy to my musical heart is the way Shostakovich's music has been taken into the standard repertory, after being dismissed for many years as Soviet Union hackwork. I confess I like him best when he is most bitterly sarcastic in his music, or most profoundly sad.

10. **Morton Feldman**

It seems to me that America's best composers—Ives, Ellington, Elliott Carter, John Cage—sound like no one else. And absolutely no one sounds like Morton Feldman. Showing a respect for the ear worthy of Webern, Feldman's music is the closest thing I know to abstract expressionism, my favorite kind of painting. Listening to Feldman is like viewing the paintings of Jackson Pollock, Mark Rothko, Franz Kline, Barnett Newman, Hans Hofmann—in a word, heaven.

The arbitrary size of this list leaves no room for Frescobaldi, Monteverdi, Louis Couperin, Francois Couperin, Elizabeth Jacquet de la Guerre, Henry Purcell, Vivaldi, Handel, Domenico Scarlatti, Schubert, Schumann, Brahms, Sibelius (all seven symphonies and the tone poems!), Schoenberg, Webern, Bartok, Ravel, Roger Sessions, Stefan Wolpe, Vincent Persichetti, John Cage, Pauline Oliveros, Tippett, Henze, Dallapiccola, Nono, Takemitsu, Boulez, Birtwistle, Alfred Schnittke, Steve Reich, Gil Evans, Wayne Shorter—the list goes on and on.

J. The Future of the Wind Band

I believe the wind band (or wind orchestra) has a glorious future ahead of it, especially if certain problem areas are improved.

Most important to me is the quality of music programmed. Too many times I have attended wind band concerts in which many of the pieces were mediocre at best. It is not uncommon to encounter truly meretricious music on wind band programs.

Surely by now there is such a wealth of good to excellent music for winds and percussion that performance of third-rate pieces cannot be justified. Equally important is a greater flexibility with regard to instrumentation. Unlike the symphony orchestra, which seldom has the same number of players on stage for an entire concert, the wind band too often seems imprisoned by its instrumentation. There seems to be reluctance on the part of some conductors to use only a fraction of the ensemble members. The primary concern, I believe, should be for the audience. The greater the variety of sound that is presented, the greater the enjoyment for the listeners. Concerts should be programmed with care for historical periods, stylistic diversity, and timbral variety. The use of soloists in concertos is also necessary for effectively diverse programming.

Wind band conductors need to be more adventurous. Too many wind and percussion concerts are mired in traditional tonality. The world of music has long since moved past nineteenth century hymnbook harmonies. There is nothing wrong with non-tonal or non-metrical music. Scores with open forms and aleatoric procedures are rewarding for performers and listeners alike. There is good and bad music composed in all styles and genres. I fervently hope that a new generation of wind band conductors will be willing to become part of the contemporary music world, seeking out the most rewarding new music to complement the best of what has gone before.

With regard to the technical abilities of today's wind band musicians, I am in awe. The level of technical execution on wind instruments has never been higher, and today's percussionists routinely perform in a manner undreamed of fifty years ago. I have encountered middle school bands that sound like superb high school groups, high school ensembles as fine as many university bands, and college ensembles indistinguishable from professional groups. Upon this technical foundation a great musical edifice will be erected. I dream of concerts in fine acoustic settings filled with the music of Mozart, Haydn, Richard Strauss, Dvorak, Gustav Holst, Vaughn Williams, Messiaen, Persichetti, Warren Benson, Varese, and Stravinsky, along with the best and boldest contemporary works from around the world.

K. Other Facets of My Everyday Life

I could not compose or play keyboard music all the time, even if I wanted to. The mind needs diversion. One must get out of doors.

In the warm months I grow organic vegetables in the backyard garden. Late afternoon usually finds me at the beach for a relaxing swim. I often break up the day's work with a bicycle ride of several miles or a long walk.

On the Shrewsbury River nearby my brother Robert and I keep our sixteen-foot sailboat, *Tom Cat.* Many of my compositions first floated into my head during long sails during spring, summer, or fall. I recommend sailing to all composers and musicians.

I read whenever I can. Poetry and fiction are my main interests, but I also read books on music, cinema, wine and food, travel, sports, and socialism. I am a great fan of serious movies, which I consider to be the greatest of all art forms. My list of favorite filmmakers includes Buster Keaton, Charlie Chaplin, Eisenstein, Renoir, John Ford, Howard Hawkes, Orson Welles, Joseph Losey, Truffaut, Godard, Andrei Tarkovsky,

Ingmar Bergman, Ozu, Fellini, Andre Techine, Tsai Ming-liang, Abbas Kiarostami, Robert Altman, and Frederick Wiseman. As one might guess, I don't care much for contemporary Hollywood movies. Baseball and soccer are my favorite professional sports.

Cities are one of my greatest enthusiasms. Although I live at the Jersey shore, I find cities to be always invigorating and inspiring. My favorite American cities are Boston, Chicago, and San Francisco, but when I say "the city," of course I mean New York. The museums, restaurants, movie theaters, concert halls, parks, broad avenues and quirky side streets, diverse neighborhoods, "unique" subway system, baseball stadiums (Go Mets!): I love them all.

My three brothers, their wives and children, my mother, and an aunt all live in New Jersey: our family is close-knit and frequently together. The congregations at the two churches where I play are an extended family as well, including many good friends. None seem to mind what I am or what I do (I try to behave).

I attend concerts whenever I can, not out of "professional" duty or interest, but because I love live music, and I try to perform in concert at least a few times every year. Music fills much of the time that others might reserve for hobbies: the care, feeding, and maintenance of harpsichords, clavichords, recorders, and organs (and teddy bears, but that's another story) are deeply rewarding. Time flies.

L. Comprehensive List of Works for Band

Sinfonia II (1972)

Gr.3 6' Manhattan Beach Music (rental)

Sinfonia III "Hymns & Dances" (1972)

Gr.5 10' Manhattan Beach Music

Commissioned by H. Robert Reynolds for the University of Wisconsin Wind Ensemble; Premiered 1973, Madison, Wisconsin, H. Robert Reynolds, conductor

Sinfonia IV "Suite for Winds & Percussion" (1972)

Gr.2 5' Hal Leonard (out of print)

Southern Suite (1972)

Gr.2 5' Hal Leonard (out of print)

The Headless Horseman (1973)

Gr.2 2' Manhattan Beach

Sinfonia V "Symphonia Sacra et Profana" (1973)

Gr.5 7' Manhattan Beach

Commissioned by the University City High School Wind Ensemble; Premiered 1974 University City, Missouri, John Kuzmich, Jr., conductor

The Child and the Kings (1973) (revised 1995)

Gr.2.5 4' Daehn Publications

Rhythm Machine (1974)

Gr.2 4' Bourne Co.

Sinfonia VI (1974)

Gr. 2.5 7' Manhattan Beach

Three Pieces for American Band, Set No. 1 (1974)

Gr.5 6' Bourne Co. (rental)

Blue Goose Rag (1975)
(arrangement of piano rag by Raymond Birch)

Gr.2	3'	Manhattan Beach

Serenade for Percussion & Band (1975)

Gr.2.5	4'	Bourne Co.

Sinfonia VII "The Continental Saxophone" (1975)

Gr.5	12'	Manhattan Beach (rental)

Commissioned for the U.S. Bicentennial Celebration by Southern Illinois University, Edwardsville; Premiered 1976, Edwardsville, Illinois; Southern Illinois University Wind Ensemble; Alan McMurray, conductor

Concert Piece for Trumpet & Band (1975)

Gr.4 (solo)	5'	Daehn Publications
Gr. 2 (band)		

Streets & Inroads (1976)

Gr.2	4'	Manhattan Beach

Sinfonia IX "Concert in the Park" (1977)

Gr.4	10'	Manhattan Beach

Commissioned by the Friends of John Rafoth; Premiered 1978, Madison, Wisconsin

Three Pieces for American Band, Set No. 2 (1978)

Gr.3	7'	Bourne Co.

Commissioned by Gilbert S. Lance Middle School; Premiered Kenosha, Wisconsin 1979; Larry Simons, conductor

Pentatonic Variations for Piano & Band ("One Week") (1979)

Gr.4 (solo)	6'	Manhattan Beach (rental)
Gr.2.5 (band)		

Commissioned by Cherokee Heights Middle School; Premiered 1979 Madison, Wisconsin; Karen Becker, piano soloist

Serenata for Trumpet & Band (1981)

Gr.3 (solo)	6'	Bourne Co.
Gr.2.5 (band)		

Sinfonia XII "Southern Heart/Sacred Harp" (1984)

Gr.5	14'	Manhattan Beach (rental)

Commissioned by the Campbell University Wind Ensemble; Premiered Buies Creek, North Carolina 1985; Jack Stamp, conductor

Sinfonia XIII "Storm Variations" (1985)

Gr.4	18'	Bourne Co. (rental)

Commissioned by the Oconomowoc High School Symphonic Band; Premiered 1986 Oconomowoc, Wisconsin; Dennis Glocke, conductor

Sinfonia XIV "Three Canzonas" (1986)

Gr.5	9'	Manhattan Beach (rental)

Commissioned by the Hanover College Wind Ensemble; Premiered 1987 Hanover, Indiana; Jon Mitchell, conductor

The Diamond Rule (1987)

Gr.4.5	5'	Allaire Music

Sinfonia XV "Ursa Major" (1987)

Gr.5	12'	Manhattan Beach (rental)

Commissioned by the Gamma Phi Chapter, Kappa Kappa Psi, Stephen F. Austin State University; Premiered 1990 Nagodoches, Texas; John Whitwell, conductor

No Sun, No Shadow "Elegy for Charles Mingus" (1987)

Gr.6	28'	Allaire Music (rental)

Commissioned by the Emory University Wind Ensemble; Premiered 1988 Atlanta, Georgia; Jack Delaney, conductor

Dreams & Fancies (1988)

Gr.2.5	7'	Hal Leonard

Peace Song (1989)

Gr.2.5	5'	Bourne Co.

Sinfonia XVI "Transcendental Vienna" (1989)

Gr.4 8' Manhattan Beach

Commissioned by the Thoreau Intermediate School Symphonic Band; Premiered 1990 Vienna, Virginia; Richard Sanger, conductor

Sinfonia XVII "The Four Winds" (1989)

Gr.3 9' Manhattan Beach

Commissioned by the Charles D. Evans Junior High School Band & Orchestra Boosters; Premiered Ottumwa, Iowa 1990

Jody "Variations on a Texas Work Song" (1989)

Gr.2.5 5' Manhattan Beach

Commissioned by Lincoln Middle School Band; Premiered 1991 Abilene, Texas

Concerto for Piano & Wind Orchestra (1990)

Gr.6 29' Allaire Music (rental)

Commissioned by the California State University-Fullerton Wind Ensemble; Premiered 1990 Fullerton, California; Mary Mark Zeyen, piano soloist; Mitch Fennell, conductor

Concerto for Marimba & Wind Orchestra (1991)

Gr.6 25' Allaire Music (rental)

Commissioned by the University of Washington Wind Ensemble; Premiered 1994 Reno, Nevada; Robert Meunier, marimba; Timothy Salzman, conductor

Grizzly Bear Rag (1993)

Gr.2.5 4' Daehn Publications

Theme & Variations (1993)

Gr.1 3' Manhattan Beach

Sonata for Wind Band (after C.P.E. Bach) (1993)

Gr.3 6' Daehn Publications

Sinfonia XVIII "Aurora" (1995)
Gr.5 10' manuscript
Commissioned by the Waubonsie Valley High School Wind Ensemble; Premiered 1996 Aurora, Illinois; Charles Staley, Jr., conductor

Freedom's Necessary Tones (1995)
Gr.2.5 5' Manhattan Beach

Three Preludes (1995)
(arrangements of organ preludes by Anton Bruckner)
Gr.3 6' Daehn Publications

Train Heading West & Other Outdoor Scenes (1997)
Gr.1.5 4' Manhattan Beach

America Verses (1997)
Gr.3 6' Manhattan Beach

Procession & Torch Dance (1997)
Gr.2 3' Daehn Publications

The Waukesha Rondo ("Rhythm Games") (1998)
Gr.3.5 8' Manhattan Beach
Commissioned by the Central Middle School Band; Premiered 1999 Waukesha, Wisconsin; Laura Katz Sindberg, conductor

Sinfonia XIX "Preludes & Grounds" (1998)
Gr.3 8' Boosey & Hawkes
Commissioned by the Berwick Middle School Band; Premiered 1999 Berwick, Pennsylvania; Brian Fish, conductor

Narrative, Ground & Variations (1999)
Gr.3.5 8' manuscript
Commissioned by the Thoreau Middle School Symphonic Band; Premiered 1990 Vienna, Virginia; Richard Sanger, conductor

Mysterian Landscapes (2000)

Gr.4 7' Boosey & Hawkes

Commissioned by the Bald Eagle High School Band; Premiered 2001 Bald Eagle, Pennsylvania; Casey Teske, conductor

El Jardin de Esperanza (The Garden of Hope) (2000)

Gr.4 7' manuscript

Commissioned by Northern Valley Regional High School-Old Tappan; Premiered 2001 Old Tappan, New Jersey; Kurt Ebersole, conductor

Sinfonia XXI (2000)

Gr.6 20' manuscript

Commissioned by Jack Stamp for the Keystone Wind Ensemble; Premiered 2001 Denton, Texas; Jack Stamp, conductor

Slow March with Celebration (2000)

Gr.2 5' Boosey & Hawkes

Commissioned by the St. Anthony Middle School 7th Grade Band; Premiered 2001 St. Anthony Village, Minnesota; Christian Ravndal, conductor

Three Pieces for American Band, Set No. 3 (2001)

Gr.6 13' manuscript

Commissioned by the U.S. Military Academy Band; Premiered 2001 West Point, New York; Lt.Col. David Deitrick, conductor

Song With Variations (2001)

Gr.2.5 3' Daehn Publications

Grand Festival Music (2001)

Gr.4 15' manuscript

Commissioned by Kenosha Unified School District No. 1 for Band-O-Rama 2002; Premiered 2002 Kenosha, Wisconsin; John Whitwell, conductor

Charlotte Doyle's Voyage (2001)

Gr.2.5 9' manuscript

Commissioned by the J.T. Lambert Intermediate School 7th & 8th Grade Band; Premiered 2002 East Stroudsburg, Pennsylvania; Kimberly Conklin, conductor

Surfboard Blues (2002)

Gr.2.5 4' Daehn Publications

chapter 3

mark Camphouse

A. Biography

Mark Camphouse is Professor of Music and Director of Bands at Radford University in Virginia, a position he has held since 1984. Prior to his appointment at Radford, Professor Camphouse held similar faculty positions at universities in Illinois (Blackburn College), Minnesota (St. Cloud State University), and Oklahoma (University of Oklahoma). While on leave from Radford during the 1998-99 academic year, Mr. Camphouse served a one-year appointment as Acting Dean of Music at New World School of the Arts in Miami, Florida.

A native Chicagoan born in Oak Park, Illinois in 1954, Mr. Camphouse completed his high school education a year early and went on to receive his formal musical training at Northwestern University, where he received the Bachelor of Music degree in 1975 and Master of Music degree in 1976. His principal teachers at Northwestern included Vincent Cichowicz (trumpet), John P. Paynter (conducting), and Alan Stout (composition). During his third and final year of high school, Camphouse was awarded a Chicago Civic Orchestra scholarship, which enabled him to study trumpet privately for two years with legendary Chicago Symphony Orchestra principal, Adolph Herseth.

Camphouse began composing at an early age, with the Colorado Philharmonic premiering his *First Symphony* at age 17. Principal commissions include those by the John P. Paynter Foundation, William D. Revelli Foundation, The United States Army Band ("Pershing's Own"), The United States Marine Band ("The President's Own"), Florida Bandmasters Association, and some of America's finest college and high school wind bands.

Mr. Camphouse won the 15th Annual National Band Association (NBA) composition contest in 1991, and was runner-up in both the 1986 and 1989 American Bandmasters Association (ABA) Ostwald competitions. His works have been performed in such prestigious venues as Carnegie Hall, The Kennedy Center, Orchestra Hall-Chicago, Royal Albert Hall-London, and conferences of the World Association for Symphonic Bands and Ensembles (WASBE), College Band Directors National Association (CBDNA), Music Educators National Conference (MENC), American Bandmasters Association, and the Midwest International Band and Orchestra Clinic.

His works for wind band are published by Kjos, Southern, and TRN music companies. They have received widespread critical acclaim and are performed frequently throughout the U.S. and abroad. Many may be heard on the Albany, Citadel, and Summit labels. Engagements as a guest conductor, clinician, and lecturer have taken him to 38 states, Canada, and Europe. He was co-founder of the New Mexico Music Festival at Taos, where he served as Music Director and Conductor of the Festival Symphony Orchestra and Wind Ensemble for five summer seasons (1978-1982). He also served for four summers as Associate Director and Music Division Head of the Virginia Governor's School for the Arts (1986-1989), and as Music Director and Conductor of the New River Chamber Winds from 1993-1997.

Mr. Camphouse was elected to membership in the American Bandmasters Association in 1999. He has served as coordinator of the National Band Association Young Composer Mentor Project since its inception in 2000. He received the 1991 Radford University Dedmon Award for Professorial Excellence (Radford's highest faculty honor), and in 1992 attained regional finalist status in the prestigious White House Fellowship Competition. Virginia Governor Mark Warner presented Professor Camphouse with a 2002 Outstanding Faculty Award, sponsored by the State Council of Higher Education for Virginia (SCHEV). This award is the Commonwealth's highest honor for faculty at Virginia's colleges and universities for demonstrated excellence in teaching, research, and public service.

Mr. Camphouse has been married to soprano Elizabeth Ann Curtis since 1982. They live in Radford with their twin 15-year-old daughters, Beth and Briton.

B. The Creative Process

Staring at a blank sheet of manuscript paper as I am about to begin sketching a new work is simultaneously a rather terrifying moment as well as an exhilarating one.

All aspects of my professional work (score study, class preparation, correspondence, and composing) arc done during the early morning hours, usually between 5:00-10:00 AM, in my office at school, never at home. Office equals work. Home equals family. In spite of that clear distinction, it is at times rather difficult to maintain a desirable balance between work and family.

The process, manner, and environment in which a composer chooses to work is simply a matter of finding what works best for them. All aspects of my creative work (composing and orchestration) are done the old-fashioned way. My basic equipment includes, ideally: a freshly tuned, real piano—not some ghastly electronic imposter, a handful of freshly sharpened number two pencils, a generous stack of freshly opened manuscript paper, and a pot of freshly brewed high-test coffee which, in the not so good old days, would be frequently accompanied by not-so-fresh Marlboro Light cigarettes...flip-top box, of course.

I do not use machines during any part of the creative process. In fact, it took me until the fall of 2000 to finally allow a computer to occupy my office for e-mail and word processing. I have a lingering reputation, especially among my Radford University faculty colleagues, of being a technological dinosaur. Guilty as charged, for the most part! I am in good company, however. It is interesting to note that the distinguished American author/historian David McCullough, who won the 2002 Pulitzer Prize for biography (his second such award over the years) uses a manual, yes—*manual* typewriter for his work. Now there is a real dinosaur...and a truly brilliant and scholarly one, at that! My using an IBM Selectric II typewriter (circa 1976) makes me, by comparison a bona fide technophile!

If a work is programmatic, the composer needs to do some homework in order to gain some basic familiarity with its extra-musical aspects. Sometimes, the composer must dig deeper, and engage in more substantive research. For example, in trying to better understand the many disturbing complexities of child abuse and neglect (the topic of my work entitled *Watchman, Tell Us Of The Night*), I spent an entire afternoon with a very impressive program and policy specialist with the National Center on Child Abuse and Neglect in the U. S. Department of Health and Human Services in Washington, DC. I returned home with countless volumes of reports, studies, and statistics about violence against children which helped me gain a much better understanding of what I now view as nothing less than a societal disgrace. Indeed, child abuse and neglect is a national tragedy of epidemic proportion.

Research for my six-movement *Symphony From Ivy Green* for soprano and wind orchestra about the extraordinary life of American humanist Helen Keller was truly fascinating. The research included visits to her birthplace, home, and church in Tuscumbia, Alabama, and interviews with some of her direct descendants.

A visit to the Ronald Reagan Presidential Library and Museum in Simi Valley, California proved to be the major impetus in my decision to create a work for narrator and symphonic band that portrays President Reagan's vision of America. Entitled *The Shining City,* the narrator's text is drawn from nine of Reagan's speeches (four while president, five post-presidential) and his very moving November 1994 letter of farewell to the American people. My rather sizeable home library of presidential biography includes nearly 30 books on the life and presidency of Ronald Reagan alone. These were especially valuable in the area of text selection and its accuracy.

With the possible exception of *Symphony From Ivy Green,* I cannot recall beginning any of my works—programmatic or non-programmatic—with a preconceived mold of the work's form or structure. I feel strongly that the work's musical material should determine form or structure and that there be harmonious coexistence between the work's intellectual and emotional elements. These two elements must evolve simultaneously, and blossom naturally. They cannot be forced.

After engaging in any necessary extra-musical research, the first of three major steps I take utilizing musical notation involves generating rough—and I mean very rough—initial sketches. In examining the file to my work honoring John P. Paynter entitled *Whatsoever Things,* there are 21 pages of sketches which, to me, now resemble unintelligible hieroglyphics. The sketches were made over a three-week period, between May 15 and June 3, 1996.

The second step is perhaps the single most important. It is putting things together by organizing, developing, and refining the best material from the sketches, in the form of a fairly clean, 3-stave quasi piano score. My records indicate the piano score of *Whatsoever Things* was written over a two week period: June 4-19, 1996.

As with all my works for band, the final, fully orchestrated manuscript score is a concert pitch, or "C" score. When playing orchestral trumpet parts, transposition was always a necessary evil, but never an overly problematic one. While orchestrating, however, transpositions become an unpleasant hassle, which I find rather distracting in what is one of the most important and most individualistic aspects of the entire creative process.

When I complete the fully orchestrated concert pitch score, I make several photocopies, (pencil reproduces very well on today's copiers) and send one off to my copyist, Douglas Richard, a very gifted member of the arranging staff of the United States Military Academy (West Point) Band. Douglas works his magic on Finale with astonishing accuracy and brevity, and generates a fully transposed score and extracts a complete set of parts.

Orchestration is an art in itself. It is very intricate work, and it has to be just right. As a result, for me, orchestration becomes the most laborious and, by far the most time-consuming part of the creative process. Miscalculations in orchestration can be deadly! I am always amazed when I hear that some composers claim to be able to compose or orchestrate on planes, in hotel rooms, or at home while watching television. The orchestration of *Whatsoever Things* (a 247-measure work having a duration of approximately 14 minutes) occurred over a three and a half month period: September 3 through December 18, 1996.

Composers must possess good proofreading and editing skills. Thoroughly proofing the score and set of parts prior to the works initial reading and/or publication, while rather uninspiring and very time-consuming work, is an absolutely essential final step in the creative process.

C. The Approach to Orchestration

The most revealing glimpse of a composer's soul can be found in his/her harmonic vocabulary. The second most revealing—and a very close second—is of the composer's use of instrumental color and concept of texture via the art of orchestration.

I both compose and orchestrate at the piano. When time permits, I like to generate a well-organized piano score of my sketches prior to beginning work on oversized score paper. I am, however from the very outset of my sketches always thinking about and "hearing" instrumental colors and textures.

The orchestration process is therefore both an integral and virtually simultaneous part of the creative process.

There are many fine orchestration texts available today. If my memory serves me correctly, I purchased my first orchestration text (Nikolai Rimsky-Korsakov's *Principles of Orchestration)* for $4.00 in 1968 as a high school freshman. I find *The Technique of Orchestration* by Kent Kennan and Donald Grantham to be especially helpful in introducing basic scoring concepts to my students. I am also extremely impressed with the recently published third edition of Samuel Adler's *The Study of Orchestration.* However, the best orchestration texts, by far, remain the actual scores of the works by the great composers.

In looking over my college transcript, I apparently was never enrolled in an orchestration or arranging class, per se. But I do vividly recall regularly carrying mountainous stacks of scores and recordings from the Northwestern University School of Music library to my dorm room. So when people ask with whom did I study orchestration, I pause, then smile, and reply (truthfully) that I studied orchestration with Britten, Copland, Ives, Mahler, Respighi, Vaughan Williams, etc., etc.!

Wind band directors need not necessarily re-enroll at a nearby college or university with professors x or y to study orchestration. By purchasing or borrowing scores and recordings, the wind band director can study orchestration with symphonic masters like Berlioz, Strauss, and Debussy, or (if you prefer) especially fine orchestrators for the wind band like Warren Benson, Percy Grainger, and Vincent Persichetti. The musical growth of the director as a result of studying the music of the great composers via scores and recordings can have a very beneficial effect on all aspects of the (director's) school band program.

I believe the time I invested over the years making music as a player—directly immersed in the sound from the vantage point of the trumpet section of symphony orchestras, wind bands, or brass quintets—was tremendously valuable in helping me develop an understanding of and appreciation for balances and interesting instrumental colors and textures. Textural sameness and blocked, one-size-fits-all scoring, whether for wind band or symphony orchestra, is dreadfully boring.

I recall very often bringing scores of works being rehearsed into the rehearsal, enabling me (during long rests and movements in which the trumpets were tacet) to follow and better understand what was happening sonically and structurally, and how this was (or sometimes was not!) being communicated to the players by the conductor.

Composing and orchestrating my first work for band in 1980 (I had composed four previous orchestral works) made one thing extremely clear to me, and that is that composing and orchestrating effectively for band is far more difficult than composing and orchestrating for symphony orchestra. Why is this? I believe the answer is quite simple. We miss tremendously that wonderfully warm, sustaining, homogeneous body of instruments from the string family. When composing for band, composers must indeed be prepared to be as creative with their orchestration skills as they are with their compositional technique. I have also found composing and orchestrating a Grade 3 or 4 work for high school band to be far more challenging than composing and orchestrating a Grade 5 or 6 work for a college, university, or professional military band.

I believe the special challenges inherent in scoring for the wind band are at least partially responsible for major 20th century composers like Aaron Copland, David Diamond, Paul Hindemith, Peter Mennin, and Walter Piston leaving us with so few works for band—fine works, certainly—but clearly not their best works. By contrast, other major 20th century composers such as Warren Benson, Morton Gould, Karel Husa, Vincent Persichetti, and Gunther Schuller took time (thankfully!) to develop an understanding of the band, and became quite inventive in their approach to scoring for it. As a result, their works for band are among some of the finest in their catalogs.

Although I came to write and score for the wind band through a solid foundation in orchestral traditions, I wish to cite several composers closely associated with the wind band as being especially influential in my developing some individuality—quasi sonic "fingerprints," if you will—with my wind band orchestration. They are Vincent Persichetti, for his rich, dark, organ-like sonorities and (sectional) clarity; the inventive, thick, and reedy textures of Percy Grainger; and the always fresh sounding brilliance of John Barnes Chance and Fisher Tull.

Young composers and arrangers who are serious about learning how to score effectively for band can learn a great deal by studying the fine, always very well crafted orchestration in works by Clare Grundman, Gordon Jacob, and Alfred Reed.

Some of my favorite color combinations include rich and sonorous passages in low-middle register clarinet with mid-upper register euphonium, lyrical solo flute and solo trumpet lines in octaves, and especially unison horn lines in their upper register. I feel it is important to try to provide some exposed and interesting passages for players on inner parts, such as bass clarinet and tenor saxophone. I also believe that the pianoforte should become a tasteful, essentially regular member of the wind band percussion section. Virtually every school and most band rooms in America have at least one available piano and, better still, someone in the band is quite probably a capable pianist. Clearly, the percussion section of the wind band has experienced extraordinary growth in the areas of size, sounds, and assignment of important thematic material. Composers must use great care in the area of chord voicing and spacing when scoring for band. This is particularly important in avoiding muddiness in low brass and low reed parts.

Some final thoughts: Have you noticed there has increasingly become a kind of both sonic and stylistic sameness among our leading American professional symphony orchestras? There used to be wonderful, individualistic and clearly recognizable differences in sound and style among our orchestras. The Boston Symphony had a certain characteristic sound and style, as did the Cleveland and Philadelphia Orchestras, the Chicago Symphony, etc. And composers were very aware of those differences in characteristic sound while orchestrating their (commissioned) works for those orchestras.

Today's increasing sameness in sound and style has produced a quasi "corporate" approach that seems to discourage individuality. This approach has really caught on among many leading orchestral players and studio teachers throughout the U.S. The end result has made orchestras less interesting to listen to, both in live and recorded performances.

There have been major changes in both the roles and expectations of the music director of today's professional symphony orchestras. The temptation of lucrative global guest conducting engagements and multiple (frequently intercontinental) music directorships, have significantly diminished the music director's podium time and ability to cultivate and refine a distinctly characteristic sound and style with a single 'home' orchestra. There has also been a corresponding diminishment, seemingly, in the ability and willingness of the music director to have a visible and meaningful presence while serving the cultural and educational needs of the community.

I hope we will never experience a sameness or quasi "corporate" approach that discourages individuality in the art of orchestration. This would be very detrimental to the joy of celebrating every composer's unique individuality in orchestration—an art that must always remain among the most highly personalized aspects of the creative process.

D. Views from the Composer to the Conductor Pertaining to Score Study and Preparation

Preparation

The conductor must do a fair amount of homework before even thinking about setting foot on the podium. The conductor should first engage in some basic research on the work and the composer. This (initial) research need not be of the highly detailed or "scholarly" variety, but simply a practical, common sense gathering of essential information about the work and the composer. Of course, I strongly encourage the conductor to dig increasingly deeper with research as the score study process unfolds.

If necessary, listen to a recording of the work (ideally, more than one, if possible) with score in hand. Re-confirm with yourself that it is a work you believe in, and that the time you and your students will invest in its preparation will be time well spent, and will contribute to the musical enrichment of your students, yourself, and to your audiences. Then lock the recording away for a good while and study the score the "old-fashioned" way.

Make initial determinations (lightly, in pencil) about melodic and harmonic content, which often lead the conductor toward a discovery of the work's overall structure and form. Be on the lookout for how the composer is developing his/her musical ideas, i.e. motivically, melodically, rhythmically, harmonically, etc. Sing through what appear to be principal melodic lines. Visit the piano and become better acquainted with the harmonic content and how it relates to the melodic material. Have a consultation with a metronome.

Get out some manuscript paper and write down some of the melodic material, and be sure to include dynamics and articulations. This approach is closely related to the one Vincent Cichowicz used in teaching orchestral excerpts to his trumpet students. He would encourage us to first obtain a score to the work to enable us to see how the (trumpet) part fit into context with the rest of the orchestra. Then, we would write the passage out by hand. (I have an entire notebook of manuscript orchestral trumpet excerpts.) As a result of writing down those trumpet excerpts, today—nearly 30 years later—I can still play virtually all of them from memory. Writing down the principal melodic material gives the conductor more of a sense of "ownership" of the work. And, of course it stands to reason that the conductor's understanding and retention of melodic shape and direction will be enhanced.

Some conductors find charting a piece (measure-by-measure, section-by-section) to be a helpful and effective way to study and prepare a score. This is fine, and as they say, "whatever works," but I have always had a bit of an aversion to that rather tedious method, primarily because it is not generally the way most composers go about creating and organizing their music. One of my guiding principles as a composer/conductor is this: when composing and orchestrating, think like a conductor; when conducting, think like a composer.

After investing a good amount of time in "old-fashioned" score study, (it is impossible to specify the number of hours, days, or weeks required to gain a solid initial understanding of the work) go back and listen to a recording(s) and see if you find that some of your perspectives about the music have changed.

Is it healthy for the conductor to listen to a recording(s) of the work? Yes, of course it is, but in limited doses. I feel that any conductor who claims to not consult recordings is either not very bright or is a liar, or possibly both! It is terribly important, however, that the conductor takes pride in the realization that his/her performance reflects his/her interpretation of the work.

Have there ever been times where circumstances prevented me from being well prepared at a rehearsal of a particular piece, causing me to "wing-it" in the rehearsal? The answer is yes, maybe a handful of times over the past 25 years. While I suppose having a 'wing-it' rehearsal once every five years, on average, constitutes a still pretty decent batting average, I can still remember a couple of those rehearsals, and although I probably "winged-it" quite well and probably fooled at least most of my students, I felt a bit "dirty" afterwards, both personally and professionally. We must make sure that under-prepared rehearsals by the conductor are the great exception to the rule of thorough preparation.

Good score preparation provides the solid foundation that enables the conductor to function effectively both as a musician and as a teacher. Only through thorough score preparation will a conductor be able to fulfill his/her most important responsibility: to be, as Maestro Erich Leinsdorf said, "the composer's advocate."

There are two especially fine books which are very beneficial for directors at all levels who are interested in improving their skills in the areas of score preparation and rehearsal technique: *Rehearsing The Band* by John E. Williamson, published in 1998 by Neidig Services, and the now four volume series *Teaching Music Through Performance In Band,* compiled and edited by Richard Miles, published by GIA.

Proportion and Pacing

Although extremely important in the mind of the composer, the elements of proportion and pacing are frequently overlooked by many conductors. The conductor, as the principal re-creator of the work, must be willing to make a determined effort to try to understand these two elements from the composer's perspective.

Proportion pertains to the work in the strategic or "big-picture" sense. The conductor acquiring an understanding of the work's architecture in the macro sense is therefore very important, especially in terms of identifying and achieving important structural, harmonic and, most importantly, emotional points of arrival in the music.

Not all climatic moments in music are of the fortissimo and beyond variety. There are sometimes soft, emotional climaxes in music which can be every bit as intense and powerful as the all-too-prevalent loud varieties. For example, the dynamic climax in *A Movement For Rosa* is clearly reached in measure 176, with the low brass marked at a triple forte level. However, the emotional climax of the work occurs in measures 187-191, where the dynamic level is at a pianissimo level. In my *Elegy*, the dynamic climax is clearly reached (with considerable Wagnerian aplomb!) with the fortissimo in measure 170. While this marks a very heroic point of arrival in the music, the emotional climax of the work is reached in measure 180, where the dynamic level is pianissimo.

Among the most vivid examples of carefully calculated, contrasting varieties of musical climaxes occur in the third movement of Gustav Mahler's *Symphony No. 4*, which is my personal favorite of his nine completed symphonies. Compare the exuberant triple forte outburst in measures 315-323 (clearly the dynamic climax of this movement) to the magical emotional climax found in measure 322, where Mahler masterfully sustains the prevailing dynamic level of triple piano (sometimes pppp!) for some 22 measures to the end of this very intimate, sublimely gorgeous movement.

Pacing, although closely related to proportion, pertains more to the smaller, more tactical things in the music in the micro sense, such as the handling of a 4-measure crescendo/decrescendo or an 8-measure accelerando/rallentando. I cannot think of a better way for conductors at all levels to develop a greater appreciation for and understanding of pacing than to encourage them to try their hand at actually composing, orchestrating, and then conducting a simple, 32-measure piece, (4-measure introduction, two 8-measure melodic phrases with two 4-measure transitions, and a 4-measure concluding section) making sure to include the entering of all tempo fluctuations, dynamics, and articulations.

Fermati should be included in matters pertaining to pacing, and the increasingly careless manner they are handled by many conductors causes me great concern. The conductor's handling of fermati, both in terms of their duration (they are seldom held long enough) and their releases should be every bit as musically appropriate as all other aspects of musical performance. I also urge conductors to please be more responsive and sensitive with their handling of one of the most powerful properties available to the composer: the use of silence.

Passion

If a conductor lacks a passion for music and music making, there is little likelihood of inspired teaching occurring in the rehearsal room. In all candor, the best solution for the band director lacking a passion for music and music making is for that individual to find another line of work, pronto!

Performances that are squeaky-clean in terms of accuracy and technically dazzling with razor-sharp precision and clarity, but devoid of feeling, expression, and emotion leave me cold. Indeed, I equate performances by ensembles and conductors suffering from those symptoms with John Nance Garner's (FDR's first Vice President) description of the office of the Vice Presidency. He found serving as Vice President of the United States to be about as meaningful and satisfying "as a bucket of warm spit."

Some conductors seem to pride themselves on not generating so much as a single bead of perspiration during rehearsals or performances. I suggest those conductors take time to view some video recordings of Leonard Bernstein or Sir Georg Solti. I recall Maestro Solti, during a guest lecture he delivered at Northwestern University stating, (with his very crisp Hungarian accent) "I do not trust a conductor who does not sweat!" Yes, it is OK to sweat while making music as a conductor. By all means, resist the temptation of over-conducting or, even worse, blatant choreography. But please, I implore conductors at all levels to really get into the music and bring more passion to both their conducting and their teaching.

I encourage conductors to invite their students to join them in actually enjoying the fruits of their (joint) labor during performances. Many times, I have found this to be very helpful (especially with high school honor bands) in reducing player tension while simultaneously enhancing player focus and attention. When performing, we should strive toward Debussy's description of his own music: to be "relaxed, but alert."

These are exciting times to be in the band profession. Our medium is one, for the most part, that looks ahead. The orchestra seems content, for the most part, to look back. Because of the contemporary nature of the band's repertoire, band conductors are only one phone call or one e-mail away from having the opportunity to communicate directly with many composers writing for band today. No matter how persistent in their efforts, Los Angeles Philharmonic Music Director Esa-Pekka Salonen and Cleveland Orchestra Music Director Franz Welser-Möst will, even with the wonders of today's communication technology, find it exceedingly difficult to send an e-mail to or have a telephone conversation with Bach, Beethoven, or Brahms!

I cannot think of any composer who does not welcome a phone call, e-mail, or letter from conscientious band directors or students who want to dig a little deeper by going directly to the source of the music. Think about the unique insights and perspectives band conductors can gain through this interaction and, even more importantly, the wonderful results that can be achieved when sharing these discoveries with students. Many conductors, after having direct communication with the composer, become genuinely inspired and bring increased levels of passion to their teaching and conducting.

The well-prepared and inspiring conductor has the conviction and pride to conceive their own tasteful and unique interpretations of a work, and the passion to achieve it. Conductors possessing those qualities understand the significance of Gustav Mahler's wonderful statement: "What is best in music is not to be found in the notes."

There are three outstanding books containing valuable information and ideas pertaining to musical passion, expression, and inspired leadership that should be on the bookshelf of every band conductor in America: *The Winds of Change* by Frank L. Battisti, published in 2002 by Meredith Music, *The Intangibles of Musical Performance* by Edward S. Lisk, published in 1996 by Meredith Music, and *The Joy of Inspired Teaching* by Tim Lautzenheiser, published in 1993 by GIA.

E. The Relationship Between the Composer and the Commissioning Party

My full-time university teaching position (quite often accompanied by an overload), full-time family activities and responsibilities, much out-of-town guest conducting/clinician activity, and the simple fact that I compose and orchestrate very slowly, all add up to the reality of my not being able to accept more than one, or (on very rare occasion) two commissions per year. I dislike having to turn down a number of quite attractive commission requests annually, but I have come to realize my "just-say-no" approach is, in the end, probably a blessing for both the commissioning party and myself.

Make no mistake, there are composers who do not compromise quality while accepting numerous commissions per year, and I must say I am quite envious of them! But then there are others who seem far more interested in padding their bank accounts rather than leaving a body of quality music that will stand the test of time and enrich future generations of musicians and audiences. The commissioning party should use care in making this important distinction.

The thought of any publisher determining a required (or even suggested) number of works for a composer to generate annually is completely alien to me and is fundamentally wrong. Very often, the commissioning party will and should have expectations for publication of the work that they have commissioned. Accordingly, the commissioning party should investigate the reputation and philosophy of the probable publisher of the work, as well as the composer.

A written follow-up to the composer within a few weeks of the initial (telephone) inquiry that broadly summarizes the conversation is encouraged. By this time, the composer should have determined if he/she is, or is not the "right" person for the job. The composer must also have a clear understanding of the musical realities of the conductor and ensemble, as well as feel comfortable with any extra musical stipulations by the commissioning party. For example, a 1994 commission by the St. Louis Youth Wind Ensemble carried with it an expectation that the composer select a contemporary social issue or aspect of the human condition on which to base the work. I responded with *Watchman, Tell Us of the Night,* which calls attention to the shockingly widespread national tragedy of child abuse and neglect.

A more formal contractual agreement should then be sent

to the composer. To best serve and protect the interests of both the composer and the commissioning party, the contract should contain very specific information pertaining to: the scope, duration, and range of difficulty of the work, due date for the completed, bound full score, responsibilities and procedures for individual part extraction, premiere performance date, and all financial details for composer payment.

Ideally, the commission should include provisions for the composer to be present at final rehearsals and/or the premiere of the work. The unique insights and perspectives that only the composer can bring, together with direct personal and musical interaction among the composer, conductor, ensemble members, and audience, always generate very positive and memorable experiences.

One of my favorite and certainly most unique sources of funding for commissioning I have experienced occurred with the Florida Bandmasters Association. In 1992, I had the honor of being the first recipient of their ongoing (FBA) commissioning project. Funding for the commission was and remains generated by band director late/penalty fees for various FBA functions. The result of this commission was my work entitled *A Movement For Rosa,* honoring Civil Rights heroine Rosa Parks. My sincere thanks to those "tardy" band directors, and may their procrastination continue to benefit fellow composers!

F. Views on the Teaching of Composition and How to Mentor the Young Composer

Teaching composition can be very challenging. On the one hand, the teacher wants very much to equip the student with many of the basic 'nuts and bolts' of compositional craft, thereby enabling the young composer to express his/her ideas in a manner that is both disciplined and imaginative. On the other hand, the teacher must use great care in not crossing a sometimes very fine line that inadvertently tampers with the young composer's most cherished possession: his/her creative identity.

Some of the most important basic "nuts and bolts" of compositional craft that can be 'taught' include acquiring clean and accurate notational skills, gaining a heightened awareness of and appreciation for various forms/structures and timbres, and constantly striving for more effective development of motivic and melodic material via a thorough understanding of contrasting harmonic languages and facility in contrapuntal technique.

Young composers should be regularly involved in re-creating music as performers. Therefore, I emphasize the critical importance of composers becoming as proficient as possible on their principal performing instrument. And if that instrument is not the piano, the young composer must add it to a list of absolute essentials that are required for continued musical growth.

I believe it is perfectly fine for a young composer to emulate the style of their "favorite" composer(s). This is very natural and has been very prevalent throughout the history of Western music. In a sense, all composers are derivative. Early Beethoven, for example, contains the influence of late Mozart. Early Brahms was influenced by Beethoven's later writing. And, of course, the music of the great film composer John Williams contains 'influences', shall we say, from just about everyone! I have discovered that, in most cases, over a period of time, a young composer's own, distinctive creative voice will begin to emerge.

A good teacher of composition should be especially helpful in guiding the young composer toward becoming proficient with perhaps the single most important aspect of developing good musicianship and, ultimately, impressive levels of creativity. This means learning how to *listen* to music—a widely diverse historical and stylistic spectrum of music—performed by equally widely diverse media. This may sound simple, but in most respects knowing *how* to listen and what to listen *for* is really the ultimate "bottom-line" in becoming both a good composer and good musician.

I encourage wind band directors who may have a "budding" composer in their ensemble to read and share an especially fine article by award-winning composer Dana Wilson, Professor of Music at Ithaca College (Ithaca, New York) entitled *Guidelines For Coaching Student Composers,* from the July 2001 issue of *Music Educators Journal.* I also highly recommend W. Francis McBeth's *Twentieth Century Techniques Of Composition For The Beginning Student,* published in 1994 by Delta Publications.

It is a great honor to serve as coordinator of the National Band Association Young Composer Mentor Project, an enterprise I conceived in the late 1990's and have coordinated since its inception in 2000. Thanks to the ongoing and enthusiastic support of caring and forward-looking individuals on the NBA Executive Committee, the Young Composer Mentor Project has become a regular (annual) event in which five young composers (ages 18-25) apply for selection to participate in several days of intensive study with a trio of mentors who thus far, in addition to myself have included David Gillingham, Timothy Mahr, Jack Stamp, and Frank Ticheli. Three of the five student participants from the inaugural (2000) session have since gone on to win composition competitions, receive commissions, and have their works published.

By 2020, one hundred gifted and idealistic young composers and several dozen dedicated and highly respected mentors will have joined me in coming together through this endeavor. And what a special joy it will be to eventually witness today's student composers becoming tomorrow's composer mentors!

I become very excited when visualizing the highly favorable impact the NBA Young Composer Mentor Project can have on the future of the wind band medium and our profession as a whole, for it is the composer—especially our young composers—who remain the true lifeline of our repertoire.

G. Individuals Who Have Been Especially Influential in My Development and Career

It seems that some wonderful and extremely influential, but less well-known teachers never quite make it into ones resume. We tend to list the more "famous" artist/teachers with whom we have studied, and in most cases, starting with the college years.

I was extremely fortunate to have had some truly outstanding private teachers and equally outstanding band and orchestra directors at all levels of my training. In retrospect, I cannot recall having a single teacher or director ("famous" or not famous) being anything less than a superb musician, educator, and personal role model.

Piano Teachers

Francis Svec, wife of our elementary school district superintendent, and Lydia Sterba, a very passionate teacher and brilliant pianist who was a frequent soloist with community orchestras throughout the Chicago metropolitan area, were among my first and most influential private teachers. Were it not for the solid foundation laid by these two excellent teachers of piano—the instrument I regard as the bedrock of musical knowledge—it is highly unlikely I would have ever acquired the many basic skills which are essential for both composition and score study.

Completing piano requirements during my first week of college enabled more time for trumpet study and ensemble participation. But in retrospect, I wish I had gone further with private piano study, especially while at Northwestern.

Trumpet Teachers

Joseph Hans Kelter was a delightful older gentleman with a decidedly Germanic background and approach to the trumpet. He was a wonderful instructor who, like my piano teachers, laid a very strong foundation of basic playing fundamentals. I received especially fine guidance from Mr. Kelter in the critically important areas of tone production, technique, and repertoire, thereby enabling later advanced private study with Adolph Herseth and Vincent Cichowicz.

I would like to try to help dispel a widely mistaken notion that I still hear occasionally in the instrumental music world. It goes something like this: "Oh, so you studied with both Herseth and Cichowicz. I hear Herseth is a great player but not such a good teacher, and I understand Cichowicz is a great teacher but not an especially good player."

For the record, I can assure everyone that my personal experiences always demonstrated that Mr. Herseth and Mr. Cichowicz were **both** great players **and** great teachers, each in their own wonderfully unique and inspiring ways. My studies with both men went far beyond valuable trumpet instruction. They were always great lessons in the art of good musicianship. The warm personal friendship I continue to enjoy with Vince Cichowicz and his wife Genie is among the most cherished I will ever have.

Band and Orchestra Directors

My District 99 (Cicero, Illinois) elementary school band director was John Peckenham, under whose direction I played between 1963-1968. He was a solid musician and very straight-ahead person.

J. Sterling Morton East High School (District 201—Cicero, Illinois) band director, Joseph J. Frantik was a fine conductor and clarinetist as well as a very gifted transcriber of orchestral works for band. I am very grateful for his providing me with some important organizational and leadership opportunities and responsibilities so early in my musical development.

The instrumental music program in the Morton High School District was unusually strong and comprehensive, and made significant impressions on me while I was still attending Abraham Lincoln Elementary School. My older brother played trumpet in the Morton Band and I can recall regularly attending their concerts under the dynamic leadership of then director of bands, David C. McCormick, who is now a member of the board of directors of The Midwest International Band and Orchestra Clinic.

One of my first, up-close encounters with great band literature occurred in the mid-1960's while observing a rehearsal of Peter Mennin's *Canzona,* under Dr. McCormick's inspired direction. I was really taken by the intensity and energy of that fine work...and still am! I also recall being fascinated with seeing and meeting real, living composers for the first time! These included Philip Rhodes and Vaclav Nelhybel, both of whom had composition residencies at Morton, in conjunction with the world premiere performances of their (commissioned) works. Their music impressed me as being so strikingly modern at that time.

Morton High School Fine Arts Division Head, Robert J. Dvorak, also a fine composer, was very kind and supportive of my growing interest in composition. I have nothing but positive memories of my high school band experiences.

I played in two orchestras during my high school years. At Morton, I played under Theodore Radek, who was one of the kindest men I've ever had the pleasure of knowing. He had a special affinity for and knowledge of the music of his native Czechoslovakia.

One time Chicago Symphony principal cellist, Dudley Powers, who for many years led the Youth Symphony Orchestra of Greater Chicago, was particularly supportive of my early compositional efforts and would generously devote rehearsal time to read new orchestral works I had composed. On one occasion, he performed one of my works (a 15-minute symphonic poem) on a special (April 1971) concert in Orchestra Hall celebrating the 25th anniversary of the Youth Symphony.

Legendary Northwestern University director of bands, John P. Paynter was a kind of musical father figure. He was an excellent conductor, superb musician, and a great teacher. I have yet to play under any conductor (band, orchestral or choral) with a better understanding of the compositional process and appreciation of the composer's intentions. I especially marveled at his impeccable abilities in the areas of score study and preparation, and the multi-faceted aspects of rehearsal planning and procedures. Every rehearsal I played under Mr. Paynter's direction was a great lesson both in conducting and in life.

My private sessions with him, via independent study courses, were especially valuable and influential in my development as a conductor, composer, and educator. I will always hold John Paynter's musical and personal integrity in the highest regard.

Composition Teachers

I was an applied (trumpet) performance major in college. As a result, my formal composition study was rather limited. Although largely self-taught as a composer—as compared with the highly specialized training received by many of my distinguished colleagues in this book—I had some private study while a high school student with Concordia University music professor, Richard Hillert. I also had four quarters of private composition lessons and seminars at Northwestern with Alan Stout, a very kind and brilliant man whose music I greatly respected.

I had hoped to study composition with Samuel Barber at the Curtis Institute in Philadelphia. Although I was accepted to Curtis as a trumpet major, my application as a composition major there was rejected. Although greatly disappointed with that rejection, I have absolutely no regrets about any aspect of the education and training I received at Northwestern. But I do sometimes wonder what direction my career might have taken had I attended Curtis as a trumpet major.

Other Wonderful Teachers and Influential Individuals

- Northwestern University School of Music professors Grigg Fountain (Choirmaster and organist of NU's Alice Millar Chapel), Margaret Hillis (founding director of the Chicago Symphony Chorus), and my wife, soprano Elizabeth Curtis, for their introducing me to important concepts of singing and the rich vocal repertoire. Elizabeth is an adjunct faculty member in the music departments of both Radford University and nearby Virginia Tech. I marvel at her excellence both as a vocal performer, (she specializes in contemporary American repertoire) and as a teacher of voice. Some of my most enlightening and liberating musical experiences have occurred while collaborating with singers. Indeed, all instrumentalists have a great deal to learn from our vocal colleagues...and vice versa!

- Northwestern University School of Music professors Arrand Parsons (aural skills) and Frederick Ockwell (orchestral conducting);

- Chicago Symphony principal percussionist and long-time administrator and resident conductor of the Civic Orchestra of Chicago, Gordon Peters (orchestral conducting);

- Northwestern University School of Music professor and former Cleveland Orchestra principal clarinet, Robert Marcellus (chamber wind repertoire);

- United States Air Force Band Conductor Emeritus, Colonel Arnald D. Gabriel for the always inspirational musical leadership he brings to countless numbers of young musicians (including this one as a rising high school sophomore in July of 1969 at the University of Illinois Summer Youth Music Camp) and audiences throughout the world;

- United States Army Band ("Pershing's Own") Conductor Emeritus, Colonel Eugene W. Allen and his wife, Claire for their always very generous and gracious support and encouragement. It was Colonel and Mrs. Allen, whom in February of 1985 commissioned *Tribute,* my first work for band to be published;

- Frederick Fennell, who during the summers of 1979 and 1980 had one-week guest conducting residencies with the New Mexico Music Festival at Taos, of which I served as co-founder and music director. The insights and perspectives I gained through feedback from his observing Festival rehearsals and performances under my direction were invaluable. Of course, the opportunity to observe rehearsals and performances of Festival ensembles under his direction proved especially illuminating. An August 1980 performance he led of the original (chamber) version of Copland's *Appalachian Spring* remains the single most magical performance of that work I have ever heard. Clearly, all facets of our profession have been immeasurably enriched through the artistry and vision of the legendary Frederick Fennell;

- Distinguished American composer and self-proclaimed "ethno-funkologist" David Amram, for his important contributions to American music, his impressive knowledge of world musics, and especially for his always-infectious enthusiasm and love of both music and life. "Hanging out" with David for five summers in Taos, New Mexico was a joy!

- English trumpeter Philip Jones, for his pioneering efforts and accomplishments on behalf of brass chamber music. While visiting my friend, Scottish trumpeter John Miller in the United Kingdom during the summer of 1975, Mr. Jones very graciously gave me permission to accompany (as an observer) the Philip Jones Brass Ensemble during a one-week performance tour of England. This proved to be a marvelous experience...a unique, up-close look at and interaction with one of the world's most distinguished chamber music ensembles. Arrangements by PJBE members of works from the Renaissance period, in particular, and recordings thereof are especially impressive in terms of their adherence to proper style and performance practice.

Among the most important opportunities for musical growth during my college years occurred on Friday afternoons, not on the Northwestern University campus, but in the heart of downtown Chicago. Orchestra Hall (now Symphony Center)—home of arguably the world's greatest symphony orchestra—became the world's greatest laboratory for those of us who really wanted to both see and hear many of the things we had studied in classes, lessons, and rehearsals during the week all come together in performance by the Chicago Symphony Orchestra. The cost for students attending this Friday afternoon "lab" was, at that time (early to mid 1970's) a whopping $1...yes, one dollar for a seat in the gallery...where Orchestra Hall acoustics were (at that time) by far the best! That Friday afternoon lab became a kind of musical heaven for me where, for example, as a young trumpet player I could see and hear what was, at that time, the world's finest (and certainly the most robust!) orchestral brass section. As a young conductor and composer, I could observe the world's finest conductors (Solti, Giulini, Leinsdorf, Kubelik) and guest soloists (Stern, Serkin, Brendel, Price) in programming ranging from the standard repertoire to world or U.S. premieres of new works by composers such as Tippett, Henze, Druckman, and Lutoslawski.

The individuals most directly responsible for providing me with rich educational and artistic opportunities and who were most influential in instilling important personal values and goals were my parents, William and Esther Camphouse. *They* were my finest and most influential teachers. Neither were musicians, but they recognized the importance of the arts. There was always good music to be heard in our home, either on the radio or phonograph. Because my parents never had the opportunity to attend college, a top priority of theirs was to make certain my brother and I received first-rate education at major universities. My father was a school custodian, and the finest and most hard-working school custodian I've ever seen. My mother was a school secretary, and the finest and most hard-working school secretary I've ever seen. They lived and experienced the most important aspect of the American Dream: providing meaningful opportunities through love, hard work, and sacrifice, to enable a brighter future and better quality of life for their children.

My brother Bill (four years my senior, to the day!) has enjoyed a long and very successful career as a public school music educator and band director in downstate Illinois at both the high school and community college levels. A University of Illinois graduate (I try not to hold that against him!), his instrumental background is also trumpet and piano. I am especially pleased that he will be able to devote more time to composing and arranging upon his retirement from teaching in 2003.

H. Ten Works I Believe All Band Conductors at All Levels Should Study

1. Samuel Barber, ***Knoxville: Summer of 1915, op. 24 for Soprano and Orchestra***

   This is Barber's most compelling masterpiece...a perfect marriage of equally evocative text (James Agee) and music. This work asks universal questions from the innocent viewpoint of a child, and makes us question our own values and place in the world.

   Runner-up: Barber, *Concerto for Violin and Orchestra, op. 14*

2. Ludwig van Beethoven, ***Symphony No. 3 in E-flat, op. 55 "Eroica"***

   Perhaps the British conductor Sir Charles Groves said it best in his marvelously succinct single sentence summation of Beethoven: "Beethoven shifts from the rule of *pattern* to the rule of *expression."* This is what Beethoven does so effectively in the *"Eroica."*

   In many respects, this work represents the dawn of the Romantic era. All of the trademarks of Beethoven's genius can be found in this extraordinarily forward-looking work. These include the dramatic enlargement of symphonic proportion, scope, and design via lengthy transitions, a

greatly expanded development section, and the scherzo replacing the minuet and trio as the standard third movement. We also find a significant increase of harmonic tension, expanded orchestration with wind, brass, and percussion instruments rising in importance, the inclusion of precise dynamic shadings, superb motivic manipulation, and finally, a wonderful, highly individualistic, overall *earthiness* in style and temperament.
Runner-up: Beethoven, *Missa Solemnis in D, op. 123*

3. Aaron Copland, ***Appalachian Spring*** *(Ballet for Martha)*

I admire equally both versions of this Pulitzer Prize winning work, composed in 1943-44 as a ballet for Martha Graham. The more intimate chamber ensemble version for 13 players best presents the Copland stylistic trademark of "lean grandiosity." But the depth of the (full) orchestral version is better suited to convey the lushness of certain passages.

When discussing the differences between his "severe" and "simple" styles, Copland said: "What I was trying for in the simpler works was only partly a larger audience; they also gave me a chance to try for a home-spun musical idiom...I like to think I have touched off for myself and others a kind of musical naturalness that we have badly needed."

The work's lively and flexible rhythms, the still fresh sounding harmonies via pandiatonicism (i.e. an important 20th century compositional technique in which each note of the diatonic scale is given equal importance. Copland was especially fond of using this technique in vertical combinations as we find in the A Major/E Major opening of

Appalachian Spring), which is an especially important ingredient in Copland's desire to achieve a kind of musical naturalness—vivid instrumental colors, and that special Coplandesque chord spacing that so appropriately conveys both the American character and landscape, all add up to this being perhaps the single most beloved and enduring 20th century work by an American composer.

Playing Mr. Copland's music under his direction on three occasions in the 1970's are among my most treasured musical memories. He was a very kind man, and his status for nearly 50 years as "Dean" of American composers was indeed very richly deserved.

Runner-up: Copland, *Music from the film score, Our Town*

4. Claude Debussy, ***Prelude to the Afternoon of a Fawn***

I share the view of Pierre Boulez that modern music was awakened with this extraordinarily innovative work composed by Debussy between 1892-94. I have always marveled at this quasi-tone poem's exquisite sense of proportion, balance, and transparencies. The music is a general impression of Stephane Mallarmé's 1876 poem.

If any one musical composition best typifies the artistic movement referred to as Impressionism, this is surely it! Moods and atmospheres are evoked through blurred harmonies, vague and misty textures, and a very intentional lack of clearly identifiable pulse and meter. There is extensive motivic development and transformation of the opening theme throughout the work. The orchestration is complex and sophisticated, but very carefully crafted to give the listener a sense of simplicity overall.

Imagine what an extraordinary contribution Debussy

could make to enrich today's wind band or (more likely with Debussy) wind *ensemble* repertory! One of my favorite statements by a composer is Debussy's assessment of his musical antithesis, Richard Wagner. Debussy said: "Wagner was a glorious sunset mistaken for a dawn." How true.

Runner-up: Maurice Ravel, *Daphnis and Chloé*: *Suite No. 2*

5. Paul Hindemith, ***Symphonie Mathis der Maler***

Not only did the 20th century's single most reprehensible figure (Adolf Hitler) frequently not listen (thankfully) to his brilliant generals, he also had Nazi Minister of Propaganda and Public Enlightenment, Joseph Goebbels angrily denounce Paul Hindemith—arguably the leading German composer of his generation—as a musical "degenerate."

Although the complete opera *Mathis der Maler* (based on the life of 16th century painter, Mathias Grünewald) did not receive its premiere until 1938 in Zurich, Hindemith had extracted from it a brilliant three movement symphony which was premiered in Berlin under Wilhelm Furtwangler in 1934. It has become an orchestral classic. The work's final 17 measures—a majestic "Alleluia" heralded by the brass section—are perhaps the most glorious and inspirational in the entire orchestral repertoire.

Runner-up: Hindemith, *Symphonic Metamorphosis on Themes of Carl Maria von Weber*

6. Charles Ives, ***Three Places In New England***
   (*An Orchestral Set*).

   The unique and visionary Charles Ives—son of a Yankee bandmaster, Yale graduate, and highly successful insurance man—composed *Three Places In New England* between 1912-1914. It would not receive a performance until 1930. In this work, we hear Ives at his pioneering best, with his employment of ingenious multi-layered textures, and "poly-everything" approach to harmony and rhythm. Quite probably his most frequently performed work, and among his first to be published commercially, Ives, after attending a rare, live (1931) performance of *Three Places In New England* quipped: "Just like a town meeting—every man for himself. Wonderful how it all came out!"

   The third movement, "*The Housatonic at Stockbridge*" (from the poem by Robert Underwood Johnson) is a strikingly beautiful and haunting tone painting...an unforgettable sonic journey of the composer and his wife, Harmony (of all names!) "taking a Sunday morning walk near Stockbridge (Massachusetts) the summer after we were married. We walked in the meadows along the river and heard the distant singing from the church across the river. The mists had not entirely left the river, and the colors, the running water, the banks and trees were something that one would always remember."

   Runner-up: Ives, *String Quartet No. 1*

7. Witold Lutoslawski, ***Concerto for Orchestra***

   Polish composer Witold Lutoslawski (1913-1994) completed his *Concerto for Orchestra* in 1954, ten years after the premiere of Bela Bartok's brilliant orchestral tour

de force of the same title. While certainly indebted to the Bartok, Lutoslawski's inventive orchestration, forward-looking yet accessible harmonic vocabulary, comparative brevity, and impressive integration of compositional ideas make his *Concerto for Orchestra* a refreshing and equally dazzling orchestral showcase. I have found both the Bartok and Lutoslawski *Concertos* to be great joys (and challenges!) to conduct.
Runner-up: Bartok, *Concerto for Orchestra*

8. Wolfgang Amadeus Mozart, ***Symphony No. 29 in A Major, K. 201***

   Although Mozart had just turned 18 when he composed this symphony, it can hardly be viewed as a "youthful" work. It displays remarkable maturity, and has a freshness and vitality that somehow sets it apart from his others. The contrapuntal writing is especially impressive, and the lean wind resources called for (only a pair of oboes and horns) provide a charming blend with some of Mozart's finest and most elegant string writing.
   Runner-up: Mozart, *Piano Concerto No. 25 in C Major, K. 503*

9. Joseph Schwantner, ***New Morning for the World*** *"Daybreak of Freedom" for Speaker and Orchestra*

   Commissioned by American Telephone and Telegraph Company for the Eastman Philharmonia, Pulitzer Prize winning American composer Joseph Schwantner composed this deeply moving work in 1982 as a tribute to Dr. Martin Luther King, Jr., who the composer calls "a man of great dignity and courage whom I had long admired." Schwantner's extraordinarily rich lyricism, gorgeous

harmonic language, and complex and highly effective undercurrent of rhythmic tension interact so dramatically and always tastefully with the powerful and timeless eloquence of Dr. King's words.
Runner-up: Aaron Copland, *A Lincoln Portrait for speaker and orchestra*

10. Igor Stravinsky, ***Le Sacre du Printemps*** *(The Rite of Spring)*

    We can trace the subject of sex in music back many hundreds of years, but with "Le Sacre," Stravinsky gave those in attendance on the evening of May 29, 1913 at the Theatre des Champs-Elysees their first taste of an X-rated production!

    The Rite of Spring, according to the composer was "a fleeting vision which came as a complete surprise...I saw in imagination a solemn pagan rite: sage elders, seated in a circle, watching a young girl dance herself to death. They were sacrificing her to propitiate the god of spring." Curiously, Stravinsky eventually decided he liked the music to *Le Sacre* better in concert version than its original (stage) version.

    With this audaciously innovative work, Stravinsky boldly set new parameters of orchestral virtuosity. Indeed, although prepared and led by two of the world's preeminent performing artists (choreographer Vaslav Nijinsky and conductor Pierre Monteux), the premiere of *Le Sacre* necessitated no fewer than 126 rehearsals! I hasten to add, however, although still fiendishly difficult for both player and conductor, today—by virtue of stunning advances in instrumental technological design and instrumental performance skills (especially in the area of technical virtuosity)—solid regional orchestras like the Roanoke (Virginia) Symphony can present a very respectable *Rite of Spring* with only eight to ten hours of rehearsal preparation.

Stravinsky also ushered in dramatic and strikingly new concepts of orchestration as well as forever changing music's harmonic vocabulary. But what, more than anything makes *The Rite of Spring* a true cornerstone of modern music? I believe it is how Stravinsky exploited, indeed revolutionized music's most primitive element: rhythm, especially through use of complex asymmetric meter and incessant syncopation.

Perhaps Pierre Boulez said it best: "*Le Sacre du Printemps* serves as a point of reference to all who seek to establish the birth certificate of what is still called 'contemporary' music."

Runner-up: Stravinsky, *Octet for Wind Instruments*

I must also include any of the nine symphonies by Ralph Vaughan Williams...especially Numbers 2 (*A London Symphony)*, 5 (In D Major), and 7 *(Sinfonia Antartica)*. Each is so personal, imaginative, and accessible. I believe Vaughan Williams (as well as Dmitri Shostakovich) played a major role in keeping the symphonic tradition fresh and alive up to the time of his death in 1958. Band directors who know only his *English Folk Song Suite, Toccata Marziale, Flourish for Wind Band,* or his *Variations* (marvelously scored by Donald Hunsberger) are getting a very narrow and really quite incomplete view of this great English composer.

I. Ten Composers Whose Music Overall Speaks to Me in Especially Meaningful Ways

1. **Samuel Barber**, for his extraordinarily penetrating warmth and lyricism.

2. **Ludwig van Beethoven**, for his profound influence on virtually all aspects of the creative process. He forever changed the way composers viewed their role in both music and society.

3. **Aaron Copland**, for his uncanny ability to chronicle the American experience, and for his multifaceted efforts in successfully establishing a global American musical presence.

4. **Claude Debussy**: texture, texture, and texture!

5. **Giovanni Gabrieli**, for the magnificent splendor of his Venetian polychoral and instrumental music.

6. **Paul Hindemith**, for his masterful counterpoint and clear sense of structure. He was one of the finest musicians of the twentieth century.

7. **Charles Ives**, a true American original! He made pioneering innovations in harmony, rhythm, and texture well prior to those made by his supposedly more "sophisticated" European contemporaries.

8. **Wolfgang Amadeus Mozart**, for his energy, elegance, and astonishing productivity in such a tragically brief lifetime.

9. **Igor Stravinsky**: Paris—May 29, 1913...nothing was ever quite the same in music after than date!

10. **Ralph Vaughan Williams**, for his rich and gorgeous harmonic language and strong, always tasteful sense of national identity.

I must also, without hesitation, give considerable mention to the twentieth century musician I most admire: **Leonard Bernstein.** Had he left us with only *West Side Story*; that alone would be ample testimony to his genius. What a phenomenal musical role model! He was a truly inspirational and influential conductor, gifted and prolific composer, superb pianist, respected author of five books, eloquent arts advocate, passionate social activist, and the finest music **educator** (in the best sense of that word) I can think of, especially via his nationally televised Young People's Concerts with the New York Philharmonic, and the Norton Lectures he delivered at Harvard. Maestro Bernstein immeasurably enriched all aspects of our profession and the lives of people everywhere.

J. The Future of the Wind Band

"If an orchestral work is over ten minutes long, you're lucky if it's performed twice, and if it's over 25 minutes, more performances (after the premiere) are a miracle."

—Pulitzer Prize & Grawemeyer Award Winning Composer Aaron Jay Kernis, talking to *The Christian Science Monitor*

The above statement speaks volumes as to why I find the future of the wind band medium to be such an especially positive and exciting one.

The symphony orchestra is a medium I both love and respect—and I always will. Principal reasons include:

- it's intoxicatingly rich and seemingly endless sonic palette;
- the great legacy of its superb repertoire spanning over three centuries;
- the magnificent acoustics and architecture of many concert halls designed for orchestral performance

Before discussing the future of the wind band, a brief personal retrospective pertaining to the symphony orchestra seems appropriate. Indeed, some of my most important and most meaningful formative musical experiences occurred more by way of the symphony orchestra rather than the band. These include:

- my initial encounter as a boy of age six (1960) with "contemporary" music. I recall so vividly hearing The Rite of Spring for the first time via a Reader's Digest L.P. box-set collection of "classical" music on our family's monaural phonograph. This was quite an ear and mind-opening experience!

- my first recollections of observing conductors were of the orchestral, not band, variety: Fritz Reiner, with the Chicago Symphony via WGN-TV broadcasts ("Mommy, who's that mean-looking little man waving that stick?"), and Reiner's one-time Curtis Institute conducting student, the wonderfully warm and exciting Leonard Bernstein, leading the New York Philharmonic during his incomparable Young People's Concerts on CBS.

- hearing my first original composition for large instrumental ensemble (a little 4-movement orchestral suite I composed and orchestrated in 9th grade) come to life one cold Saturday morning in January of 1970, in the old, creaky and drafty Fine Arts Building on Michigan Avenue, during a reading by the Youth Symphony Orchestra of Greater Chicago. Wow!...hearing your first orchestral work come to life...what a memorable and truly invaluable experience for a young composer!

Later that year, I entered that little suite in a Young Artist Competition sponsored by the Chicago Symphony Orchestra. It was never performed, but it did receive an "honorable mention" award, which proved to be an incredible incentive for me to continue with my creative work.

My approach to trumpet performance also had a decidedly orchestral influence as a result of advanced and intensive private study with Chicago Symphony Orchestra members Adolph Herseth, with whom I studied between 1970-72, and Vincent Cichowicz (1971-76). I must, however specify that as a trumpet player, it was through my elementary school *band* experience that I played my first solo passage in public (March 1964) on my school-owned Conn "Director" model trumpet (complete with Conn 4 mouthpiece). The memorable masterpiece was *Forest Glen Overture,* from the Kinyon-Powers Book.

Conducting my first complete orchestral program in concert performance in July 1978 with the New Mexico Music Festival at Taos Symphony Orchestra was certainly a milestone event. The program consisted of Tippett's *Suite in D for the Birthday of Prince Charles* (a work for which I have a genuine interest in eventually transcribing for wind band), Copland's *A Lincoln Portrait* (former U.S. Senator Fred Harris, narrator), and Tchaikovsky's *Symphony No. 5.*

I continued to compose orchestral works during my high school and college years. Most received multiple performances, but none were ever published. I did not compose my first work for band until 1980, which coincided with my first tenure-track faculty position as a college band conductor. I have been composing regularly, indeed almost exclusively, for band since 1985. Why is this? It is related to what brought a composer of the stature of Aaron Jay Kernis to make such a rather troubling statement in *The Christian Science Monitor* about today's symphony orchestras. Let me try to explain.

Symphony orchestras today are plagued by paralyzing labor/management disputes, obsolete marketing techniques, and good faith but largely failed efforts in responding to a host of rapidly changing socioeconomic realities. The symphony orchestra has become a quasi-museum...a glorious museum, dedicated overwhelmingly to preserving the great masterpieces of the *past.*

Today's wind band, out of historical necessity, continues to look *ahead.* More than ever in the band's comparatively brief but increasingly impressive history, there now exist especially great opportunities to secure today's *finest* composers to create not a token, minor work for the band, but rather to generate a *number* of works of the highest caliber, that give us their very *best* creative efforts. Regrettably, this has not always been the case.

We need to accelerate our efforts in getting the word out to today's finest composers the following simple and I believe compelling truths:

- today's wind band = commissions;
- today's wind band = multiple performances;
- today's wind band = a favorable environment for publication.

And perhaps most importantly, today's wind band provides the composer with especially exciting opportunities to make a significant contribution to the artistic and educational enrichment of *all* segments of a community, especially for our young people in school band rooms across America.

The distinguished American musician, educator, and community advocate, Dr. David C. McCormick, in a recently published article entitled *Band, the Medium with a Special Mission,* states:

> "The wind band medium can and should take the lead in helping 21st century society make art music a more central part of life. In doing so, the band has duel roles of stimulating creation of fine new art music and bringing serious music of various historical periods to the masses of society. No other medium can perform that second role as well as the band, a long heritage that needs to be revitalized. The future is bright for school, college and community bands to introduce wider and wider audiences to new music along with music of the past, and lead those audiences to realize enhanced qualities of life with art music. The music world needs that infusion of new interest. A more musical community is a healthier community."

> "Society needs musicians with evangelistic zeal to aggressively bring art music to the masses, and that is just what the band medium and its leaders (most of whom are superb salespeople) do so well. It is the band's heritage."

> "Of all performing media, the symphony orchestra seems destined to attract the largest audience that will

> pay to hear serious music. It seems destined to continue attracting an audience weighted to upper socioeconomic levels of society, an audience that is accustomed to formal events. That audience has been and will continue to come from older age groups, and from clienteles that have resources to provide financial support for ensemble's employing large numbers of performers. But the symphony orchestra does not seem destined to evangelize the world on behalf of music. That role can and must be taken by the band."
>
> "We need to revitalize the band as the medium to reach out and lead communities to place high value on music, to reach out and develop audiences for the entire art of music in all media. We must capitalize upon the band's long and unique heritage of bringing serious music to both the sophisticate and the masses."

I certainly mean no disrespect, nor do I suggest there should be any diminishment in the recognition of and appreciation for our distinguished wind band conductor predecessors and all that they accomplished for our medium and profession. I do, however, believe it is vitally important that we not merely strive to accomplish the same things our mentors and role models did, nor in the same manner. My generation of composers, conductors, educators, and performers must, on our watch, make a determined commitment to do an even better job. And I believe that is just what *they* (the Hindsley's, the Paynter's, the Revelli's, et al.) would want and expect from our generation!

- A symbolic (and moral) imperative: The establishment of America's first, full-time (52-week season) professional wind band. Free from the insular world of academe and devoid of important but non-musically related duties inherent in our superb military bands, this multi-faceted enterprise will have many artistic similarities with those of a major professional symphony orchestra, but will be far more involved with and responsive to the complex needs and realities of an urban community while simultaneously addressing matters related to globalization.

The creation of this enterprise will also prove to be an important first step of taking action to correct what is clearly a moral dilemma of there being so few available, meaningful employment opportunities for the legions of outstanding wind, brass, and percussion players upon their graduation from leading colleges, universities and conservatories. Formation of an enterprise of this magnitude will require extraordinarily innovative design and visionary leadership. This endeavor could prove to be perhaps the single most important legacy my generation can leave to the wind band profession.

- We must continue to strive for improved balance in the school band curriculum. I have always felt long-time University of Minnesota director of bands, Dr. Frank Benscriscutto said it best in the January 1984 issue (Vol. 38, no.6) of *The Instrumentalist.* He said, "Marching and competition are 'American' and are useful, good and enjoyable if kept in balance. However, these ingredients are candy-coating over the soul-enriching vitamins present in the core of music itself." How true! I believe it is important and healthy for band directors at all levels to occasionally re-evaluate their priorities, program emphases, and focus.

- We must examine carefully and find ways to increase minority student participation in school band programs. There are tragically few African American children involved in school band programs today. This is undoubtedly due in part to there being so few African American band directors currently in the profession to serve as mentors and role models for children of all racial and ethnic backgrounds. Stimulating greater interest in school band participation is especially important among Hispanic American children. Indeed, this will soon become a *demographic imperative*. The ethnic and racial make-up of the American mosaic is changing rapidly. We must recognize and address these racial and ethnic participatory imbalances now, if the band is to remain at all relevant to our changing society. Failure to do so will have far reaching negative consequences for school band programs and the whole of instrumental music education throughout America in the next 25 years.

- Music that promotes the "faster, higher, louder" syndrome is, regrettably, alive and well in far too many of our school band rooms. It is growing like a cancer, eating away and destroying important elements of musical sensitivity such as the shaping of phrases, nuance, balance, and style. I am also very concerned with the widespread detrimental effect inferior, formula-style, so-called "educational" band music (what an incredible misnomer!) has had on virtually all aspects of a young player's aesthetic and technical development. In many respects (and this is not an exaggeration), I find the innocuousness of airport terminal *men's room* music to be more musically satisfying than some of our school *band room* music!

Clearly, it is time for school band directors to stop spending tax-payer dollars on comic-book music! Directors can and should be more discriminating with the music they purchase. The GIA series, *Teaching Music Through Performance In Band,* is an absolutely terrific resource for band directors at all levels, and is especially helpful in guiding the director toward literature that is enriching. I am especially pleased to see Volume 4 in that distinguished series being devoted to young band and beginning band literature.

- Simply stated, we currently have too many music degree granting institutions in the United States. By all means, we should continue to provide numerous and meaningful performance opportunities for students at our colleges and universities. However, we must begin to do a far better job of providing a good arts education and a greater appreciation for the arts among our non-music major college students, who will become our future tax-payers, band boosters, school administrators, civic/governmental leaders; in short—our audience! This is where we are failing. We are failing to educate, develop and build the audiences of tomorrow.

Colleges and universities today are accepting too many students with mediocre abilities as well as questionable attitudes about both the art of music and the teaching profession. Young people who "like band" and/or "like music" in high school should certainly be encouraged, and in the most positive manner, to continue their active participation in music-making at the college level. But my quarter century as a college music professor has shown in most cases that they should not be encouraged to *major* in music in college. Liking band and liking music is just not enough! Young people interested in having a career in music must be hopelessly in love with music in every way. They must have a genuine *passion* for music! We must, once and for all, stop advising our young people to major in music education "as a back-up." Good grief, I abhor that mentality, and it has caused serious damage to our profession! Clearly, we need music educators who are, first and foremost, excellent musicians who also have a passion for teaching. Period!

We certainly need to encourage our young people to dream great dreams, and aim high—that's the American way, and I'm all for that! But, it is also extremely important that we always be *honest* with them at all phases of their development.

Epilogue: Some Final Thoughts

If I have a particular strength to offer our profession, it is not as a composer, per se. Nor is it as a conductor, per se. Nor is it as a teacher, and it certainly is no longer as a trumpet player. I have discovered there are better compositional craftsmen, more technically proficient conductors, more dedicated pedagogues, and much finer trumpet players in this world than I. But, if I had to identify one thing about me that I do take genuine professional pride, it would be the perspectives I possess and, hopefully, the integrity I bring to my work by simply trying to be a good ***musician***. That is a very special word to me. I am indeed very proud and feel it is a great privilege to be a musician. And I am especially proud and feel it a great privilege to count my ten fellow chapter contributors and Mallory Thompson among my friends and colleagues. Each are truly unique, enormously dedicated, and leading citizens of an extraordinary community of good musicians.

Frederick Fennell concludes his important 1954 book, *Time And The Winds* with the following statement: "The future course of the development of the wind ensemble as a form of musical art rests completely in the hands of the composer—for it is he who writes *The History of the Use of Wind Instruments.*"

Nearly half a century has passed since Fennell's statement, and while it remains true that the composer is the only purely creative figure in music, the challenges, needs, and opportunities facing the wind band are suggesting to me that the future course of the wind band as a form of musical art (now) rests completely in the hands of...the consummate musician.

This shared responsibility—a new partnership among an extraordinary community of our finest musicians, comprised of composers, conductors, performers, and teachers—will require leaders with vision. These leaders must have a deep understanding of and appreciation for *both* the creative *and* re-creative processes, as well as a keen awareness of and sensitivity to the needs and realities of contemporary society.

Leaders possessing the above mentioned qualities, together with the highest levels of artistic and personal integrity can best guide the wind band medium toward a brighter and more artistically meaningful future.

K. Other Facets of My Everyday Life

Since I average 20 weekend guest conducting and clinician engagements per year, it is really nice to all pile into the van as a family (Old English Sheepdog, West Highland Terrier, and

Blue and Gold Macaw included) and escape to our summer cottage in the Lake Geneva, Wisconsin area. While not at all fancy, the cottage, which was built in the 1920's by my great uncle, a successful Chicago artist/illustrator, has always been a special place for our family and will remain so for generations to come.

Living in Virginia, there are a number of nice, fairly close-to-home scenic/historic trips we enjoy taking when time permits. Our favorites include absolutely anywhere on the Blue Ridge Parkway, Colonial Williamsburg, Washington, DC, and Monticello (Thomas Jefferson's home, just outside of Charlottesville). Although we live 300 miles from the Atlantic coast, we always manage to spend one week on the Outer Banks of North Carolina, which are great any time of year. We also have enjoyed several cross-country trips, which always prove to become great and memorable family adventures.

As a hobby, I enjoy flag collecting and fly 3x5 foot state, international, and historic flags on our side yard flag pole. Flags are colorful symbols having often fascinating histories. And people in our neighborhood are always very curious and intrigued with some of the less familiar flags.

In my leisure time, I enjoy reading—almost exclusively non-fiction, especially U.S. history and presidential biography. Theodore H. White, David McCullough, and David Halberstam are among my favorite author/historians. While I have a quite sizeable collection of books on music, scores and recordings in my Radford University office, I must confess that my home library of non-music books is far greater in number than my office music holdings. I'm not quite sure what this means!

As one who is constantly fighting "the battle of the bulge"—i.e. my ongoing saga of trying to shed 15 to 20 pounds—the one form of vigorous physical exercise I truly enjoy is racquetball. I have been playing racquetball on a fairly regular basis for the past eight years, and I try to play at least twice per week. It is a great game and great stress reliever. One of my daughters has become a fine racquetball player and is rapidly becoming a fierce competitor. And I can assure the reader that any rumors of my ever losing a racquetball game to fellow composer-conductor colleague, Jack Stamp are, of course completely false! About the only other sports-related things I enjoy are keeping up with my favorite pro-ball teams: the Green Bay Packers, Boston Celtics, and especially the New York Yankees.

My television viewing is very limited, due to both time factors and the lack of quality programming. I am a news "junkie," (newspapers, magazines, NPR radio) and whenever possible, I like to view CBS *Sunday Morning* and the various news interview shows. The one prime time show we try to watch regularly is *The West Wing,* which in most respects represents what television can and should be in terms of providing the viewer with a strong cast delivering thought-provoking entertainment. When I am up late, perhaps while unwinding after a concert, I'll tune in to Jay Leno, but I must say I really continue to miss Johnny Carson and (especially) Doc Severinsen and The Tonight Show Band.

Our twin daughters, Beth and Briton, are as strikingly different as their mother and father. Fortunately, in most respects, they take after my wife far more than me! We are truly blessed with having two such beautiful, bright, and talented children. Having children certainly helps keep things in proper perspective and also helps remind us what is *really* important in life.

L. Published Works for Wind Band

Tribute for symphonic band (1985).

Commissioned by The United States Army Band, Colonel Eugene W. Allen, leader and commander. Runner-up, 1986 American Bandmasters Association Ostwald Award. Duration 6 minutes; grade 5; TRN Music Publisher.

Elegy for symphonic band (1987).

Commissioned by The United States Marine Band, Colonel John R. Bourgeois, director. Runner-up, 1989 American Bandmasters Association Ostwald Award. Duration 13 minutes; grade 6 TRN Music Publisher.

To Build A Fire for symphonic band (1991).

Based on the short story by Jack London. Commissioned by The United States Army Band, Colonel L. Bryan Shelburne, leader and commander. Winner, 1991 (15th Annual) National Band Association Composition Contest. Duration 17 minutes; grade 6; TRN Music Publisher.

Essay for symphonic band (1992).

Commissioned by Bowling Green State University Band Alumni for BGSU director of bands Mark S. Kelly, in commemoration and celebration of his 25 years of service to the University. Duration 11 minutes; grade 6; TRN Music Publisher.

A Movement For Rosa for symphonic band (1992).

Honoring Civil Rights Heroine Rosa Parks. Commissioned by The Florida Bandmasters Association. Duration 12 minutes; grade 5; TRN Music Publisher.

Watchman, Tell Us Of The Night for symphonic band (1994).

A musical tribute to the survivors of child abuse and neglect. Commissioned by The St. Louis Youth Wind Ensemble. Duration 15 minutes; grade 5; Neil A. Kjos Music Company.

Declarations for symphonic band (1995).

Commissioned by the Bishop Ireton High School Wind Ensemble—Alexandria, Virginia; Garwood Whaley, director. Duration 8 minutes; grade 6; TRN Music Publisher.

Whatsoever Things for symphonic band (1996).

Commissioned by the Revelli Foundation for the 1997 Honor Band of America (Ray Cramer, conductor) as the inaugural commission of the Paynter Project. Duration 14 minutes; grade 5; Southern Music Company.

Three London Miniatures for symphonic band (1997).

Commissioned by Regina B. Stott for the Woodward Academy Band—College Park, Georgia; Marguerite Wilder, director. Duration 8:30; grade 4; TRN Music Publisher.

Symphony From Ivy Green (Symphony No. 3) for soprano and wind orchestra (1999).

Text from the writings of Helen Keller. Commissioned by Marrietta M. Paynter for soprano Elizabeth Curtis and the Northwestern University Symphonic Wind Ensemble, Mallory Thompson, conductor. Duration 26 minutes; grade 6; Southern Music Company.

Pacific Commemoration for symphonic band (1999).

Commissioned by Michael Burch-Pesses and the Pacific University Wind Ensemble on the occasion of the 150th anniversary of the founding of Pacific University; Forest Grove, Oregon. Duration 8 minutes; grade 5; TRN Music Publisher.

The Shining City for narrator and symphonic band (2001).

Text from the speeches and writings of Ronald Reagan, 40th President of the United States. Commissioned by James F. Keene and University of Illinois Bands in conjunction with the Mark H. Hindsley Commissioning Project. Duration 21 minutes; grade 5; Neil A Kjos Music Company.

In Memoriam for symphonic band (2002).

Commissioned by the Revelli Foundation in memory of long-time Bands of America friend and colleague L.J. Hancock, Director of Bands, Norwin High School; North Huntingdon, Pennsylvania. Duration 4:30; grade 4; TRN Music Publisher.

chapter 4

david Gillingham

A. Biography

David Gillingham earned Bachelor and Master Degrees in Instrumental Music Education from the University of Wisconsin-Oshkosh and the Ph.D. in Music Theory/ Composition from Michigan State University. Dr. Gillingham has an international reputation for the works he has written for band and percussion. Many of these works are now considered standards in the repertoire. His commissioning schedule dates well into the first decade of the 21st century. His numerous awards include the 1981 *DeMoulin Award* for *Concerto for Bass Trombone and Wind Ensemble* and the 1990 *International Barlow Competition* (Brigham Young University) for *Heroes, Lost and Fallen.* Dr. Gillingham's works have been recorded by Klavier, Sony and Summit Records. His works are regularly performed by nationally recognized ensembles including the Prague Radio Orchestra, Cincinnati Conservatory of Music Wind Ensemble, The University of Georgia Bands, University of North Texas Wind Ensemble, Michigan State University Wind Ensemble, Oklahoma State Wind Ensemble, University of Oklahoma Wind Ensemble, Florida State Wind Ensemble, University of Miami Wind Ensemble, University of

Illinois Symphonic Band, Illinois State Wind Symphony, University of Minnesota Wind Ensemble, Indiana University Wind Ensemble and the University of Wisconsin Wind Ensemble. Also, nationally known artists, Fred Mills (Canadian Brass), Randall Hawes (Detroit Symphony) and Charles Vernon (Chicago Symphony Orchestra) have performed works by Dr. Gillingham. Over sixty of his works for band, choir, percussion, chamber ensembles, and solo instruments are published by C. Alan, Hal Leonard, Southern Music, Music for Percussion, Carl Fischer, Moon of Hope, MMB, T.U.B.A, I.T.A., and Dorn. Dr. Gillingham is a Professor of Music at Central Michigan University and the recipient of an *Excellence in Teaching Award* (1990), a *Summer Fellowship* (1991) a *Research Professorship* (1995), and most recently, the President's Research Investment Fund grant for his co-authorship of a proposal to establish an International Center for New Music at Central Michigan University. He is a member of ASCAP and the recipient of the *ASCAP Standard Award for Composers of Concert Music* in 1996, 1997, 1998, 1999, 2000, 2001, and 2002.

B. The Creative Process

I believe the creative process to be highly personal. The thought of having an audience during this process or anyone in the same room is unthinkable. Therefore, I must be alone and away from distractions for a reasonable amount of time, whether it is at the crack of dawn, between classes, during weekends, or workday evenings. The time of day is of no consequence. The length of time, however, is crucial. I must have a block of time that is adequate for me to focus entirely on the music. If I am between classes, an hour is often an insufficient amount of time to "get back into" the project. The actual creative process is one that transcends words. For me, it begins with a particular mood while sitting at the piano improvising. Sometimes I preface my work by playing music I admire, such as a Beethoven piano sonata, or a Bach chorale. Once I have ignited the "spark" or the idea, it is as if one electrode in the brain sends a signal to another electrode and the spontaneity continues like a snowball rolling down a hill.

For the past several years, I have preferred composing at my office/studio at Central Michigan University where I have a grand piano with a specially built Plexiglas writing board that attaches to the music stand so that the music paper is at chest level just above the keyboard. I also have appropriate hardware in the office which includes a Kurzweil 2000 synthesizer, and a MacIntosh G4 computer with a large portrait monitor whereby I can image a whole page of 11 X 17 inch score as it would appear on a music stand. In the "old days," when I was a struggling doctoral student at Michigan State University, I wrote everything by hand. We would begin with a condensed pencil score that was eventually meticulously copied on vellum with a manuscript pen. Finally, it would be transferred onto paper through an ammonia process machine not much smaller than a piece of John Deere farm equipment! Having "paid my dues" doing it the old way, I have quickly jumped onto the proverbial technological band wagon and embraced the use of *Finale* along with a synthesizer for my compositional work. Everything, however, does start by hand in my "sketch book" sitting at the piano. But, the quicker I can get to the "electronic score," the better. I see no value in leaving behind "autograph" scores for people to analyze. My music, when performed, is my individual "signature" whether it is being read from hand manuscript or computer generated manuscript.

I seldom compose away from the piano. To paraphrase Stravinsky, "Rarely do melodies and themes come to me away from the piano and, if they do, I often kick myself for not having pen and manuscript handy to write the ideas down." The whole spontaneity of the process occurs at the piano. This is my instrument, and is therefore the easiest to transmit my ideas through. Furthermore, this instrument seems to enhance the creative process. Playing by ear before I began formal piano lessons has helped my improvisatory skills at the piano over the years and, as a consequence, has greatly helped my ability to compose.

As a younger composer, I heard only the timbre of the piano when I composed at the piano. Now, however, it is easy for my ear to perceive ideas at the piano as various instrumental timbres. This is certainly not an innate ability and has been acquired through years of writing for band and orchestra as well as various chamber ensembles. Therefore, while at the piano, I not only compose, but I score simultaneously. Couple this with computer technology and the process is streamlined.

There can be no substantial creativity without the proper mindset. Perhaps this explains why so many of my works for band are programmatic. If the music tells a story, or if it reflects an image, there is a mood or a mindset that must be operative during the creative process. This is why I need large blocks of time to become reacquainted with a piece. It takes time to shift gears and find that particular mood. Even if the piece does not have any programmatic connotations, there is always a mood or a mindset that sets the tone and direction of the work.

C. The Approach to Orchestration

When I was in the 266th Headquarters Army Band in Vietnam from October of 1970 to January of 1972, I became interested in writing for band. I set out to compose what I thought was going to be a wonderful concert march. The piece consumed my time for months. Finally, I was given the opportunity to conduct the work in a reading session. It was a scoring disaster! Though I was a mere couple feet away from the flutes and clarinets, I couldn't hear them. They were simply scored too low. This was a humble beginning and it motivated me to work hard at correcting what I perceived to be a weakness in my writing. Later, while working on my doctorate at Michigan State University, I was particularly impressed at how my composition teacher, Jere Hutcheson, scored. His scoring was everything but traditional and his orchestra and band works featured a huge palette of instrumental colors, many of which were odd combinations. Particularly admirable was his use of percussion color. This influence was so profound that I wrote my first percussion ensemble work (*Paschal Dances*) featuring many of the sounds, techniques, and colors used by Hutcheson. This affinity for percussion color, as one might surmise, found its way into my band pieces. Thus, I consider percussion color a most vital and integral part of the overall sound of the band. Another scoring influence has come from the monumental orchestral works of the romantic period, which feature robust and dramatic brass and shimmering woodwinds.

Over the years I have developed a sort of "scoring gospel according to Gillingham." I have developed a philosophy and technique of scoring as a result of my great love of orchestral works and my desire to make the band sound more orchestral. Because of the use of multiple (more than two) clarinets and flutes, the band has taken on a stereotypical "squeeze box" sound. This has likely come about because of transcriptions that replace the violins with tutti clarinets. Of course, there is a need and a place for this type of scoring, but I don't think it should dominate the whole band repertoire.

In my discussion of the band in my scoring class, I preach the "A-B-C's": *Autonomy, Balance,* and *Color. Autonomy* emphasizes the individuality of each instrument and stresses the use of the individual color of the instrument, rather than its membership of a large group. I often treat the woodwinds (and brass) as "orchestral" winds in pairs and often as solos. I reserve the tutti scoring for the sections requiring volume, strength, and depth. *Balance* is the traditional concept of making sure instruments project with cognizance of their tessitura strengths and weaknesses. Balance, of course, can always be corrected by adjusting dynamics, but when this doesn't work, it is a scoring problem. My first "march," with flutes scored within the staff, is a perfect example of disregard for balance. The final principle, *color,* is perhaps the most important. Choosing appropriate colors is paramount in the scoring process. I have always maintained that average melodic, harmonic, and rhythmic material can be greatly enhanced by great scoring. This is certainly not to say that I encourage average melodic, harmonic, and rhythmic material! Let it suffice to say that scoring is an essential part of the creative process whether you are writing for a solo instrument (yes, you can still think in terms of the color of the various parts of the instrument's tessitura), or for a large ensemble such as the band.

The color of the percussion family intrigues me and is an essential element of all my band scores. It is an ever-expanding plethora of sounds. I am in continual search of new "sounds" and new combinations of the standard instruments. Many of the combinations and sounds that I have incorporated into my band works were suggested by the late Robert Hohner, Professor of Percussion at Central Michigan University, or by many of his students. Such sounds have included water-dipped crotales, suspended cymbal on the timpani, crotales on roto-toms, mallets playing on the strings of the piano, bowed cymbal, bowed tam-tam, the stick end of the mallet on the bars of the marimba, bowed marimba, bowed vibraphone, bowed crotales, and, my all-time favorite, the brake drum. Many of my band works utilize the color of the marimba, which has such a warm and mellow tone. It can be a "life saver" in very quiet sections. I also have an affinity for the combination of bells and vibraphone.

Many have said that my scoring "signature" is my feature of the low brass (including the horns) on lyrical chorale-like melodic lines. I do, in fact, have a deep affection for that section. After all, I grew up playing euphonium in band.

D. Views from the Composer to the Conductor Pertaining to Score Study and Preparation

All conductors are aware of the value of score *preparation.* This preparation can differ depending on the composer of the work. Beyond the usual marking of metrical changes, tempi, and entrance cues, I would make the following suggestions for preparation of my scores.

The conductor should have a clear idea of the formal structure of the work. Many of my works are programmatic and therefore the structure coincides with a certain sequence of events. Basically, there are two types of forms: 1) those based on the return of materials, and 2) those which are through-composed with no return of material. Knowing this formal structure will aid the conductor in the "pacing" of the events.

Analyze the score for motivic and thematic material. Motivic and thematic material are the life and soul of my music. Not only is it crucial that the conductor be familiar with the melodic/motivic material, but he/she must be aware of which instrument or instruments carry these lines. It is a sort of "who's on first/who's on second" situation. Armed with this knowledge, the conductor should be able to effectively rehearse the work in respect to volume and balance.

Pay particular attention to metric modulation. I have an affinity for the use of this metrical formula whereby a former rhythmic value equates to a new rhythmic value. This rhythmic formula is a precise mathematical way of changing tempos. Unfortunately, it has become the source of many questions and confusion among band conductors.

Know the tonal plan of the work. Conductors should be aware that until rather recently, most of my band scores were in "C" and untransposed. It seemed that this was the trend of the past century and I was under the impression that conductors preferred this format. After a number of complaints, I have returned to the transposed format. Be aware, however, that because the tonality of many of my works shifts rather freely, I seldom use key signatures, and one could easily mistake a score without a signature as one in "C." This being said, I can safely say that most of my music is tonally-based and the conductor should be able to ascertain tonal centers throughout the piece. Even when there are key signatures, the conductor should be aware that these signatures are merely a convenience for the composer—so that he/she doesn't have to go through the work of placing all those sharps and flats in front of the notes. With the advent of computer notation these days, this becomes a moot point! Suffice it to say, however, that the key signature is not a precise predictor of the tonality (i.e. three sharps could indicate A-Major, f#-minor, b-Dorian, c#-Phrygian, etc.). With all of this being said, conductors should indicate all of the tonal centers in the piece. Since I perceive key centers as colors and moods, the conductor will then have a better understanding of the emotional character of the work.

The harmonic structure is another indicator of the style of the composer. Though I certainly don't advocate that all band directors become theoreticians and analyze pieces chord by chord, I do suggest that the conductor have at least some familiarity with the chord vocabulary of the composer. For example, a four-note cluster sonority could be perceived as "wrong notes" in one of my works only because the surrounding section may be quite tonal. Knowing that I often use such sonorities for percussive attacks or for mood changes would certainly give the conductor a clue as to whether the notes are intended or not intended. There is also a predilection in my music to have unison horns in their high register playing notes that are clearly non-harmonic. I absolutely relish the intense degree of tension created by these notes! Unfortunately, more times than not, conductors will second guess me and perceive the notes as simply mistakes in the score.

It is important that conductors can detect textural changes in the music. A case in point would be a fugato development, which I have been known to use at times. Understanding the "prime players" in such a texture is extremely important. Each entering instrument must be heard and then must diminish in volume when accompanying the next entrance.

One last key element in score preparation is an understanding of the orchestration. As formerly pointed out, the percussion timbre has a high degree of importance in my band scores. Additionally, one will find chamber-like scoring and a tendency toward low brass chorale-like writing. Knowing this, the conductor can zero in on and carefully rehearse the sections featuring those timbral combinations.

An understanding of the *proportion* of the work can be achieved by an analysis of the formal structure of the work. After the conductor has prepared the score, he/she should have full understanding of the form. As I stated in the aforementioned paragraphs, many of my works are programmatic, and this sequence of events will aid in gauging its proportion. Each segue or transition into each event or section is also important. If these sections cannot be linked together in a convincing fashion, then the whole proportion of the work will be confusing to the listener.

Pacing the work can be problematic. Despite a conductor's knowledge of the form, melody, harmony, metrical scheme, and texture, putting it all together so that it comes across as music can sometimes be difficult. I believe that the pacing is related to the formal structure in that each event or section must occur "in its own time" not too soon and not too late. Also, each event must achieve the proper emotional emphasis. To do this, careful attention must be paid to tempo, tempo changes, and dynamic contrast. Furthermore, it will be necessary to maintain proper balance so that there is a clear differentiation between the melodic line and the harmony.

How does one convey the *passion* of the music? Understandably, this may be the most difficult task for the conductor. We have all heard performances of our pieces in which, despite a flawless technical presentation, the passion was noticeably absent. I think this occurs for two possible reasons: 1) the technique takes precedence over the musicality/passion, or 2) the conductor is not aware of where the "musical moments" occur in the piece. These musical moments are places where there is a sort of apex or pinnacle of emotion. Some pieces only have one such moment and some have them in multiples. Just as a phrase has a point of destination, so does a piece of music. I have been truly blessed to have worked with a number of wonderful conductors who have been able to extract the passion from my music. I would love to name them all here, but my fear is that I would inadvertently leave someone out. Hurting the feelings of one of my dear friends would be devastating. My point, however, is that these conductors have become my friends. They have come to know me as a person. I have had the pleasure of working with them and their ensembles on many of my pieces. They are never reluctant to pick up the phone and call me and ask questions about my music and the "rhyme and reason" of its existence. Therefore, getting to know the person behind the music may be the easiest path for a conductor to take in conveying the passion of the music.

E. Discuss the Relationship Between the Composer and the Commissioning Party

The relationship between the composer and the commissioning party must either start out as or become one that is personal. I don't believe that the composer should be elevated to the level of "godliness," towering above all the rest of humanity. A commissioned piece of music should result from an equal partnership between the composer and the commissioning party. That being said, it is important that the commissioning party not exert any control over the artistic direction of the work. When a composer is selected for a commission, it is usually because the commissioning party has an admiration for the entire output of the composer and not just one single work. A composer can never duplicate what he or she has done previously in a new work. If the composer can do this, then perhaps the composer is composing by "formula" and therefore composing for the wrong reason. Therefore, I do not consider it apropos for the commissioning party to dictate any sort of artistic authority over the composer. I do feel, however, that the commissioning party can make suggestions as to the programmatic direction of the piece. Recently, I was commissioned by the Florida Bandmasters Association and it was suggested that I might consider depicting the colorful history of the Seminole tribe in Florida. The idea was intriguing, and I began to research the history of the Seminoles. The resulting piece, *Council Oak,* tells the story of the Seminole tribe in Florida using authentic Seminole songs. It is also appropriate for the commissioning party to apprise the composer of instrumentation limitations, weaknesses of particular sections, and the technical level of the ensemble. As composers, we must be aware that commissioned pieces are "tailor made" creations for the commissioning party. It would be irresponsible for a composer to disregard the technical limitations, the instrumentation, or weaknesses of the ensemble for which the work is being written. All but one of my commissioning experiences have involved some wonderful collaborations between myself, the conductor, and the ensemble. The one disappointing experience occurred when the commissioning party did not follow through with a performance or a recording of the work. This occurred early in my career when my commissioning experience was quite "green" and resulted because of a one-sided relationship where the commissioning party wanted to control the artistic direction of the work. Nevertheless, I have learned from this sour experience and all of my successive commissions have been memorable and worthwhile. Especially notable have been my experiences with junior high and high school ensembles. Because of the technical limitations of these groups, my artistic integrity has been challenged. One can't simply "pull out all the stops" as one can when writing for college or university ensemble. Creating music of depth and substance at this level becomes an uphill battle, but the rewards are tremendous!

F. Views on the Teaching of Composition and How to Mentor the Young Composer

My philosophy of teaching composition at the college or university level may be considered somewhat nontraditional. My role as a "teacher" of composition is as much a "cheerleader" as it is an educator. I am there to pat the students on their backs and tell them that their music is progressing in the right direction. When it does not progress in that direction, I need to tell the student what to do to change that direction. While I think it is crucial for the composition teacher to educate the student in all of the compositional trends and techniques of the past century and of the current decade, I do not think it is appropriate for us to force the student into a stylistic "box." By this, I do not think it serves us well as teachers of composition to force the student to write music that will ultimately receive the "stamp of approval" from those in the compositional world who feel they are on the "cutting edge." On the contrary, we, as composition teachers, should work toward the end of helping the student develop his/her individual "voice." We must lay out all the wares of composition on the table in front of the student and let him/her pick and choose what methods can best be incorporated into the student's individual style. How is education being served if we "mass produce" composition students by dictating exactly what needs to be part of their style based solely on the current trends of the world of composition? Of course, we are there to push, encourage, guide, correct, advise, and give them all the tools they need to become successful composers.

As a mentor, I tell students that they should only pursue a degree in composition if it is for the right reason. This reason, in my opinion, is that there is music inside of them that they feel obligated to release. I have been "releasing" music from my inner self since I was a child, and even though my original career path was that of a teacher, I eventually discovered that composition would one day dominate my life. Some of the wrong reasons for pursuing composition are: 1) "I want to become a star," 2) "I want to have my works published so that I can make lots of money," and 3) "I want to impress people with the most shocking and innovating music they have ever heard." Music needs to flow from the inner self onto the paper (or computer!). My greatest joy as a composer has come from those particular moments when I have realized that I have created something that I know couldn't have possibly come from my head (which supposedly is filled with a vast knowledge of compositional craft), but has come directly from my heart.

G. Individuals Who Have Been Especially Influential in Your Development and Career

First and foremost, my parents have exerted the most influence on my career. As far back as I can remember in my life (3-years old), my parents have nurtured my musical career. They paid for my music lessons, encouraged me, and sympathized with all the "ups and downs" of being a struggling musician. They are also responsible for making me the person I am. My ethics, morals, and spiritual beliefs are largely the influence of my parents. For this, I will never be able to thank them enough during my lifetime. Hopefully, the music I have created will reflect my gratitude. My siblings, Jim and Bonna, have also been supportive. Both of them were involved in music in high school, and they have carried their love for music into their adult lives.

There are other people who have also had significant roles in guiding my career. When I was growing up on a large farm in Rosendale, Wisconsin, my aunt and uncle and cousins lived upstairs. I recall many "get-togethers" with my aunt, uncle, and cousins where we would stand around an old pump organ and sing through old hymns accompanied by my Aunt Jeanne. My Aunt Jeanne, Uncle Wayne and my cousins Jane, Lyndel, John, and Paul were supportive of my musical career all through my life and those old hymns have found their way back into some of my works.

While in high school, my band director, Ralph Crain, encouraged me to become a band director. While in undergraduate school at the University of Wisconsin-Oshkosh, my theory teacher, Roger Dennis, became another major influence on my life. He was an excellent teacher whose techniques I have attempted to emulate in the classroom. Also influential at Oshkosh was my piano teacher, James Kohn. He pushed my technical skills to the limit and taught me how to find passion in music.

After receiving my Bachelor of Music degree, I took a "forced" hiatus in the army, first with the Fifth Army Band in Chicago, and then with the 266th Headquarters Band in Vietnam. This stint in the Army was tremendously important in my life. I met many wonderful musicians in both of these bands and started growing my "writing wings," as a staff arranger and then composing my first original work for band (which, by the way, was a failure!).

Upon my release from the Army, I finished my Masters in Instrumental Music Education at UW-Oshkosh, taught middle school band for four years, and then traveled to East Lansing, Michigan, to work on my Ph.D. in Theory/Composition at Michigan State University. Roger Dennis, my theory teacher, was solely responsible for encouraging me to pursue the doctorate and for getting me admitted to the program at Michigan State. While at Michigan State, Jere Hutcheson helped me grow as a composer. I have already mentioned his influence earlier in this chapter. My first work for band was published while I was at Michigan State. Kenneth Bloomquist, director of bands, was responsible for opening this window in my career. While at MSU, I also had the good fortune to meet H. Owen Reed, but had the misfortune of not being able to study with him—he was retired. My moment with Owen Reed would come later.

My first college teaching job was at Spring Arbor College (now Spring Arbor University) in Michigan where I met a wonderful colleague, Ken Bauman, director of bands. I am grateful for him as a mentor and a most supportive colleague.

After coming to Central Michigan University in 1984, I was awarded a Summer Fellowship where I was successful in begging Owen Reed to take me on as a student in the summer of 1992. He and his wife spent their summers at Canadian Lakes, a mere thirty-minute drive from the campus of Central Michigan University. Words will never be able to describe what a memorable experience that summer was. Here was a man who had known Roy Harris, Aaron Copland, and Leonard Bernstein! He generously shared many of his compositional "secrets" with me. Once in a while he would take me fishing (of which my skills were nil) and he would relate stories about his life. I reaped the benefits of that summer, coming away as not only a better composer, but also a better person because of my relationship with this great American composer.

Finally, there are many band conductors in this country with whom I have had the honor and privilege of working. There are too many to mention here, but suffice it to say that their support and friendship have enhanced my career more than they will ever know. And most importantly, my wife Linda, who has been a constant source of inspiration and support for the past 28 years.

H. Ten works I Believe All Band Conductors at All levels Should Study

There are certainly a multitude of works from the band, orchestra, vocal, and chamber repertoire that should be studied by all band conductors. It is impossible to narrow this list down to ten works. I can, however, list at least ten works that have had a profound influence upon my compositional study and career. They are as follows (not in any order of preference):

1. Bartok, *Concerto for Orchestra.* Not only is this a musical masterpiece, but it is a masterpiece of orchestration.

2. Holst, *Suite in F for band.* This is a gem in the band repertoire with classic form and inspired melodic and harmonic material.

3. Jacob, *William Byrd Suite.* The suite is a wonderful example of effective scoring of masterpieces of early music.

4. Grainger, *Lincolnshire Posy.* To me, this work is representative of the sheer genius of Percy Grainger. The scoring is inspired and the passion derived from English folk songs is unequalled.

5. Stravinsky, *The Rite of Spring.* All band conductors should be familiar with this work. It is a towering monument of the last century and contains a wealth of compositional techniques identified with "modern music."

6. R. Strauss, *Don Juan.* To my mind, the scoring of this work is unequalled during the Romantic to early twentieth century. The programmatic format has greatly inspired my own compositions.

7. Beethoven, *Symphony No. 5.* Obviously, this is one of the greatest musical compositions ever written. One can study the melodic, harmonic, and rhythmic material and come away a richer man. But, to me, the work is a study of the passion of the human soul.

8. Copland, *Symphony No. 3.* Not only is this one of the finest American works of the past century, but it also seems to express the American ideal better than any other work by

an American composer. Multiple performances of this symphony never fail to leave me in awe.

9. Brahms, *German Requiem.* The genius of this musical work is only transcended by its spirituality and, upon hearing a performance, is about as close to God as one can get on earth.

10. Crumb, *Black Angels for Electric String Quartet.* The colors exuded by this work are mind-boggling. The ambience is mesmerizing and the emotion is tremendously intense. This was the first piece of so-called "contemporary" or "avante garde" music to which I was exposed. It has had a profound effect on my compositional style.

I. Ten Composers Whose Music Overall Speaks to Me in Especially Meaningful Ways

At risk of leaving out someone really important, the following composers come to mind as having a profound influence on my life as a composer. I am grateful to (again not in any particular order):

1. Ludwig van Beethoven—for the sheer emotion I derive from his music.

2. Richard Strauss—for his scoring genius.

3. Joseph Schwantner—for his unique way of creating a romantic sound through the use of extended techniques.

4. David Maslanka—for the depth and sophistication of his music.

5. Aaron Copland—for being a role model for the "American sound."
6. Paul Hindemith—for his innovative harmony and his tenacity to hold on to tonality.
7. Bela Bartok—for his rhythmic creativity, scoring, and tenacity to take the path less traveled.
8. Peter Tchaikowsky—for the sheer excitement of his music.
9. Wolfgang Amadeus Mozart—for his perfection of formal structure, and
10. J. S. Bach—for his belief that his talent was a gift and that all of his works were dedicated "to the glory of God."

J. The Future of the Wind Band

My prognosis for the wind band is that it can look forward to a healthy future. In the past twenty-five years, I have seen some interesting developments. The band repertoire has gradually changed from a reliance on orchestral transcriptions to compositions written expressly for the band. There has been a philosophical change in instrumentation to distinguish between the chamber-like wind ensemble and the large symphonic band. The wind ensemble has precipitated a large body of music that is more "orchestral." Perhaps most important, the literature for the band, symphonic band, and wind ensemble has reached a level of sophistication equal to that of the orchestral repertoire. There are a large number of first-rate composers who have chosen to write nearly exclusively for the band. They have taken this path since they are almost guaranteed a performance, and the level of playing, at least at the college or university level, is professional. Many composers enjoy multiple performances. And why shouldn't they? Their pieces are dramatic, sophisticated, and engaging. The College Band Directors National Association has also helped to elevate the image of band music with its ambitious commissioning project, enlisting Pulitzer Prize-winning composers such as John Harbison, Michael Colgrass, and Joan Tower to write for band.

Despite all these positive advances, a stigma remains over bands, band music and band composers. I was once told that I "could never be recognized as a great composer if I continued to write for band." This said by a prominent band conductor. What does this say when there is this type of derogative attitude among our own ranks? The bulk of our general audience still perceives the band as an "outdoor ensemble" that plays concerts in the park consisting of Sousa marches and transcribed light classics. Make no mistake, Sousa marches and transcriptions are part of the heritage of the band, but the repertoire has been ever expanding over the years. Certainly the CBDNA Commissioning Project is helping the image of the band. We are moving forward and band composers will continue to distinguish themselves. Perhaps one of these years, a work for band will be awarded the Pulitzer Prize. It is only a matter of time and time is on our side.

K. Other Facets of My Everyday Life

About five years ago, I was literally a "jack of all trades and master of none." In addition to composing, I taught theory and composition full time, directed the men's chorus, sang in a District Championship barbershop quartet and was the organist at a local church. All of this in addition to spending quality time with my wife and two children! I remember my wife saying one day, "Dave, you have to decide what you are going to do when you grow up." She was right. I needed to focus on one thing, or a least upon less than what I was doing. I chose composition. Since then, I have enjoyed increased success in that area. Still, I find some time for other things. My family always comes first and I strive to do "family-oriented" activities on a weekly basis. This might be something as simple as going to a shopping mall to something more strenuous like cross country skiing (with the Gillinghams this is quite the "comedy of errors"). In the summer I enjoy gardening. Our family often takes at least one trip to Beaver Island in upper Lake Michigan. Beaver Island is sparsely populated and there is an abundance of nature and nature trails. When weather permits, my wife and I enjoy walking. If there is any "spare" time left, I am a big fan of Dean Koontz, and I can easily get immersed in one of his latest novels.

L. Comprehensive List of Works for Band

Symphonic Proclamation (1977)
Grade: 5/6
Publisher: Jenson Publications, Inc., 1979 <OUT OF PRINT>
Premiere: Nov. 16, 1977; Michigan State University Symphonic Band, Kenneth Bloomquist, cond.

Intrada Jubilante (1979)
Grade: 4
Publisher: C. Alan Publications, 1999
Premiere: May, 1979; Webster Stanley Junior High Band, Roger Lalk, cond.

Concerto for Bass Trombone and Wind Ensemble (1980)

Grade: 6
Publisher: Carl Fischer, Inc., 1986
Premiere: June 4, 1981; Michigan State University, Stanley DeRusha, cond., Curtis Olson, Bs. trombone.

Concerto for Woodwind Quintet and Wind Ensemble (1983)

Grade: 4/5
Publisher: C. Alan Publications, 2000
Premiere: Jan. 13, 1995, MENC, Indianapolis, IN; Powers Quintet, Central Michigan University Symphonic Wind Ensemble, John E. Williamson, cond.

Revelation (1983)

Grade: 4
Publisher: Hal Leonard, Inc., 1989
Premiere: May 22, 1983; Grand Ledge High School Symphonic Wind Ensemble, Michael Kaufman, cond.

Chronicle (1984)

Grade: 6
Publisher: Carl Fischer, 1986
Premiere: Apr. 18, 1984; Eastern Michigan University Concert Winds, Max Plank, cond.

Heroes, Lost and Fallen (1989)

Grade: 5
Publisher: Hal Leonard, Inc., 1991
Premiere: May 7, 1989; Ann Arbor Concert Band, Ann Arbor, Mi.; Victor Bordo, cond.

Concerto for Alto Saxophone and Wind Ensemble (1990)

Grade: 6
Publisher: MMB Music, 1990 (rental)
Premiere: Mar. 17, 1990; Central Michigan University; CMU Wind Ensemble, John Williamson, cond., John Nichol, A. Sax.

Vintage (1991)
Grade: 4
Publisher: T.U.B.A. Press, 1991
Premiere: Jan. 18, 1991; Ann Arbor, Mi.; Big Rapids H.S. Band, Kent Boulton, cond., Ed. Mallet, euph. soloist. MSBOA Midwestern Conference.

Prophecy of the Earth-band with pipe organ (1993)
Grade: 4
Publisher: C. Alan Publications, 2000
Premiere: May 20, 1993; Dallas, TX., J. J. Pearce H.S. Band; Matthew McInturf, cond., Paul Riedo, organ.

Apocalyptic Dreams (1995)
Grade: 6
Publisher: Southern Music Co., 1996
Premiere: Mar. 2, 1995; Univ. of Georgia Symphony Band, H.D. Satterwhite, cond.

Quintessence (1997)
Grade: 5
Publisher: C. Alan Publications
Premiere: Feb., 1997: Illinois State University—SU Wind Symphony, Stephen Steele, cond. ISU Brass Quintet; David Collier, perc.

Concertino for Four Percussion and Wind Ensemble (1997)
Grade: 5
Publisher: C. Alan Publications
Premiere: April 17, 1997: Oklahoma State University; OSU Wind Symphony Joseph Missal, cond.

A Light Unto the Darkness (1997)
Grade: 4
Publisher: C. Alan Publications, 1998
Premiere: April 16, 1998; University of Oklahoma; Mt. Pleasant H.S. W.E., Roger Sampson, cond.

Sub-Saharan Rhythm (1998)
Grade: 4
Publisher: C. Alan Publications, 1998
Premiere: March 19, 1998; Traverse City East J.H. Symphonic Band, Peter Deneen, conductor.

A Crescent Still Abides (1998)
Grade: 5/6
Publisher: C. Alan Publications, 1998
Premiere: May 7, 1998; Hofstra University Wind Ensemble, Peter Boonshaft, cond.

Galactic Empires (1998)
Grade: 5
Publisher: C. Alan Publications, 1998
Premiere: Mar. 12-15, 1998; Bands of America Festival, Indianapolis, IN.

New Century Dawn (1999)
Grade: 5/6
Publisher: C. Alan Publications, 1999
Premiere: July 6, 1999 at the 6th International WASBE conference; Oklahoma State University Wind Ens., Joseph Missal, cond.

Internal Combustion (1999)
Grade: 5/6
Publisher: C. Alan Publications, 2000
Premiere: December 1, 1999; New York State Honor Band, Jerry Junkin, cond., NYSSMA Convention.

Be Thou My Vision (1999)
Grade: 4
Publisher: C. Alan Publications, 2000
Premiere: October 26, 1999; Indiana University Wind Ensemble; Ray Cramer, cond.

When speaks the signal-trumpet tone (1999)
Grade: 6
Publisher: C. Alan Publications
Premiere: Mar. 30, 1999 University of Georgia Wind Ensemble; Fred Mills, trumpet; H. Dwight Satterwhite, cond.

And Can It Be? (2000)
Grade: 4
Publisher: C. Alan Publications, 2000
Premiere: Feb. 20, 2000; California All State Honor Band, H. Robert Reynolds, cond. California Band Directors Assoc. Convention, San Jose, CA.

Lamb of God (2001)
Grade: 5
Publisher: C. Alan Publications, 2001.
Premiere: Jan. 26, 2001; Illinois Music Educator Association All-State Conference. Southern Illinois University-Edwardsville Wind Symphony, John Bell, cond.

With Heart and Voice (2001)
Grade: 4/5
Publisher: C. Alan Publications, 2001
Premiere: May 20, 2001; Apple Valley High School Wind Ensemble (Apple Valley, MN), Scott A. Jones, conductor.

Council Oak (2001)
Grade: 4
Publisher: C. Alan Publications, 2002
Premiere: Jan. 12, 2002. Florida Bandmasters Convention, Tampa, Fl. Florida State Honors Band, John Whitwell, cond.

Proud and Immortal (2001)
Grade: 4/5
Publisher: C. Alan Publications, 2002
Premiere: Oct. 16, 2001; Oklahoma State University Wind Ensemble. Joseph Missal, cond.

Au Sable River Festival (2001)

Grade: 4
Publisher: C. Alan Publications, 2002
Premiere: May 20, 2002; Grayling H.S. Band (Grayling, MI). David Gillingham cond.

Bells of Freedom (2002)

Grade: 1
Publisher: C. Alan Publications, 2002

A Parting Blessing (2002)

Grade: 4
Publisher: C. Alan Publications, 2001
Premiere: Pending: May, 2002; Apple Valley High School Wind Ensemble, Craig Kirchoff, conductor.

Works for Chamber winds and percussion:

Serenade for Winds and Percussion (Songs of the Night)(1990)

Grade: 6
Publisher: C. Alan Publications, 2000
Premiere: March 5, 1990; MENC Convention, Washington D.C. Univ. of Georgia Wind and Perc. Faculty. H. D. Satterwhite, cond.

Waking Angels (1996)

Grade: 5/6
Publisher: C. Alan Publications 1997
Premiere: Mar. 1, 1997; CBDNA National Convention, Athens, GA. University of Georgia Wind Symphony, Dwight Satterwhite, cond.

chapter 5

david r. Holsinger

A. Biography

In 1999, having served 15 years as Composer in Residence to Shady Grove Church in Grand Prairie, Texas, award winning composer/ conductor David R. Holsinger relocated to Cleveland, Tennessee, where he teaches conducting and composition, and serves as Director of the Wind Ensemble at Lee University.

Holsinger's compositions have won four national competitions, including a two time ABA Ostwald Award. His works have also been finalists in the NBA and Sudler competitions. Educated at Central Methodist College, Fayette, Missouri, Central Missouri State University, Warrensburg, and the University of Kansas, Lawrence, Holsinger was also honored with an honorary Doctorate and the Gustavus Fine Arts Medallion, from Gustavus Adolphus College in St. Peter, Minnesota. In the summer of 1998, during the Texas Bandmasters Association convention in San Antonio, the United States Air Force Band of the West featured Holsinger as the HERITAGE VI composer. This prestigious series celebrating American wind composers was founded in 1992 and had previously honored Morton Gould, Ron Nelson, Robert Jager,

W. Francis McBeth, and Roger Nixon. An elected member of the American Bandmasters Association, Holsinger's recent honors include being inducted as a National Patron of Delta Omicron Music Fraternity, receiving the Distinguished Music Alumni Award from Central Missouri State University, the Christian Instrumental Directors Association 1999 Director of the Year Citation, Phi Mu Alpha Sinfonia's Orpheus Award, and biographical inclusion in both *The Heritage Encyclopedia of Band Music,* Vol. I and III, and *Program Notes for Band.* During the past ten years, Holsinger has served as visiting Composer in Residence at eleven American colleges or universities, and held the Acuff Chair of Excellence in the Creative Arts at Austin Peay State University, Clarksville, Tennessee.

In addition to his university duties, Holsinger spends much of his energies as a guest composer and conductor with All State organizations, professional bands, and university ensembles throughout the United States. When not composing or conducting, he plays with his HO train layout.

* * * *

My birth date is December 26, 1945. By all indications, I was born in an unwed mother's home in Kansas City, Missouri. Early in 1946, I was adopted by Marvin and Hannah Holsinger, who lived in a small farm community 50 miles east of the city. Among the things my parents knew about my birth parents was that both were high school students from Iowa, and each came from musical families. This information made a lasting impact on my parents, and when I was not quite five-years old, I began taking piano lessons with Mrs. Trenchard, the local piano teacher. My mother insistently declared that for the first year she had to "beat me to the piano," and after that, she spent a lifetime, "beating me away from the piano!" I mention all this to, in some small measure, explain the seed of my musical fervor, which has nothing to do with deep seated hostility toward John Thompson, Book One. It just seems that music was the center of my life for as long as I can remember.

As an only child, growing up on a farm in Hardin, Missouri, was not a bad life. I had my dogs, my .22 rifle, and I was alone and could be anything or anybody I imagined. One day a cowboy, next day a soldier...Superkid, able to leap tall buildings and jump off the garage roof, towel tied around the neck for lift, sailing through the air . . . usually suffering the inevitable broken body part. Other than that occasional setback, life was great on the farm. As expected, I helped my Dad with fieldwork. Of course, he had to suffer the plight of having a son who had to have three or four "music breaks" a day. Whatever chore I was assigned was always subject to interruption as I left the tractor and scurried to the farmhouse to play piano for a half an hour or so. He probably should have hired extra help.

I loved music. I sang myself to sleep every night. I took jazz lessons on the Hammond organ from the organist for the Kansas City Athletics. I knew how to "improvise" in Junior High. I was in every music and drama group in school. Everybody said I'd make a wonderful music teacher when I grew up and went to college.

I've attended Central Methodist College in Fayette, Missouri, Central Missouri State University in Warrensburg, and the University of Kansas at Lawrence. At the last two schools mentioned, the study of composition was my primary goal. However, it was an incident at that first small college that set me on the course I travel today.

In the 1950's and 1960's, Central Methodist College was a hotbed for music education graduates. Although very small, with fewer than 1000 students, the college seemed to produce an inordinate number of very good instrumental and vocal educators for the state's public schools. Almost every music teacher I had in public school had been a graduate of CMC. Somewhere along the way, I just knew it was the place for me. I went to Central Methodist to become "the music teacher."

However, I discovered one thing about my career choice very early in my education. In comparison to all my classmates, their desire to be a music teacher was *considerably greater* than my desire to be a music teacher. But, music was all I knew and, of course, everyone back home *did* have my future all figured out. Who was I to argue? I was having a great time being a college guy, so why buck the system? In the spring of my junior year, everything changed.

Like a number of small colleges in the Midwest, the Central Methodist Band and Choir always had a spring tour, usually consisting of seven days of travel with three concerts a day at schools or churches. One group headed east, the other west. In the fall of 1965, our band director announced that we would have a guest composer traveling with us on the upcoming spring tour. His name was Vaclav Nelhybel, and he would be conducting two of his recent works, *Trittico* and *Chorale*. The pieces arrived. The music was big and brash, loud and gritty. They were vibrant and full of thunderings and poundings, and we couldn't wait for this man to show up on our doorstep! My classmates and I were all young and egomaniacal in those days. The first thought in our collective mind was "we're hot players and we're going to show this guy what music is all about!"

Two days before the tour, Vaclav Nelhybel walked into our band hall, stepped on the podium, lifted his arms, and as I watched that first slashing downbeat of the baton, I realized I didn't have a clue what *his* music was all about. I had absolutely no idea how "personal" music could be. In that one electrifying instant, I saw brutality, beauty, angst, anguish, joy, triumph, sorrow, exhilaration, devastation, despair, hope, faith . . . all in the eyes of one man conducting HIS music. For seven days we rode the bus and played the schools. At the close of the final tour concert, I sat in the back of an empty stage and wept. I was overcome by the transformation I knew was happening in my life. I had now come face to face with my future. I wanted to be a composer.

The following week was spring break. I went home to the farm, set down at the piano and proceeded to work, morning, noon, and night, writing my first composition. I don't remember the exact day my mother ran screaming from the house, but nevertheless, at the end of the week, my first composition emerged; a work for band I entitled *Prelude and Rondo.* A few years later, it was to become my first published work.

In 1967, I graduated from Central Methodist and immediately moved to Central Missouri State to begin a master's degree. From that point, life seemed to gather that uncompromising acceleration none of us are ready for, but we all experience. I "joined" the army; I married; I won my first composition contest, which was sponsored by the Federation of Music Clubs of America. My wife and I moved to Europe where I was stationed in Germany; I won my second composition contest at Kent State University. I returned to civilian life and back to school. I played trumpet, keyboards, and sang in a rock band for five years. (Baby #1). Several more of my compositions are published to good reviews. I teach high school music and I go back to school at the University of Kansas, (Baby #2), and win my first Ostwald prize in composition. (Baby#3).

I accepted Jesus Christ as my Savior, and I moved to Texas.

I know that, at this juncture, many are asking themselves, "Aren't serious composers supposed to suffer more?" Let me point out that for the first seven and a half months we lived in Texas, I worked as a laborer in a drapery factory, cutting out blackout drape ten hours a day, six days a week. Every evening I would come home with my hands so swollen that it was impossible to play the piano. However, during that period, I composed *The Deathtree* for the U.S. Marine Band, which would later become the centerpiece of *The Easter Symphony*. I was also commissioned and wrote *In the Spring, At the Time when Kings Go Off to War*, which shortly thereafter, became my second winning entry in the American Bandmasters Ostwald Prize. (OK, it appears that even my suffering has gone well! So much for the "hard-knock" life).

Of the past 20 years, I have spent 15 at Shady Grove Church in Grand Prairie, Texas, in the center of the Dallas-Ft. Worth metroplex. During my tenure there, I served in many capacities as a music minister. However, for the most part, I was a composer in residence. I served a wonderful pastor named Olen Griffing, who understood that my passion to compose was a ministry that extended beyond the walls of his church. Therefore, it was his heart to be my "patron" and help me succeed in that evocation.

At the time of this writing, I am serving my third year as the Director of the Wind Ensemble and a teacher of composition and conducting at Lee University in Cleveland, Tennessee, at the foothills of the Smokey Mountains near Chattanooga.

B. The Creative Process

As a "maturing" composer, I realize that "personal emotion" is a primal factor in my output. I easily "wear my heart on my sleeve," compose music that is experience motivated, and make no apologies for compositions that are written, expressly, to be "in your face." I wish I was a glib and inspiring wordsmith, but I'm not. I speak best with music. I'm just a composer guy.

I don't produce a lot of music in a year. It's not that I'm a slow and meticulous composer, but rather, my output is a direct product of my lifestyle. I accept only three or four commissions a year, because I have only the months of July through December in which to write. Somewhere along the way, 12 or so years ago, I was invited to guest conduct an All-State Band. Up until that invitation, I had perhaps conducted a half dozen regional and local bands in the Dallas-Ft. Worth area. I'm not sure how it happened to this day, but suddenly I was considered a fairly adequate conductor/motivator. This newfound career became extremely time-consuming. From January to June, I find myself on the road Thursday through Sunday conducting, and Monday through Wednesday I am teaching at the university. All the other days I like to spend time with my wife and family. Do you see the math problem here?

As with that very first composition written over spring break of 1966, some things have not changed. I am basically a "binge" composer. Whereas many composers set aside that special time of the day when they are most apt to feel the muse rising, I, on the other hand, grab any chance I can get and then "go around the clock." Music is easy. When it's there, it simply pours out. This is not to say that I don't have a "process." I do. But I have also always had a good intuition about the movement of music. In fact, that intuition was probably the greatest detriment to my composition study as a young man. Many times, to the consternation of my teachers, I tended to leap over the process and depend on my intuitive gifting to complete the work. Basically I had the ability to make my music sound like, say Stravinsky, without really understanding the specific principle or craft of composition that Stravinsky represented at any given juncture of his career. I could imitate, without being able to offer explanation. Why some of my teachers just didn't kill me on the spot still begs explanation!

So what is my process? At its inception, it is a "visual" process. I need a "picture" to paint. This explains why I write very little absolute music, but rather find myself exploring "story" music; writing compositions that depend on "word painting" even when no text appears in the finished product. I need a title before beginning a piece. I knew the story line for *To Tame the Perilous Skies* for weeks. It was intended to be a composition celebrating the 50th anniversary of the Battle of Britain, but until the actual title was birthed, no note was put on the page. Silly quirk.

I wised up about studying the compositional process and using the intuitive gift to my advantage. Consider again, Stravinsky. Here was a man who never settled for the "status quo." He is an example to my students of a composer who watched and examined as the winds of change blew through a half century of compositional exploration. He carved, he dissected, he pulled aspects from each "process" that sped by, and he put them in his own personal compositional toolbox. And then, after they all rattled around for a time, he pulled them out, he molded them to his specific compositional genius, and suddenly his music was old and new at the same time. The label may have said "neoclassic," but the flavor was Stravinsky.

Later, the process might be "twelve-tone," but the essence was first and foremost "Stravinsky!"

I, as a student of composition, learned an important lesson studying the result of that evolution. I believe, over the past 20 years, I have managed to combine chosen concepts of the craft of composition with the limitlessness of intuition and establish a "style" of writing that fits my personal perspective of what music should be.

I compose at the piano, at the keyboard, and at the computer. My writing, for the most part, is linear.

I have had two great teachers of composition. I say "great" not because they were world renowned, but rather because they were EXACTLY the teacher I needed at the time I studied with each of them. The first was a man named Donald Bohlen, a student of Ross Lee Finney at Michigan, and at the time I met him, a "die hard" serialist! He was my composition instructor at Central Missouri State. To say that we were at opposite poles of the musical spectrum would be grossly understating the case. I learned more from this man in nine months than I had in the previous four years of college! He opened my ears and eyes to a 20th century of new sounds and compositional methods I had no idea even existed, much less an understanding of how they worked.

The second great teacher I had was Charles Hoag, Professor of Composition at the University of Kansas. From Donald Bohlen and Charles Hoag I learned that, regardless of the process I choose to utilize in my composition, that process must be *defendable.* At any given point, one must be able to identify and trace the development of any single idea or flow of idea, but from Charles Hoag, I learned a very special lesson. Hoag taught me that I need not be ashamed of the choices I make. We are all bits and pieces of every composer, teacher, mentor, and musician with which we have associated. However, we do not need to be carbon copies of anyone. No matter what the process we choose, whether we are conservative, radical, or somewhere in between, it is *okay* to have a *personal* voice in the process. I am aware that even if I chose to compose in the most mathematically intricate synthesis dealing with structure, pitch density, registral display, and timbral selection, I would also be cognizant that it was a "personal" decision and it was MY voice that said, "*I* have decided this is the *way* it is going to *be*...."

Back to more practical matters. I have used Finale Software, MAC version, for a long time. My serial number is *very* small. When I started using the software package, the manuals weighed 14 pounds! The screen on my original Macintosh Classic appeared to be only about six inches square. (I spent more time waiting for "redraw" than breathing). I probably only use 60% of the software's capabilities, but what I do use, I use very well! Just call me "Mr. Computer Whiz."

Working the DVD in the den is still a mystery.

C. The Approach to Orchestration

It is obvious to me that orchestration is as much a product of the composer's style as are the choices he or she makes compositionally. In that regard, I consider myself a fairly "white bread" orchestrator!

I am so impressed with people who really deal in the color palette available. Philip Spark's use of muted brass in his second *Dance Movement* is incredible. I very rarely think of using mutes. Fellow composer Jim Barnes, who I consider a master instrumentationalist, is constantly aware of the instrumental color spectrum he deals with. He is consummately mindful of the soloistic qualities of each instrument. The scores of his major works reverberate with vivid timbral hues. I hardly ever write solos or think about soloistic qualities. Mark Camphouse's instrumentation choices always seem to forge a grand and glorious, almost Mahler-esque orchestral canvas. I think we're fortunate he chose to compose for bands rather than orchestra!

Instrumental color is as much a signature of band composers as is their content. Let's face it, Percy Grainger *sounds* like Percy Grainger. There is a distinctive quality in his instrumental choices that, in combination with his musical style, sets his music apart. No one scored four-part horn sections better than Claude T. Smith. I'm not sure what he did, but his horn writing always sounded different than anybody else's horn writing. That particular sound became just as much a musical signature as his whimsically notorious use of the 7/8 measure. (I can't help but think that Claude was amused at the band world's almost "mystical cult worship" of an asymmetrical measure).

Even though at times I wish my orchestrations were ripe with refined timbral explorations, I know that what I do is exactly what my music demands. The choices I make are a direct product of the music I write. My high woodwind parts are always extreme, because I want edge and enunciation in their lines. The doublings I use are not meant to acoustically produce new sound spectrums. They are employed to *dominate* the spectrum. I am aware that my music is very mid-voiced, therefore more and more, I score for only one or two F Horn lines. I more often than not double my horns with trumpets rather than alto saxes, because I want that brassy edge to be paramount. The saxophones, over the years, have become the section I use as the "engine" of my orchestration, considering their flexibility and brashness. I also consider the versatility of the instruments. My clarinets can be penetrating and edgy or full and reverent. My reviewers refer to "no mercy" horn lines, and yet at times, I ask those same players to be the timbre of weeping.

One aspect of my orchestration has very little to do with color. It has everything to do with the individual musician seated in the ensemble. When Vaclav Nelhybel conducted the Central Methodist Band, I was a baritone player in the ensemble. (I was never good enough to be classified as a "euphonium" player!). One of the dynamics of that meeting was that I had a great part to perform in the compositions. In fact, it seemed that everyone in the band had important lines to play. No one seemed to think of themselves as "filler" material. I was always very aware of that feeling of "essentialness" when I began writing and scoring music as a young composer. In an *Instrumentalist* review of one of my early works, *Hopak Raskolniki,* John Paynter stated, "Every player has an exciting part to play." Knowing that every musician involved feels that he or she was important to that performance has really been an influence in my writing and scoring for a great many years. One of my pet exhortations is, "When the piece is over, you should feel like you've been somewhere!" Every musician needs to feel like a vital cog in the machinery of a performance.

Most of my instrumentation choices over the years have probably been more the product of intuition than learnedness. Consider again my first composition, *Prelude and Rondo.* After finishing the music, I was faced with the daunting task of scoring it for band. So I bought some ready-made band score paper, which in itself was a bit unnerving. (What the heck is a basset horn? I scratched that one off). It was likely at about that same moment I realized that I hadn't really paid all that much attention to Professor Anderson in orchestration class. But then again, we didn't spend a great deal of time with "band" instruments in class. After all, here it was, 1965, and it was obvious to me that Kent Kennan was unaware that the saxophone had been invented and was in everyday use! The book only listed about 12 percussion instruments, including the flexatone, which was there only because it appeared in both a Khachaturian piano concerto and Schoenberg's Opus 31 *Variations*. Not necessarily a ringing endorsement! In reality, the best instrumental choices available to me were the accumulated sounds I had experienced while sitting in a band for the past ten years. So I just started fitting music to the family of instruments I felt best portrayed the character of each particular section. My moment of confusion came with the F horns. Do they go up a fifth, or down a fourth? Obviously, not being the sharpest knife in the drawer, I decided to write the horns wherever they fit the best, so as not to crowd the music above and below them on the ready-made band paper staves.

Since confession is good for the soul, I admit in writing, to my ignorance some 30 years ago, that yes, many of the measures of F Horn in *Prelude and Rondo* are actually transposed to the wrong octave. Of course, when conductors enthusiastically expound on the "wonderful" horn-writing in said piece, I am always quick to reply, "What can I say...stroke of genius, I suppose...." Perhaps ignorance IS bliss.

I probably shouldn't leave this subject before discussing my percussion writing, which to many, seems to be one of the hallmarks of my compositions. Again, we're talking accidental fame! Once, while visiting Dr. Francis McBeth at his home, we were sitting around the front room sharing stories. Dr. McBeth began to recount an incident with his composition class. He described how many of his young composers insisted on waiting until their pieces were completed before even considering writing percussion into the score. "David," he said to me, "I told them how foolish that was....I said, only *bad composers* would do such a thing!" You know what's coming, don't you? For the slightest of split seconds, Dr. McBeth was almost speechless, as I indicated that that was exactly the process I utilized in my own work. Again, however, my percussion scoring is a direct product of my compositional process. I write many linear lines containing diverse rhythmic elements, all which run somewhat amuck, but fortunately in the same direction most of the time. I need to "live" with the density of this rhythmic collage in order to really understand what the percussion underpinning of the music should be. Before moving to the computer age, there were times when I had inked the score and copied all the parts before I was ready to add that final layer of percussion to the fabric of the composition.

I love percussion. I consider them vitally important to the energy of my works. My mallet writing directly affects the enunciation of my woodwinds. My timpani parts are notorious for being almost scalar in content. I think timpani players deserve more than four pitches per composition! (What are those tuning pedals for, anyway?) My auxiliary writing is meant to enhance the tonal choices that exist. I spend hours in "rock 'n roll" pro shops, just fooling with all kinds of noisemakers to see if there is a new addition that will fit my particular compositional palette. The percussion section is the only family of instruments still growing and developing. As long as one can find two different rocks to hit together, we will always have an evolving and diverse list of ingredients available for the percussion texture.

Admittedly, there is *one* drawback to this course of percussion writing. Most directors, when filling out their band rosters, usually prefer to have five to seven players in the percussion section, covering all aspects of that section, including mallets, timpani and all the non-tuned instruments. Because I'm working with a "separate entity" in my process, I tend to get carried away with the diversity of instruments available, and inadvertently, my percussion writing generally calls for eight to twelve players on a good day!

Call up the reserves.

D. Views from the Composer to the Conductor Pertaining to Score Study and Preparation

I conduct a new band every weekend. As a conductor, my first priority is to get everyone on the "same page" as quickly as possible. Anyone who is involved in the clinic situation week after week devises a system of "preparation, proportion, and pacing" concerning rehearsal procedure. My rehearsal and score discovery are very similar.

With a typical honor band, after a brief period of individual warm-up, I address the "intellectual properties" of music expression with three concepts. At the beginning of the first rehearsal, I verbally address these concepts and demonstrate them with very concise scale exercises. The first concept states that "notes do not weigh the same," and therefore, smaller notes must always "lead" to larger ones or stronger ones. Anytime a player finds a figure of smaller note values moving to large note values, the movement must be made with a slight crescendo.

The second concept is that "music always moves forward, not note to note, but rather, point to point." It is well and good that we start each phrase with a strong and centered attack. However, if we have no idea where the phrase is going, we'll be musically wandering around, simply moving from note to note, until we accidentally find a resting place. I encourage the players to look well ahead in their music even at the onset and realize that they can find the destination of each phrase on their own. Even lines that seem disjointed, and not at all linear, still move forward to a defined point on a regular musical basis. Small rhythmic fragments and pitchbursts also move forward. This is a musical concept that is all-inclusive. I often use the example of getting on an airplane to come to the concert venue. I know where I'm starting, but it is personally more important that my baggage and I get to my destination of the weekend. I am more concerned with where I am going than from whence I came! Conductors should always move forward, point to point!

The last concept of performance qualities I want the musicians to consider is actually an old concept I first observed in the VanderCook booklet on expression in music. I don't remember the exact wording, but Mr. VanderCook suggested that lines that ascend should always crescendo and descending lines should decrescendo. In context, I believe he was referring primarily to those transcribed violin parts that called for clarinets and flutes to zoom up and down in scalar delight or trepidation, whichever came first. In my more modern interpretation, the concept states, "The contour of any given line dictates the dynamics of that line." I want my players to consider that the dynamic marking at the beginning of a phrase affects only the first note of that phrase, and that the successive contour of the line will, in fact, widen or "flex" the boundaries of that dynamic range.

This explanation takes ten to twelve minutes. At that point we begin playing the music.

I will probably be chastised for the following, but I think that spending the first hour of an "honor band" rehearsal tuning and balancing a B-flat chord is more detrimental to the weekend than it is helpful. I have watched, at times in despair, as conductors spend an hour *or more* at this chore, all the while draining the energy and enthusiasm of the ensemble. This lengthy exercise, preferred by some, is generally considered by most young musicians a vehicle in which the conductor "demonstrates" his musical superiority over the subjects under his baton. I assume that because it is an "honor" ensemble that most of the members have some level of comprehension about balance, blend, and intonation. I would rather address these issues as we move through the *actual* music we are going to play for the weekend, then sap them of their strength, going about a task on a chord that will probably never reappear in the same voicing, length, or style for the rest of the rehearsal span. These players came to play. I came to conduct. I want them enthusiastic and I want them filled with energy. We tune. We play.

So, after ten to twelve minutes, we begin to address the music. I ask the musicians, however, to divide each run through into specific "missions." The first time through the piece, their mission is simply to find the correct notes and the correct rhythms. I play the piece with however many stops and starts it takes from beginning to end so the players can have a concept concerning where the composition is going. Of course, during that first run-through, I elaborate on "musical" elements, but I emphasize that their first mission is to the notes and rhythms. (I count on "musical osmosis" to take place throughout the rehearsal).

The second time through the work is section by section, however, not necessarily in numerical order. I do this so the student musicians will have a concept of musical "destinations" occurring within the fabric of the piece. In each successive run-through, the mission becomes more and more centered and miniaturized. We travel a road that leads from the total to the fragment. However, with each mission, no matter how large or how small its concept, we are always aware of the musical weight of note values, the forward direction of our music, and the contour of the individual lines and their musical interplay. Ninety percent of the final run is spent being aware of direction of the lines and fragments and consistency of the articulation of the line or fragments, and how all that affects the "musical" performance.

It is in this same manner I address a new score. I come to the table with some preconceived ideas on musicality. We all do. In fact, the emphasis of those preconceived ideas on musicality affect not only my conducting, but also my composing. I write with the hope that the conductors will have somewhat the same musical leanings as I. Whether they do or do not is out of my control, but you can't blame a guy for dreaming!

My first view of a new score is an "Igor's view," a scroll view of the entire shape and movement of the composition. My first "mission" is to understand the broad view of the work's direction. The second view of the score is by sections, noting transitions, "character" changes, instrumental entrances, style deviations, "special" moments that jump from the page. In each successive tour of the score, my mission miniaturizes. My eye becomes more acute to the idiosyncrasies and the similarities. In each pass, I move from total to fragment, not unlike the process I ask my players to use in their exploration of the new music they find on their stands.

And yet, with all that, for the musician and the conductor, we are only touching on the foundational stones of the music's potential. Now comes the search for the intangible. Music is black and white and red all over! The one intangible to all music is the red part, the "heart" or "passion" of any particular piece. Passion in music is always associated with emotion. I think that conductors will only recognize the passion in a work if they can find the "personalness" in the composition.

Music is very personal. A composition is a direct outpouring of the "personal passion" of the composer. I, as a composer, write about the world around me. I am affected by a range of influences, from my children's escapades to stories from the Bible. I have realized recently that "personal passion" does not necessarily mean an emotional criteria, like joy, happiness, sadness, anger, etc. Certainly Iannis Xenakis' passion for mathematics is as obvious in his works as Schoenberg's angst for his people in *A Survivor from Warsaw*. Music is a reflection of the composers' deepest heart cry. Understanding the personal motivation in a composer's work is paramount in understanding the "passion" of the composition.

On a personal note, like Xenakis, mathematics has always elicited an emotional response from me as well. I remember crying in math class on a number of occasions.

E. The Relationship Between the Composer and the Commissioning Party

The majority of the compositions I write are commissioned works. My relationship with those who are commissioning a piece has changed greatly over the past 25 years. Two things have helped this change: 1) It's 25 years later, and 2) I'm 25 years older.

I still remember my first commission. 1976. I couldn't believe someone was really going to offer me money to write music. Of course, in hindsight, I can't believe they offered me *so little money* to write *soooo much music*! "Wow! $500 for 15 minutes of music!?! Gosh, that's almost $30 a minute!...." (Again, "Dull Knife Syndrome" rears its ugly head)! I do remember that I was smart enough to know that when the band director said he expected full rights to the publication and/or rental of the piece, I had the presence of mind to call a friend and ask.

Claude said, "No." Thanks Claude.

In this day and age, commissioning a work for band is not the mystery it was 25 years ago. Everyone is much more educated to the procedures and expectations of both the commissioning agent and the composer. One aspect to the advantage of the band director who wants to commission a composition is that he knows the players on the playing field. Let's face it, in the band world in 2002, composers are a "dime a dozen!" We're everywhere! There exists today a myriad of successful composers with individual styles and strengths who write on innumerable levels of technical, intellectual, musical difficulty, and sensibility. The wind band is a mecca for aspiring composers today. It is a major musical entity fueled and maintained by the constant flame of *new music*, year in and year out. The band director knows what he likes and desires for his players, and contacts the composer whom he believes can best fit that projection. He has, to a degree, a concept of what that finished product will be, prior to his inquiry.

For many composers, commissioning is the lifeblood of their vocation, and each is prepared to facilitate this procedure. I have a "fee scale" for commissions, as do most composers. The price of the commission is basically dependent on the size and scope of the musical organization, length of the proposed composition, and difficulty or grade level of the music. Any special circumstances are dealt with separately.

Since I assume that the band director who contacts me knows my musical style, I also assume that he is putting the "artistic creative integrity" of his piece in my hands. The information I need from the commissioning agent should include: Projected length and grade level of the composition; the size and special needs or special talents in the ensemble; the reason for the commission (Is it to honor a person or special occasion? Should it be based on an existing musical theme and why?); a general idea of the "type" of piece the commissioning agent desires; when the piece needs to be delivered; when is the work expected to be premiered and are there special circumstances concerning the first performance? For their contract, the commissioning agent does receive first performance privilege.

Occasionally I have been bestowed with too much information. Once, after asking a project chairman what "type" of piece was envisioned, I received a two page, single spaced e-mail, containing an entire outline for about 240 measures of music which consisted of directions like, "The piece should open with an eight measure fanfare-like figure in the trumpets and high woodwinds. The first theme should be in tonic key, with 32 bar phrases, accompanied by three part trombone, in an agitated rhythmic style, probably doubled by either the horns or saxophones...etc...." I *really* wanted to suggest that a committee made up of "band method" students at his local university could probably put this piece together, but civility getting the best of me, I simply emailed back that all I really needed to know was: "fast" or "slow."

I am always interested in the "why" and "for whom" the commission is dedicated and will always attempt to artistically paint the appropriate musical portrait that will honor the spirit and letter of the commission.

For your information, I now charge more than $30 a minute.

F. Views on the Teaching of Composition and How to Mentor the Young Composer

I was a bad composition student. My main problem was that after I wrote my first piece, basically on my own, I thought I *was* a composer, when actually I was supposed to be a *student* of composition. I haven't been a teacher of composition very long, but to be a good teacher, I have found that even at age 56, it is still necessary that I be an inquisitive student of the craft. I need to be aware of what my weaknesses were at age 19 and make sure that my young charges do not fall into the trap of overestimating the skillfulness and artistry of their giftings. They should take advantage of the strengths they do possess and channel that exuberance into an intelligent and defendable course. It is my hope that they will be lifelong explorers of their craft.

I believe every student needs to develop his or her individual *process*. I am, obviously, very wrapped up in that word. The "process" has nothing to do with the musical language that the student chooses for his or her composition. It doesn't matter if their language is tonal or micro tonal. What I want for the student is that he or she develop an "order of attack" when exploring the beginning and development of a new composition. That, for every idea, the young composer realizes there is an immense variety of possibilities in the expansion of the idea, be it harmonically, melodically, or rhythmically, that must be examined. Not until all the "first choice" possibilities are excluded can one move on to the next idea set. I find my students are constantly amazed at the number of permutations one can explore in a small musical thought regarding fragmentation, linear contour, pitch order, registral displacement, and harmonic alterations. I am always quick to point out that Beethoven appeared to get some good distance out of "Dot-dot-dot-Daaaah!"

Some of my weakest pieces have too many ideas.

All my students are undergraduates and infants in the composition world. My emphasis on the development of a *process* may seem over controlling, but at the same time I am also attempting to have the student realize that, because it is the 21st century, they do not live in a "Common Practice Period Theory Box." *Nor* do they live in a "pandiatonic" theory box, or a "minimalistic" theory box, or an "aleatoric" theory box, or an "atonal" theory box. They can live in a *box of their own voice*, but it is essential that they push outward on the parameters of their boundaries in order to keep growing, always mindful that these expansions must be *defendable*! My first obligation to these students is not that I prepare them to be composers, but that I prepare them for graduate school composition. I want them to come to the graduate school table much more prepared than I was 35 years ago.

How do they know where to find their place in the world of composition? This is probably the biggest hurdle I face with my particular student body. I teach at a school where most of the students come from middle class America...the same place I grew up 50 years ago. I do for them what Donald Bohlen and Charles Hoag did for me. They made me listen to the sounds of the past three-quarters century. They told me how important it was to know the historic foundation of my craft, and I in turn, endeavor to do the same for my students.

It is important to know what and why the world of music has moved as it has during the 1900's. I think it is important that the student composer be aware of those last few movements of *Pierrot Lunaire* where diatonic pitch order began to become indistinct and the tonal language of the past began to dissolve as Arnold Schoenberg's soloist intoned, in pitchless, contoured speech inflections, the prophetic words, "Your light [O moon], so fever swollen, will pierce me *like music from afar....*" What an ominous beginning to an age of musical experimentation unlike anything that had been seen before. I'm a fan of Schoenberg's. I have composed only one work utilizing the 12-tone system, and I would never encourage my students to move exclusively into that realm without a thorough understanding of its complexity. But I get excited examining that process, begun by Schoenberg, and brought to fruition by Webern and Berg, eventually ending as dramatically as it began. The examination of that tonal evolution, from beginning to closure, is mind boggling. I direct my students to study the evolution of pitch order and synthetic scales. We explore and listen to the music of Messiaen and discuss the Modes of Limited Transposition. I attempt to introduce them to as much of the diversity of the 20th century as possible in a composition seminar hour once a week, where all composition students meet together. We look and listen to scores; from Bartok to Penderecki, Druckman to Tower, Crawford-Seeger to Wuorinen. We look and study the diversity of sound mass, improvisational music, indeterminate and determinate aspects in scores, and recordings. We dwell on the deeply moving manifesto music of Karel Husa and enjoy the silliness of Tom Johnson's unplayable score, *Celestial Music for Imaginary Trumpets.* And in all these wanderings, we seek to understand each composer's "process."

I encourage my students' awareness of the fundamental importance of form and structure in music. Whether one deals in a formal structure that is rooted in germinative development or a series of abstract shapes held together by repetitive linking sections, it is a Biblical principal that no building will stand without a proper foundation. I like to point out that Arnold Schoenberg, for all his fervor to establish a new tonal language and a system of pitch order, could not find a way to dispense with the established formal structures of the 1800's. *Klavierstuck, Op. 33a* is, irregardless of its 40 measure length, composed in Sonata Allegro Form, both in thematic content and row relationship. Concurrently, however, I think that writing a "sonatina" in 2002 is a music theory assignment and not a composition project.

Because my students are undergraduates, I do have one parameter I insist they observe. I generally don't allow any project piece to be over 60 measures in length for the first two years. There are exceptions, but this is intended to force the student composer to hone his or her selective skills in order to produce a work of conciseness and quality. Plus it gives us time to explore composing in a number of different art forms, i.e. chamber music, art song, mixed ensembles, and vocal ensembles, over that period of time.

I know that one of these days I, too, will probably experience "the kid I was" who will realize that I didn't say he couldn't write something in 36/4, quarter note at mm. 44, twenty minutes long, and stay under my 60 measure limit. Unlike my teachers, I will probably just shoot him on the spot!

G. Individuals Who Have Been Especially Influential in My Development and Career

The general public tends to view "creative" people as deep, dark-souled, dreary thinkers who choose to live in sensorial isolation, free from the invasive wiles of the ordinary world-dwellers who would poison the ebb and flow of freethinking creativity and spontaneity...fat chance of that happening with three kids running around the house! Trust me, *no* man is an island. Admittedly, we are shaped by the deposits left in our lives by those we have chosen to know and interact. Obviously I as a composer have been influenced on a personal level by Nelhybel, Bohlen, and Hoag. I, as a musician, have been guided by several band directors, whose diversity of influence and taste has culminated in the conductor I am today.

My first college band director was a man named Kenneth Seward. He may well have been the most overtly passionate musician I have ever known. He was a stickler for "right notes in the right places," but in addition, to a nearly fanatical degree, he was a *pursuer of the passion* of music. When Seward was through with you, you felt like you had wept over every note you'd played and that you, personally, were the most intense, passionate, and world-changing musician ever to walk the earth! *I am king of the world*!

Then I met my next best friend.

The Director of Bands at Central Missouri State was Dr. Russ Coleman. Let's just say that Russ Coleman had a "settling influence" on my raging ego. We all need someone to "sit" on us, occasionally. He did. But he also became my most faithful advocate and supporter, both professionally and personally, and in turn, one of my few life long friends.

I also have high regard for Robert E. Foster, Director of Bands at the University of Kansas. Here, too, is a gentleman who 20 years ago, looked past my quirks, and let me ride full gallop through the ranks of his band! He gave me means and opportunity to move into the "big-time" band world and has become a good friend and colleague, a person whose advice I am quick to heed.

Early in my career, even though at the time I didn't have a close personal relationship with them, both Francis McBeth and Claude Smith always seemed to know what I was doing, promoted my music to others, and constantly gave me encouragement in my writing. The late Pete Wiley, founder of TRN Music, decided to take a chance on a piece called *Havendance* with his budding company, and as the years passed, he became that unofficial older, wiser "Uncle" for me.

The value of the friendship and camaraderie of fellow composers should never be underestimated. Of course, composer get-togethers have undergone one drastic change in the past decade. Where we used to talk about the next big piece, we now somehow always get sidetracked about the next big computer. Instead of motives and movements, we're buried in music software analysis and hard drive capabilities. We used to be intelligent people, all drawn together in a great spiritual mist, lost in the wonder of soaring melodies, rhapsodic harmonies, and the emotionally fulfilling soul fruits of our musical journey. Now our conversations are motivated by "Ram Envy!" It's a strange world.

Of course, when it comes to the *most* influential person in this composer's life, that distinction goes to **my wife** and the **mother of the children**! Let's face it, composer's wives could write their *own* book! My wife, Winona, has endured 32 years of composer idiosyncrasies and has lived to tell about it. My wife insists that nothing seems to jumpstart the creative process more than a deadline. She occasionally wonders aloud how the same mind who knew about the commission six months before couldn't perhaps have started the piece six months ago, but rather, has to wait until the last minute to find "inspiration!" I have no retort. She's right. I know that nothing really ignites that creative spark more than when my wife comes to me, leans over, and whispers those three special words in my ear:

"Let's talk redecorating."

H. Ten Works All Band Conductors at All Levels Should Study

We are a society dominated by *the list*. We have the ten best, the ten worst, the ten most likely, and the ten least likely to appear on any list whatsoever! The Wind Band World holds its own in this whirlwind competition. Everywhere I turn I am confronted by yet another list of the most important works for conductors to know. Trust me, I've seen a ton of them. I have

Foster's "fifteen landmark" pieces list, Stamp's "If you had to pick twenty pieces" list, Cramer's list, Junkin's list, Haithcock's list, Mallory's list, and Kirchhoff's list. I even have a four-year old repertoire list from Gene Corporon that lists 988 works! Does this mean that now, four years later, I should expect to be confronted with a magnum opus entitled, "The 1500 Greatest Works for Winds and Best Restaurants in Denton, Texas?"

And now, our editor has asked each composer to list ten works *we* think band conductors should study. I'm not sure I have the expertise to write such a list. True, I've been conducting for years, but 60% of that has been my own music. I haven't been a university level conductor all that long. Consider this. Three years ago, most of my 1967 college classmates retired, and I moved to Lee University to begin, in most people's opinion, my first *real* job! To be perfectly honest, I'm still working on *everybody else's* list at present!

I will say one thing about the importance of all these lists. The wind band area is the most volatile area for the creation of new music in the world today. This is wonderful news for composers and conductors alike. However, it does breed in us, a certain laissez-faire attitude toward the music of the past. We tend to forget our foundations. We tend to forget the masterworks that put us on this popular plateau in the first place. We tend to leave behind the landmark works of the past decades, in order to always be on the cutting edge of *new*.

Lists keep us honest unto ourselves. They insure that we will not forget the Persichetti's, the Hindemith's, the Schoenberg's, the Schmitt's, the Hartley's, the Holst's, the Grainger's of our recent heritage or the Ferdinand Paer's, the Franz Krommer's, and the Rimsky-Korsakov's of our distant past.

Let's hear it for lists.

I. Ten Composers Whose Music Overall Speaks to Me in Especially Meaningful Ways

I'm a pushover. I love drama and movement in music. As a young college musician, I probably wore out three LP's of *West Side Story* and *any* Aaron Copland ballet recording before I was 21. For years, Leonard Bernstein's music epitomized that excitement and vitality I wanted to express as a musician. My music today still alludes occasionally to Coplandnesque spatialness and Bernstein's symphonic dance rhythms. I loved the Stan Kenton rendition of WSS. I became so captivated with the "neophonic ensemble" that I would rewrite all the charts for my high school jazz band into that formula. Jazz Festival judges hated to see us troop on stage. All my groups had a French Horn section and a percussion battery that looked like center stage at an Emerson, Lake, and Palmer concert! I can't tell you how many times our critique began with those ominous words, "Mr. Holsinger, you *do* know this really *isn't* jazz, don't you?..." I didn't care. It was new and dramatic and exciting! (*Okay,* truth be told, it was "rebellion," pure and simple!).

As a composer, I have been "struck dumb" a myriad of times in my lifetime. The first time I heard and watched the score to Penderecki's *Threnody for the Victims of Hiroshima* and Arnold Schoenberg's *A Survivor from Warsaw,* my heart ached. I was stirred at the heroic expansiveness of Husa's *Music for Prague,* and I sat stunned and emotionally emptied listening to the final moments of Alban Berg's *Wozzeck.* In recent years, I couldn't listen to David Gillingham's *Heroes Lost and Fallen* without that chest-tightening breathlessness one gets when confronted with the helplessness of personal tragedy.

I have been beguiled by the sensitivity of *Gesang der Jünglinge* for tape and children's voices by Karlheinz

Stockhausen, and listening to Cathy Berberian's sensuous performance of Luciano Berio's *Visage*, a "classic" of electronic music. David Cope's observation that Berberian "vocally creates an emotional gamut virtually without peer in the history of music"[1] is still true to this day.

Vocal music of the 20th century, especially that music where composers are more or less inventing their own musical language and the means of notating it, has a special allure to me. This is probably an extension of my fascination with Penderecki's "cluster bands" and Xenakis' "sonic clouds" notation. I have actually prepared two unconventional notational works for chorus during a short stint as a high school choral director. The first was Daniel Pinkham's *In The Beginning* for prepared tape and chorus, and Folke Rabe's *Rondes* for mixed choir, a work featuring both determinate and indeterminate improvisational notation. (A wonderful source for vocal notation examples is *The Handbook of Choral Notation*, edited by Frank Pooler and Brent Pierce and available from Walton Music Corporation, New York). The influence of this non-conventional vocal notational has manifested itself in a number of my own band compositions, *Ancient Hymns and Festal Dances, The Omnipresent Otserf, In the Spring*, and *Ballet Sacra.*

I am in awe of the music of George Crumb. How does he think that way?

I'm a sucker for any kind of programmatic drama music. I become very "singular" in my listening choices. After listening "exclusively" to a CD of Prokofiev's movie score to *Alexander Nevsky* for six months, my wife has forbidden it from ever

1. David Cope, *New Directions in Music,* 6th ed. (Dubuque: Wm. C. Brown Communications, Inc., 1993) p. 229

being included in the CD case in either one of our cars. Same deal with Andrew Lloyd Webber's *Jesus Christ Superstar.* Admittedly, I do tend to obsess!

As a conductor, I am more and more appreciative of our mid-20th century band composers. I am grateful for the music of Gustav Holst, Clifton Williams, and John Barnes Chance. I appreciate more and more the quirky genius of Percy Grainger. I probably wouldn't have liked him as a man, but I do enjoy his gregarious output. Personally, I think Peter Mennin's *Canzona* is a marvelously constructed composition and one of the greatest pieces composed for band. I wish I'd written it.

I've also recently discovered a composer whose music I find rather delightful to play. A march guy named John Philip Sousa....Who knew?

J. The Future of the Wind Band

I enjoy writing chamber works. I have dabbled in composing for orchestra. But 30 years ago I made a conscious decision to compose primarily for band. It is an ensemble I love.

I see the band and band repertoire as *the next big thing.* I know, I know, bands have been around since before the Crusades. We have a heritage that spans centuries, and although it's not quite as glamorous as the orchestral heritage, the band just always seems to be an ensemble more comfortable with itself. I am the first to admit that our history of truly lasting masterworks probably is just getting off the ground, but I am excited with the future of band repertoire and the composers it is beginning to draw into its environment. The primary orchestral repertoire today features works that are 75 to 200 years old. A century from now, the orchestra will feature a repertoire 175 to 300 years old. It won't have changed because the late 1700's, the 1800's, and the very early 1900's were the golden ages of orchestral literature. Yes, I know that there is new music written for the orchestra year in and year out, but I also know that even 100 years from today, the future of the symphonic orchestra will still be in the hands of a generation of "social" listeners who view the orchestra hall as a center of convivial function, musical grace and purity, and even if Eric Whitacre decides to re-score *Godzilla Eats Las Vegas* for electric chamber strings, just the title alone will not do the season subscription sales any favors!

But the wind band is "every man's" ensemble. It is the ensemble of the school-age child, who finds in its training an appreciation of the discipline, beauty, and passion of music, and perhaps of the fine arts in general. It is the ensemble of the masses. The wind band celebrates the victories, the triumphs, and the memories of a nation. The wind band waves the flag on the Fourth of July. The wind band accompanies the songs of the holidays. The wind band leads the cheering for the home team! The wind band is a primary vehicle for new music on the academic level. Every university and college has a band, and that organization is accessible to not only the public, but also to the composer, whether he or she be a student or a professional. The wind band constantly opens it doors and invites new music to flourish.

Personally, I see the wind band as an ensemble that, regardless of its centuries of recorded history, has just passed puberty! In the past 30 years, I have watched as composers have begun to stretch the musical parameters of this ensemble. I have watched and listened as conductors of these ensembles have become learned men and women of music, passing on to the next generation not only a list of past triumphs, but also a heritage of promise to future generations of new wind conductors and musicians.

I think we're hitting the teen years. And we are preparing to excitedly watch as OUR ensemble begins to mature into adulthood. How big and strong will he grow? What will he achieve? Will he grow up to be brave and adventurous or timid and introspective? Will he expand his talent or lose his treasure? Whose lives will he touch and change? Where will he be 25 years from now? How will he impact the future generations? Parenting is so stressful.

On the other hand, if wind bands start playing "rap," the end is near.

K. Other Facets of My Everyday Life

My wife Winona and I have three children. The oldest, Haven Rebecca, is in theater and choreography; the first son, Niles, is in the ministry, and our youngest, Grayson, is presently in college, leaning toward business and the restaurant world. Winona is also a band director, and presently teaches conducting, music survey, assists me with the Wind Ensemble, and serves as our instrumental department's inventory and instrumental library manager in the School of Music at Lee. This information is presented to answer the age-old question: Should band directors marry? Yes, they can, but they must be very careful. The only correct answer to the question, "Did you like the way I interpreted that work today?" is "I loved it."

I have a hobby. My basement is filled with model trains. I have lots of track, sculpted mountains, tiny trees and bushes, buildings, houses, cars and trucks, and little people glued to miniature grass and concrete. When we moved to Cleveland, my wife was adamant with every realtor that we find a house where there was room for me to rebuild the layout that I had to tear apart upon leaving the Ft. Worth-Dallas area. In retrospect, she had a deeper understanding of my hobby's significance than I.

This hobby information is offered as an answer to yet another important compositional question, "Do I ever get writer's block?"

Several years ago, Winona passed a book on to me by Mihaly Csikszentmihalyi, former chairman of the Department of Psychology at the University of Chicago, entitled *Creativity*.[2] As the book sleeve states, it is an examination of the flow and psychology of discovery and invention, based on histories of contemporary people who know about it firsthand. The book begins with a description of what creativity is, reviews the way creative people work and live, and concludes with ideas about how to make your life more creative. After reading the ten dimensions of complexity and ten pairs of apparently antithetical traits that are often present in creative people, I am thankful that my wife figured all of them out years ago. I'm a blessed man.

However, getting back to my trains, one section of the book deals with creative surroundings. Dr. Csikszentmihalyi discusses how creative people gain control over the immediate environment and transform it to enhance personal creativity. He points out that Jonas Salk liked to work in a studio where, in addition to the material he needed for writing on biology, there was a piano and an easel for painting. Csikszentmihalyi's

2 Mihaly Csikszentmihalyi, *Creativity* (New York: HarperCollins Publishers, Inc., 1996)

supposition is that surroundings influence creativity in different ways, in part depending on the stage of the process. During preparation, when one is gathering thoughts and problematic elements, an ordered, familiar environment is necessary for concentration. At the next stage, when thoughts about the problem are in an "incubation" mode, a different environment may be more helpful. The author states that, "this distraction allows the subconscious mental processes to make connections that are unlikely when the problem is pursued by the linear logic learned from experience."[3] After the unexpected connection results in an insight, the familiar environment is again more conducive toward completion of the project.

Do I get "writers block?" Of course I do. I sit before the computer screen dealing with little black dots and little white spaces, fragments and shapes, complex time designs, working at a miniature world inside a large formal structure, and suddenly, nothing seems to fit. I rise from my chair, walk down two flights of stairs, and begin "to build a tree." I begin dealing with miniature fragments and shapes, trying to match the complexity of natural design, working at a miniature world inside a large formal structure. It is not unusual that in the midst of "play," the answer to my problem two floors above is formulated and solved. My world of distraction is still very much akin to my world of creativity in terms of micromanipulation, but it really doesn't have to be. If I remember correctly, Jim Barnes goes fishing and Francis McBeth tinkers with his cars or catalogs his Indian arrowhead collection. Do they get "writers block?" I'm sure they do, but

3 Mihaly Csikszentmihalyi, *Creativity* (New York: HarperCollins Publishers, Inc., 1996) p. 146

each has found that special distraction that still fuels creative "subconscious processes."

I would encourage composers and conductors alike to seek out that balanced environment. Contrary to popular "public school band" thinking, 100% stress 100% of the time will only add up to about 50% of a life! And widows are not comforted by 25 years of Division One trophies!

L. Comprehensive List of Works for Band

I have been fortunate over the past number of years to have had my complete wind works recorded in a collection of CD's by Mark Custom Recording of Clarence, New York. To this date there are eight CD's available. In compiling this list of works, I have placed an asterisk (*) after those titles that were commissions, however, to conserve print space, I would encourage the reader to simply go "online" and peruse the label notes of those recordings to identify the commissioning agents.

Grade Six Compositions:

The War Trilogy: 1971 (1971) TRN Music / 10:00m.

In the Spring At the Time When Kings Go Off to War* (1986) Southern Music / 11:42m.

Kansas City Dances* [Tuba solo/Wind Ensemble] (1989) TRN Reserve / 9:27m.

Ballet Sacra* (1990) TRN Music / 15:50m.

To Tame the Perilous Skies* (1992) TRN Music / 13:21m.

The Song of Moses* [Band/Choral] (1994) TRN Music / 12:43m.

Gmyway's Revenge!* (1994) TRN Music / 12:27m.

The Easter Symphony*
I. Kings(1996), II. The Deathtree(1986), III. Symphonia Resurrectus(1997) Southern Music / 52:12m

Battle Music* (1999) TRN Music / 6:17m.

Ballet Exaltare* (1999) TRN Music / 15:15m.

Scootin' on Hardrock* (1999) TRN Music / 8:35m.

Symphonic Movement* (2000) TRN Music / 9:00m.

Praises!* [Ballet in six movements] (2000) TRN Music / 24:00m.

Grade Five Compositions:

Liturgical Dances* (1981) Southern Music / 8:30m.

Scrappy Bumptoe's Picture Cards and Ragtag Diary* [B5] (1981) TRN Music / 13:20m.

The Armies of the Omnipresent Otserf* (1981) Carl Fischer, Inc. / 10:23m.

Nilesdance (1987) TRN Music / 6:11m.

On the Grand Prairie Texas (1989) TRN Music / 11:05

Helm Toccata* (1991) TRN Music / 9:16

Consider the Uncommon Man* (1992) / TRN Music / 7:06m.

Sinfonia Voci* [Band/Choral] (1994) TRN Music / 6:21

American Faces* (1994) TRN Music / 5:53m.

Graysondance* (1995) TRN Music / 7:38m.

Canticles!* [Band/Choral] (2001) TRN Reserve / 17:31m.

Cityscape I [Festive Hours Neon Night]* (2001) TRN Music / 5:35m.

Grade Four Compositions:

Prelude and Rondo (1966) C.L. Barnhouse / 7:02m.

Hopak Raskolniki (1980) C.L. Barnhouse (1995) TRN Music / 4:18

Partita Allegro [WwChoir] (1980) C.L. Barnhouse / 4:25m.

Havendance (1985) TRN Music / 5:48m.

On Ancient Hymns and Festal Dances* (1987) TRN Music / 8:16m.

At the Strongholds of EnGedi* (1996) TRN Music / 4:33m.

A Little Mystery Music* (1996) TRN Music / 4:13m.

Texas Promenade* (1997) TRN Music / 5:14m.

Homage: Three Tapestries* (1997) TRN Music / 8:15m.

Fantasy on a Gaelic Hymnsong* (1998) TRN Music / 5:36m.

Abram's Pursuit* (1998) TRN Music / 4:53

Two Wedding Marches [B5] (1999) TRN Music / 7:00m.

Festiva Jubiloso* (2000) TRN Music / 4:31

Riding With the Frontier Battalion* (2000) TRN Music / 4:09

A Little Adventure Music* (2002) TRN Music / 6:20m.

Every Morning New* (2002) TRN Music / 4:18m.

Providence Unfinished* (2002) TRN Music / 4:34m.

Grade Three Compositions:

The Gathering of the Ranks at Hebron (1988) TRN Music / 5:17m.

On a Hymnsong of Philip Bliss (1989) TRN Music / 4:45m.

On a Hymnsong of Lowell Mason (1990) TRN Music / 5:16m.

On an American Spiritual (1991) TRN Music / 4:15m.

On a Hymnsong of Robert Lowery (1992) TRN Music / 5:40m.

On a Southern Hymnsong* (1993) TRN Music / 4:43m.

Lake Canterbury Regatta (1993) TRN Music / 2:11m.

Mobbusters! (1994) Wingert Jones Music / 2:07m.

In Praise of Gentle Pioneers* (1996) TRN Music / 4:52m.

Deerpath Dances* (1996) TRN Music / 4:13m.

A Jolly Walk in Hibbertland (1998) TRN Music / 1:45m.

Prairie Dances* (1998) TRN Music / 3:00m.

Adagio (1998) TRN Music / 4:35m.

The Pride of Buxmont* (2000) TRN Music / 2:34m.

Fanfare for the Glorious NayCart* (2002) TRN Music / 2:58m.

Grade Two Compositions:

Fort Canterbury March (1989) TRN Music / 2:08m.

If You Must Doodle, Doodle Somewhere Else (1990) Wingert Jones Music / 1:33m.

Scaling the North Wall (1990) TRN Music / 2:12m.

The Peasant Village Dance (1990) Wingert Jones Music / 1:39m.

The Case of the Mysterious Stranger (1990) TRN Music / 2:45m.

The March of the Combat Patrol (1991) TRN Music / 2:00m.

A Childhood Hymn (1991) Wingert Jones Music / 3:12m.

The Cluster Bluster Fluster March (1991) Wingert Jones Music / 1:36m.

Gypsydance (1994) Wingert Jones Music / 1:39m.

Von Grrrhart's 613th Regimental March (1994) TRN Music / 2:03m.

On the Cul-de-sac, Three O'clock, Friday Afternoon (1998) TRN Music / 5:00m.

chapter 6

karel Husa

A. Biography

Karel Husa, Pulitzer Prize winner in Music, is an internationally known composer and conductor who was Kappa Alpha professor at Cornell University from 1954 until his retirement, and Lecturer in Composition at Ithaca College. An American citizen since 1959, Husa was born in Prague on August 7, 1921, studying at the Prague Conservatory and Academy of Music, and later at the National Conservatory and ecole Normale de Musique in Paris. Among his teachers were Arthur Honegger, Nadia Boulanger, Jaroslav Ridky, and conductor André Cluytens.

Husa was elected Associate Member of the Royal Belgian Academy of Arts and Sciences in 1974 and to the American Academy of Arts and Letters in 1994. He has received honorary doctorates from Coe College, the Cleveland Institute of Music, Ithaca College, Baldwin-Wallace College, St. Vincent College, Hartwick College, the New England Conservatory, Masaryk University, and Academy of Musical Arts (Czech Republic). He has been the recipient of many awards and recognitions, including a Guggenheim Fellowship and awards from the American Academy and Institute of Arts and Letters, UNESCO, the National Endowment for the Arts, the Koussevitzky Foundation, the Czech Academy for the Arts and Sciences, the Lili Boulanger Award, Bilthoven (Holland) Contemporary Music Prize, a Kennedy Center-Friedheim Award, and the first Sudler International Award for the *Concerto for Wind Ensemble.* His *Concerto for Cello and Orchestra* earned him the 1993 Grawemeyer Award. In 1995, Husa was awarded the Czech Republic's highest civilian recognition, the State Medal of Merit, First Class, and in 1998 he received the Medal of the City of Prague.

His *String Quartet No. 3* received the 1969 Pulitzer Prize and, with over 7,000 performances, his *Music for Prague 1968* has become part of the modern repertory. Another well-known work, *Apothesis of this Earth,* is called by Husa a "manifesto" against pollution and destruction. His works have been performed by major orchestras all over the world. Two works were commissioned by the New York Philharmonic: the *Concerto for Orchestra* premiered by Zubin Mehta and the *Concerto for Violin and Orchestra* written for concertmaster Glen Dicterow and conducted by Kurt Masur. The *Concerto for Trumpet* was commissioned by the Chicago Symphony Orchestra and Sir Georg Solti for performance with principal trumpeter Adolph Herseth. Among his recent compositions are the *String Quartet No. 4* (an NEA commission for the Colorado Quartet), *Cayuga Lake* (for Ithaca College's centennial celebration), and *Les couleurs fauves* for wind ensemble (written for Northwestern University).

Karel Husa has conducted many major orchestras including those in Paris, London, Hamburg, Brussels, Prague, Stockholm, Oslo, Zurich, Hong Kong, Singapore, Tokyo, New York, Boston, Washington, Cincinnati, Rochester, Buffalo, Syracuse,

Louisville, and others. Every year he visits the campuses of music schools and universities to guest conduct and lecture on his music.

Much of Husa's music is available on recordings issued by CBS Masterworks, Sony, Vox, Louisville, Supraphon, Phoenix, Crystal, CRI, Everest, Grenadilla, Sheffield, Mark, and other labels.

B. The Creative Process

When I sit in front of music paper, there are times I can work with no problem...the ideas and composing seem easy. Other times, I have to force myself to find any possibility, even a few notes, arbitrarily chosen in order to start some construction of themes, harmonies, or rhythms.

Reading poetry often helps, or looking at paintings or photographs of nature or space. Sometimes I may improvise at the piano...sort of a brain cleaning, mostly to escape telephone calls, correspondence, and other happenings of "daily" life.

I like to walk alone, to see the ever-changing colors of the ocean, lake or mountains; to listen to birds and their interesting melodies and rhythms, and even sing (inside) to myself, because I *have* to write!

Sometimes, I have to remember the techniques of the last eight hundred years, including Bach's counterpoint and his use of the four notes B-A-C-H to write monumental music, to admire Debussy for his fabulous colors as well as his incredibly precise construction, in order to write the composition I was commissioned.

I often use cells of three or four notes, in some ways resembling the Schoenberg theory, although not twelve-tone. The techniques of composing are logical in the same way buildings are, be it the Eiffel Tower or a great cathedral.

I believe composers should bring something personal, unusual, original, and in some respects different from existing works. I do not mean that "all things be put up-side down," but even composers from the same era can be distinguished, for example, Dvorak from Brahms, Ravel from Debussy, etc. Also, our music should reflect today, not yesterday. And we cannot dismiss the avant-garde, because it brings us new ideas and possibilities.

I like to challenge the performers musically as well as technically. Today's performers have excellent technique and are sophisticated enough to understand our ideas. This enables us to profit from their artistry and obtain new sounds. We can hear what new sounds the brass and percussion brought us in the 20th century. This does not mean I do not respect tradition. On the contrary, we have to build our own language and not use the ones of our fathers and grandfathers, as great as they were.

I do not compose at the piano, perhaps because my first instrument was the violin. I have learned the piano as well. Composers can imagine sounds as well as construction. Naturally, I verify that all I have written for the piano is playable. And also, I can get ideas by improvising at the piano. I believe, however, that a composer can get the view of a work from the score in the same way a conductor should be able to.

I do not compose on the computer, although when I was still teaching up until 1992, I encouraged my students to learn this process. My time though is limited. Perhaps it is because I did a lot of drawing and design when I was young that I am able to hand-write music quickly. When I was in Paris and money was "short," I wrote not only scores to my compositions, but parts as well. In any case, today either the publisher or the commissioning party takes care of the copying costs.

Lastly, I have no special hours to compose, so once I start a piece, I work on it every free moment I have. It is in my head and I have to get it on the paper. I think about it constantly, and only when finished can I relax. It is an incredibly satisfying feeling to complete the last measure. After that comes another test of nerves—the first reading and the first performance!

Like all people, I watch world events on television. I see the space shuttles from Cape Canaveral from our windows and meditate on our both incredibly beautiful and utterly cruel world on our one of billions of planets....

It is hard not to bring some of these pictures into my music.

C. The Approach to Orchestration

I enjoy orchestrating for any group—orchestra, band, or small ensemble. It reminds me of painting. After one has made pencil sketches or other drawings, one plays with colors. Each instrument and every possible combination within and outside of each section gives endless coloring.

I do not see much difference in scoring for an orchestra or a band. The large ensembles we have here are close to the symphony orchestras. Naturally, we do not have strings in bands (except usually one string bass), but the saxophones, many clarinets, and larger brass fill in for the strings. Speaking of strings, one string bass seems to me a little weak against the large, powerful ensemble. When bands were smaller, one could hear the instrument, but three or four would be helpful today. Already more than 50 years ago, Stravinsky asked for four in his *Concerto for Piano and Wind Orchestra.* I feel the same amount is needed for instance in my *Apotheosis of this Earth,* otherwise the pizzicatos especially ring too thin. The bass lines simply sound more powerful with four instruments. It is interesting to note that the Spanish and French bands use also two or more violoncellos to reinforce the euphonium line. (Some American military bands often do so as well).

Because I compose (conceptually) for band the same way I compose for orchestra, this may be the reason why my music may sound unusual and seem difficult. I treat all instruments equally, without worrying about the abilities and possibilities of instruments such as alto clarinet, contrabass clarinet, or bass saxophone. If we write challenging parts for the players, they will learn them. These instruments have distinct sounds and colors. Also, the saxophones today are excellent. We have saxophone teachers in most every college/university, so why not write challenging, even sometimes virtuosic parts for them?

I treat the percussion as a section, and an important one. I write difficult, often soloistic parts for the percussion. Percussionists are players who study as long as players of other instruments. In turn they bring new sounds and, like saxophones, enhance my music for band.

The power as well as gentleness of an ensemble of winds and percussion is distinct. It is up to us to explore all of their possibilities, colors, and techniques. One has to appreciate the interest of bands and their directors in contemporary music. They are looking for new works more than our orchestras, whose literature extends back some 300 years, which they and the audiences love. Interest in new music is not as needed with orchestras. The same happens with chamber music. Therefore, the band is a wonderful champion of the living composer.

D. Views from the Composer to the Conductor Pertaining to Score Study and Preparation

A musical score should contain as many indications to the conductor as possible. If we look at the 20th century works of Stravinsky, Bartok, Hindemith, or Copland, their thoughts are very precisely indicated. These include tempos, metronome markings, dynamics, ritardandos, accelerandos, fermatas, mutes, mallets for percussion, etc. So the intentions of the composer should be clear, and the conductor should do exactly what is indicated. This is true, but only to a certain degree. There is also the art of interpretation, and we cannot ask the conductor and performers to be machines. Beethoven criticized the metronome markings and omitted them in the *Ninth Symphony*. Debussy, as I understand it, said that the metronome is good for the first measure. And Bartok, late in his life, told his son that his metronome markings should not be taken too seriously.

The conductor needs to know the studied work perfectly and it has to be in his/her mind, practically from memory, although one does not need to conduct without a score.

When I was learning a new score, I first tried to listen to a recording or tape, reading the music at the same time, just to get a first impression. Then I analyzed each movement, first in large segments (introduction, main sections, concluding section), then more closely, including the phrasing, beginnings and endings of melodic lines, rhythmic patterns, inside lines or supporting (coloring) notes, pizzicatos (they have to be cued, otherwise they do not sound together), ritardandos, accelerandos, fermats, etc.

I marked cues not only for the important phrases, but especially for players who had long rests. (They need to be assured of their entrances). I used color and large signs so that I could see them well, without looking too closely at the score. I believe the conductor has to be involved with all members of the ensemble, not only the players in the front. The conductor needs to have eye contact with the percussion, harp, piano, bass and contrabass clarinets, contrabassoon, etc., as they often need reassurance. Most of the time, when a conductor makes a mistake, he/she should apologize.

Solo passages have to be worked out in sectional rehearsals and private lessons, as there is no time to spare in full rehearsals. I am not sure stopping every five or six measures helps in the first rehearsal. The players get a better view of the music if the sections can be read without interruption. In certain cases, it is helpful to explain some facts about the work, or analyze some passages. But these should be to the point and short. In my music, it would be the *Music for Prague 1968* and *Apotheosis of this Earth* where the Prefaces should be read. In *The Vivid Colors* (*Les couleurs fauves*), the influence of 20th century Impressionist painting could be mentioned, and in the *Concerto for Wind Ensemble* my intention to write a piece in which most of the performers are soloists—by themselves or in small sections—as I believe the players of today are excellent enough to be soloists. I admire Bartok's *Concerto for Orchestra* and wanted to write a composition with the same aim for the band.

Previously, I have mentioned that while today's scores are a great help to the conductor, not all information about the music is indicated in the score. If I may cite some examples, for instance from the *Music for Prague 1968*: The last movement (Toccata and Choral) has no problem as the music is propelled nearly by itself as is the first movement from letter C to the end. But the Introduction is very difficult with all the annotation, the numerous entrances of instruments, dynamic shadings, demanding solo passages, etc. This all has to be "coordinated" by the conductor, who has to create a gray, desolate, but calm picture before the "explosion" at letter C. This effect does not come by itself, especially with the nervousness of the slow beginning. In the second movement (Aria), it is up to the conductor to obtain the long saxophone's solo (doubled by low woodwinds), indicating the phrasing, intensity and breathing, and to build progressively into the climax under the pulse of the vibraphone and marimba, as in a funeral-march procession. The players cannot judge this intense, tragic Aria by themselves, nor can they hear the proportions of sounds. Only the conductor can verify the dynamics, intensity, and gradation.

And the same applies to the Interlude: the tempo, entrances, intensity, and the ever-ringing "bells" must be coordinated by the conductor, while the dialogue between the snare drum and vibraphone goes on. In addition, some of my extreme dynamics, such as pppp, do not work in some concert halls, especially those with dead acoustics, and the conductor has to adjust some of the softest sounds.

The *Apotheosis of this Earth* poses another problem: the long, 9-minute crescendo from the starting glockenspiel note until measure 133 can only be "monitored" by the conductor. The soft, slow beginning solos are always difficult, as the players are nervous and have difficulties producing a soft sound. Long notes make the problem even greater. The decision of how slow and how soft depends on the conductor, and he/she is the only one to judge how to progress, i.e. where to go faster than the composer indicates, where to make bigger crescendos, how to measure the overall dynamics, and when even to accelerate (although it is not in the score) in order to not break the intensity and keep the motion going. These are decisions that must be made by the conductor. Music is not only written notes; they have to be brought to life by the performers.

There is another place in this work I should mention—the third movement Postscript: I did not anticipate my requiring wind ensemble members to speak would be so problematic. The problem is that I have written the dynamic level of the sentence "This Beautiful Earth" soft, i.e. piano. It has to be spoken loud, so that the syllables and words are not covered by the instruments that have to play piano. If the conductor starts to rehearse this sentence from the beginning, and the players get used to the idea, it would be better accepted. I know *Apotheosis of this Earth* is difficult to rehearse, but in concert performance, the message is understood by the audience, and finally by the performers as well. In the orchestral version, I have added in a chorus, because singers are accustomed to the importance of proper enunciation. The wind ensemble can use the chorus too, and the players therefore will not need to speak. Perhaps in the future, players will be more accepting of this unusual task!

Like any other profession, conducting takes years of study. Today we have many first-class conductors and teachers, and many outstanding programs in the schools, enabling young people to have great opportunities while learning this art. The technique of conducting (expressing with one's hands) is a necessary tool which, together with score reading ability and understanding the process of creating music leads to the conductor being able to properly interpret the music and convey the composer's ideas to the performers. This art takes years of learning. We composers are fortunate to have such devoted advocates. I am sincerely grateful to conductors and bands for their interest in my music, and for bringing my billions of notes in the score to life!

E. The Relationship Between the Composer and the Commissioning Party

I cannot say much about the commissioning process. In virtually all cases, I have been given a free hand. The only exceptions would be in the area of ensemble size/instrumentation and duration of the piece. Many commissioned works are for specific occasions, such as the Bicentennial of the United States (the ballet *Monodrama, Sonata No. 2 for Solo Piano, An American Te Deum*) or in memory of a young boy (*The Steadfast Tin Soldier*), or the New York Philharmonic's 150th Anniversary. Virtually in all cases, I have been given the freedom to use my own ideas.

I remember that in the New York Philharmonic's other commission, the *Concerto for Orchestra,* the approximate duration mentioned was 18 minutes, but I wrote 39 minutes. Maestro Zubin Mehta was completely understanding and performed the whole work, even extending the rehearsal time.

With a solo concerto, I try to provide some new ideas in order not to repeat what has already been written. Let us say for instance, with the violin, so much technique and virtuosity has been explored over the years, and yet, new paths can be found. When I wrote for the Colorado Quartet, I knew I could include many new and unusual technical devices, for they are true virtuosi of their instruments. On the other hand, when I was asked to write a composition for amateur string players (*Four Little Pieces*), I found it a challenge to compose a piece in which the violin, viola, and cello play only in first position. In most cases, the commissions have been worked out by either my publisher or representative, and the commissioning party.

F. Views on the Teaching of Composition and How to Mentor the Young Composer

When my composition students were beginners—and I have taught beginners at Cornell University and Ithaca College—I showed them techniques of composing from ca. 1200 to the present. I asked them to try these techniques themselves, to copy the masters and listen to their works with the score. (This reminds me of watching young painters as they copied *Mona Lisa* in the Louvre museum in Paris.) One has to learn the art of composing and listen to, perform, and analyze the existing masterpieces.

With graduate student composers it is different, as they have acquired various techniques. At the graduate level, I focused more on matters of style, personal ideas, and proportions, although the techniques, especially those of the present composers are studied, and each new and important work is analyzed.

The students of today have an incredible advantage over composers of the past, including me. For instance, when I studied in Prague in the 1940's, we were practically without recordings and scores of contemporary composers such as Stravinsky, Schoenberg, Bartok, and Berg. You would only learn from going to concerts in order to hear new music. In a way, I consider myself lucky, because it is in concerts that one learns an immense amount.

I was amazed when I came to Cornell and finally saw the modern scores in the library. At the same time, I admired the incredible genius (especially in orchestration) of Berlioz, as he could not study the scores of past or of then living composers, and yet put together *Symphonie Fantasique, Requiem,* etc. Berlioz is, however, an exception.

In teaching composition, I would discuss with my students the length of phrases, dynamics, orchestration, proportion, intensity, constructions, colors, and above all the importance of ideas and originality. While excellence in compositional technique is required (all important works have that), the individuality of the composer is what we all look for. The score has to have something unusual...something different from others, especially in lieu of what has already been composed before.

I believe the teacher should be demanding, but also supportive, encouraging, and sincere. Everyone needs to be given the chance to try. And then it is up to them to succeed.

G. Individuals Who Have Been Especially Influential in My Development and Career

My mother was, first and foremost, the most influential individual in my life. She respected the arts, although her education stopped at the age of 14 when she started to work. Together with my father, she bought me a violin when I was eight years old. They paid for two lessons per week, although they wanted me to be an engineer. My mother was always so encouraging in practicing; so positive. I enrolled at the technical school when I was 18, but they were closed due to the protestation against the occupation of Czechoslovakia by the Nazi regime.

Soon after, in 1940, I met the Czech composer Jaroslav Ridky and took lessons from him in theory and composition. I also took lessons in painting from Czech artists. It was through Professor Ridky's incredible belief and encouragement that helped me to enter the Prague Conservatory in 1941, which remained open because of its lower status than the universities.

Professor Ridky may have believed in some of my abilities, but as I have realized, he wanted to save me from going to work in the ammunition factory in Dresden, Germany, where as a university student I was supposed to go. He, together with my mother, was such a wonderfully positive person in my life. He was the one who made me a composer.

In 1946, I left for Paris to learn more about the world and music. In 1951, Professor Ridky died. My mother passed away in 1955, six months after my arrival in the United States (in 1954) to teach at Cornell University in Ithaca, New York. My sister and father were supportive too, but my mother and Professor Ridky gave me what a young person needs: hope and belief.

Two great personalities I met in Paris also touched my life in an incredible way. The composer Arthur Honegger, with whom I studied for about three years, and the eminent teacher and superb musician, Nadia Boulanger, with whom I did not study, but who had read and heard my scores and was most supportive and helpful in France. She recommended me to the music department at Cornell University in 1954. And here in the United States, Elliot W. Galkin, musicologist, conductor, and director of the Peabody Institute of Music, was unselfishly helpful. We had met in Paris in the fifties in a conducting class at the Conservatory.

A composer must have an understanding family. When I would come home from school or rehearsals, or from travels and needed to write music, my wife and children understood my dilemma. They were most helpful at all times and sacrificed a lot for my profession. They had to live with a composer, and this is not an easy task. I am therefore deeply grateful to my family and so many friends and unnamed persons who have liked my music.

H. Ten Works I Believe All Band Conductors at All Levels Should Study

1. *Messe de Nostre Dame* by Guillaume de Machaut. This highly sophisticated work makes us understand how knowledgeable composers already were in the 14th century.

2. *L'Orfeo* (opera in 3 acts, composed in 1607) or *Vespero della Beata Vergine* (1610).

   These works present the glory of music and the beauty of voice, string and wind sonorities.

3. *The Six Brandenburg Concertos* (especially No. 2), to hear the virtuosic passages demanded by Bach on string, wind, and brass instruments in order to understand how composers today build on techniques of the past.

4. *Symphony No. 41 "Jupiter"* by Wolfgang Amadeus Mozart. A masterpiece of construction and monument of perfection in the art of composition.

5. *String Quartet, opus 132* by Ludwig van Beethoven. This quartet contains passages judged to be "absolutely unplayable" according to the players of the time. Today, it is performed by students at conservatories all over the world. It is probably one of the first inspirations of such exalting and mystical writing.

6. *Three Nocturnes* by Claude Debussy presents a radical break in composing. They are imaginative and magnificently scored, inspired by colors and poetry. There are virtuosic passages for the whole orchestra.

7. *The Rite of Spring* by Igor Stravinsky is spectacularly daring in rhythm and orchestral colors splashed all over the score. This is the work that became the symbol of great art of the 20th century to all composers.

8. *Piano Concerto No. 2* by Bela Bartok, which contains some of the most imaginative ideas in orchestration and power as well as of beauty.

9. *A Survivor from Warsaw* by Arnold Schoenberg, for daring and powerful subject matter and sounds. This work is especially effective in live performance... similar to seeing Picasso's *Guernica.*

10. *Sinfonietta* by Leos Janacek contains some of the most individualistic, original writing and scoring from the orchestral repertoire. The joy, excitement, and hope found in this work come from the pen of a then old composer. This is a unique example of 20th century independent writing.

I. Ten Composers Whose Music Overall Speaks to Me in Especially Meaningful Ways

1. J.S. Bach for his religious and philosophical content, incredibly daring harmonies, contrapuntal writing, and his cathedral-like constructions.

2. Mozart, for his genial approach to composing and his elegant melodies.

3. Beethoven, for his powerful music, for example, the first movement of the *Fifth Symphony,* which is a "cataclysmic" force. Also his masterful construction, exaltation, and revolutionary ideas.

4. Debussy, for his amazing sense of proportions and colors, not only in large works, but also in his solo, chamber, and vocal music. His orchestration is magical.

5. Mussorgsky, for his grandeur, poetry, power, magnificent harmonies, and sense of epic proportions.

6. Janacek, for his uniquely beautiful melodic and harmonic language, orchestral innovations, sense of drama, and conveying passion and tragedy.

7. Bartok, for masterful, elegant writing and new ideas for any medium, as well as sophisticated and superb orchestration, and for his modesty and human feeling.

8. Stravinsky, for being a musical genius of the 20th century and for his innovations in all musical forms, orchestration, individual writings in solo, chamber and orchestral music, and for his sense of daring, thus opening possibilities for all composers.

9. Smetana, for being the first Czech genius who elevated Czech music among the finest ever composed, and for writing the majestic cycle, *My Country.*

10. Ives, for his audacity and unimaginable force to compose in addition to his business profession. And for his vision and sometimes "raw" beauty of expression as we find in *The Concord Sonata.*

11. Messiaen, for his visions, deep religious convictions, exquisite instrumentation, and beautiful images of love and birds.

J. The Future of the Wind Band

Today's modern concert band is an excellent ensemble. It has a wide range of colors, and the combination of winds, brass, and percussion makes it an exciting ensemble for which to write. The players in our top music schools and conservatories are excellent, and the level of playing in our smaller colleges and universities is surprisingly good, due to the fact that practically every high school in the country has a band, and children take private lessons.

When I came to this country in 1954, I was surprised by the quality of the Ithaca College and Cornell Bands. And, they played mostly contemporary music. I thought it would be fun to write for them. The occasion arose when I was asked in 1966 to compose a *Saxophone Concerto* with a concert band. Since that time, I have written approximately 15 works for band, mostly commissions.

At present, bands have much music to play. In the last fifty years, many composers in this country have written for bands, among them Copland, Hindemith, Schoenberg, Milhaud, Grainger, and Persichetti. Composers alive today are also writing for band because the possibility of being performed is much greater than with other ensembles.

And the performances are good to excellent. Bands do not have the rich repertoire of the classical, romantic, and early 20th century periods (unless we use transcriptions). It has marches, waltzes, serenades, partitas, and cassations from great composers of all periods.

I always found that the young performers in universities wanted to be challenged, and when given the chance to understand new music, they responded very positively. So many band directors also champion our music and we are all grateful to them and to the performers for their interest and work. Through their art, our music lives. The band is an ensemble of rich colors, with incredible range, power, and flexibility. The band is also capable of sounds of gentleness, elegance, exaltation, and glory.

The band is an ensemble that will be here as long as we learn how to play wind, brass, and percussion instruments, and as long as we love to share with others. This is the most important aspect, i.e. making music together, especially in these times when so much trash—and not just musical trash—is being thrown on us and our young people.

Bands, with orchestras, choirs, chamber groups, and vocal and instrumental soloists, will keep our music alive. All art is struggling these days. All ensembles, especially professional ones (orchestras, operas, chamber groups), are looking for audiences. The old generation, which was interested in music and art, is dying off. The present generation is interested in other music, but I believe the youngest generation is again interested in values of art: not only the kind made "fast, in five minutes," but the painstaking kind, such as the great pyramids, cathedrals, or the endless hours taken by Rembrandt to create a painting, or Beethoven to compose the *Missa Solemnis,* or Walt Whitman to write *Leaves of Grass.*

K. Other Facets of My Everyday Life

When I was young, in Prague, I spent nearly every night either at concerts or in opera houses. The only way to hear music was to actually be there or on the radio, but we preferred "live." I also was interested in painting and poetry, as well as sports such as tennis, ice-hockey, soccer, and skiing.

In Paris, between 1946-52, I had to abandon sports, (except for tennis), yet operas and concerts remained every night. Between 1952-54, I began to travel and conduct, and also being married and having a family, we spent time together. In 1954, my first year at Cornell University, I spent a lot of time preparing courses, learning better English, how to drive a car, and how to live in a new country with our family. (I did only a little writing, mostly short, easier compositions such as *Eight Czech Duets, Twelve Moravian Songs, Four Pieces for Strings* and *Festive Ode*). Later, I started to conduct the Cornell orchestras, and guest conducted in Europe.

There really was no time for hobbies, except playing badminton from time to time with our children. In 1965 we bought a summer home on the shores of Cayuga Lake (30 minutes from home) and spent summers boating, swimming, canoeing, etc. At the same time I was composing. By the late 1960's and early 1970's, in addition to European travels, I began to guest conduct and lecture in the U.S., mostly on new music as well as my own. When our first daughter was old enough to baby-sit her sisters, my wife would join me on my travels, especially to the Orient as well as to Europe.

During the school years, I did not have much time for composing. I wrote music mostly during vacations (Thanksgiving, Christmas, Easter) and during summers. As I got older, my sports activities started to disappear. From time to time, I watch tennis and hockey on the television. In Florida, where my wife and I now live during the winters, I am swimming in addition to walking every day.

L. Works Premiered by the Commissioning Ensemble/Conductor

Al Fresco (1974)

Commissioned by Ithaca College. First performance: Ithaca College Concert Band, the composer conducting, Ithaca, NY, April 19, 1975.
Duration 12 minutes, grade 4, publisher: AMP-G. Schirmer.

An American Te Deum (1976)

Commissioned by Coe College. Text from writings by Henry David Thoreau, Ole Rolvaag, Otokar Brezina, folk, traditional, and liturgical sources. Includes mixed chorus with 20-50 hand bells. First performance: Coe College, Cedar Rapids, Iowa, December 5, 1976.
Duration 45 minutes, grade 6, publisher: AMP-G. Schirmer.

Apotheosis of this Earth (1971)

Commissioned by the Michigan Band and Orchestra Association. Mixed chorus (optional). First performance: University of Michigan Symphony Band, the composer conducting, April, 1971.
Duration 25 minutes, grade 6, publisher: AMP-G. Schirmer.

Concerto for Alto Saxophone and Concert Band (1967)

Commissioned by the Cornell University Wind Ensemble. First performance: Sigurd Rascher, saxophone, Cornell University Wind Ensemble, the composer conducting, Ithaca, NY, March 17, 1968.
Duration 20 minutes, grade 6, publisher: AMP-G. Schirmer.

Concertino for Piano and Winds (1984)

(small wind ensemble of approximately 35 players) Commissioned by the Florida Department of Cultural Affairs. First performance: College Band Directors National Association Conference, University of Central Florida Wind Ensemble, the composer conducting, Orlando, FL, January 27, 1984.
Duration 15 minutes, grade 4-5, publisher: Schott International.

Concerto for Percussion and Wind Ensemble (1970-71)

Commissioned by Ludwig Industries. First performance: Baylor University Symphonic Wind Ensemble, Gene C. Smith and Larry Vanlandingham, conductors, Waco, TX, February 7, 1972. Duration 18 minutes, grade 5 (accompaniment), grade 6 (soloists), publisher: AMP-G. Schirmer.

Concerto for Trumpet and Wind Orchestra (1973)

Commissioned by Kappa Kappa Psi and Tau Beta Sigma Biennial Convention. First performance: National Intercollegiate Band, Raymond Crisara, trumpet, Arnald Gabriel, conductor, Storrs, CT, August 9, 1973.
Duration 14 minutes, grade 6, publisher: AMP-G. Schirmer.

Concerto for Wind Ensemble (1982)

Commissioned by Michigan State University Wind Symphony. First performance: Michigan State University Wind Symphony, East Lansing, MI, the composer conducting, December 3, 1982.
Duration 22 minutes, grade 6, publisher: AMP-G. Schirmer.

Les Couleurs Fauves (1996)

Commissioned by alumni and friends of the Northwestern University School of Music for John P. Paynter, in honor of the 40th anniversary of his appointment to the faculty. First performance: Northwestern University Symphonic Wind Ensemble, the composer conducting, Pick-Staiger Concert Hall, Evanston, IL, November 16, 1996.
Duration 17 minutes, grade 6, publisher: AMP-G. Schirmer.

Divertimento for Brass Ensemble and Percussion (1958)

First performance: Ithaca College Brass Ensemble, Robert Prins, conductor, Ithaca College, Ithaca, NY, February 17, 1960.
Duration 15 minutes, grade 3-4, publisher: AMP-G. Schirmer.

Divertimento for Symphonic Winds and Percussion (1974/95)

Arranged for symphonic winds and percussion by John Boyd. First performance: Indiana State University Symphonic Wind Ensemble, John Boyd, conductor, Terre Haute, IN October 25, 1995.

Duration 15 minutes, grade 3-4, publisher: Ludwig Music.

Fanfare for Brass and Percussion (1981)

Commissioned by the Portland Opera Brass. First performance: Portland Opera House, March 7, 1981, Fred Sautter, conductor.

Duration 6 minutes, grade 5, publisher: AMP-G. Schirmer.

Festive Ode (1955)

For mixed or men's chorus and orchestra or band. A Cornell University Centennial Commission, text by Eric Blackall. First performance: Cornell University Chorus, Orchestra and Band, Thomas A. Sokol, conductor Ithaca, New York, October 9, 1964.

Duration 4 minutes, grade 3, publisher: Highgate Press.

Midwest Celebration (Fanfare) (1996)

For three choirs of brass and percussion (8 horns, 9 trumpets, 9 trombones, tuba, 5 percussion) commissioned by The Mid-West Clinic in celebration of the 50th anniversary convention. First performance: Northshore Concert Band Brass Ensemble, the composer conducting, Chicago Hilton and Towers, December 17, 1996.

Duration 6 minutes, grade 5- 6, publisher: AMP-G. Schirmer.

Music For Prague 1968 (1968)

Commissioned by Ithaca College. First performance: Music Educators National Conference, January 31, 1969, Washington, DC, Ithaca College Concert Band, Kenneth Snapp, conductor.

Duration 19 minutes, grade 6, publisher: AMP-G. Schirmer.

Smetana Fanfare (1984)

Commissioned by San Diego State University for the Festival of Czech Music. First performance: San Diego State University Wind Ensemble, Charles Yates, conductor San Diego, CA, April 3, 1984.

Duration: 3 minutes, grade 4, publisher: AMC-G. Schirmer.

chapter 7

timothy Mahr

A. Biography

I was born in Reedsburg, Wisconsin on March 20, 1956, the second of five sons of Donald and Jeneane Mahr. We moved to La Crosse, Wisconsin when I was three, and my parents still live there. Early piano lessons from my mother preceded the time I inherited my uncle's old trombone in the summer of second grade. I was let into the lesson program at the elementary school about two years ahead of schedule. This led to a succession of experiences that found me performing with the bands at grade levels above my own—all the way through performing with the local university concert band while still in high school. Additionally, I was blessed with teachers all along the way who pushed me as well as nurtured me, both in and outside of music. I loved being able to play "The Jolly Coppersmith" on my trombone in 3rd grade. I was hooked.

I recall being completely overwhelmed by J.S. Bach's "Little Fugue in g minor" in 7th grade. It was in our music class textbook and I can still remember the excitement of finding out that our church organist had a copy of it that I could borrow. I still find it to be an amazing work, and although I now respect it for reasons that were at the time beyond my twelve-year-old mind, I'm glad that this music and my other early favorites still engage me with a gripping language that speaks to my heart and gut much more than to my intellect.

Working out arrangements with my older brother, Tom, of Blood, Sweat, and Tears tunes for our jazz band while in 9th grade coincided with my first attempts at composition. These works were pretty bad piano ballads for the young women in my life who spurned my affections and works for small brass ensembles to be performed by my buddies and I in church services.

While I was in 9th and 10th grade, I was a member of the Blue Stars Drum and Bugle Corps. We were a championship-level Division I corps, and the variety of experiences afforded me through this involvement had a direct impact on my development as a musician and young man. To this day, I can look back on my time with the corps and realize that I do things and hear things a certain way because of the stimulating experiences I encountered.

My time at La Crosse Central High School found me actively involved in the music scene. Opportunities to conduct, compose, arrange, write marching drills and improvise all presented themselves, and I knew I wanted to be a band director when I was a junior. I attended the University of Wisconsin–La Crosse during my senior year in order to take music theory courses.

I decided to attend St. Olaf College (1974–78) after visiting it my senior year as a tag-along companion to a friend who was checking it out at the time. On this trip I observed a St. Olaf Band rehearsal under the direction of Miles Johnson and caught a performance in observance of the college's centennial that involved many of the music department's ensembles. That was all it took to convince me that it was the place for me. The most important thing that happened to me in my college years was my involvement in the band program as a trombonist and student conductor. I listened and observed carefully, then internalized and dreamed the sound of those bands. To this day I readily acknowledge that my model for band sound and my respect for excellent repertoire came about from my time in this program, most notably my three years with the St. Olaf Band under the direction of Miles "Mity" Johnson.

I earned a BM degree in Music Theory/Composition after three years and finished the BA in Music Education at the end of my senior year. In mid-August, 1978 (the longest summer of my life) I finally landed a job as the Director of Bands at Milaca High School in Milaca, Minnesota, a small, rural community of nearly 3,000 people at the time. During those three years, I led a band program that numbered about 110 students while making the normal amount of mistakes for a beginning teacher. I lived 11 miles outside of town at the edge of a state forest, and wrote music in my spare time.

I pursued the MA degree in trombone performance from 1981–83 at The University of Iowa. I felt it was important for my growth as a conductor and composer to become a more accomplished performer on my instrument. During the second year I was a teaching assistant with the UI Bands and also started work within the DMA program in Instrumental Conducting.

I was fortunate to have been the right person in the right place at the right time in the spring of 1983 when I was awarded an assistant professor position as Director of Bands at the University of Minnesota, Duluth. I taught there for ten years, with an interruption during 1987–88 to spend a year in residency for my DMA program back in Iowa City. I taught composition as part of my load during my final years at UMD.

I interviewed for my present position at St. Olaf College in December, 1993, was offered the job, and started teaching in Northfield in the fall of 1994. In addition to conducting the St. Olaf Band and teaching courses in conducting and music education, I teach three levels of composition courses each year along with an occasional independent study in the subject. I find that these courses and their inherent lessons contain opportunities for some of the most stimulating thinking I do each week.

I defended successfully my DMA Essay in the fall of 1995. My essay was titled *An Annotated Bibliography and Performance Commentary of the Works for Concert Band and Wind Orchestra by Composers Awarded the Pulitzer Prize in Music 1943–1992, and a List of Their Works for Chamber Wind Ensemble.* I found the subject fascinating.

Opportunities over the past eighteen years to guest conduct many band festivals, all-state bands, intercollegiate bands, and college/university and community bands have served as laboratory experiences for me as a composer.

My career as a composer of band music began humbly while I was still a college student. I wrote a work entitled *Adagietto* for the Austin High School Symphony Band (Austin, Minnesota) in late spring of 1978. A brief exploration of the medium, it was intended to be a gesture of appreciation to its conductor, Conrad Muzik, who had been my supervising teacher for my student teaching experience. I can still remember the thrill of having the entire band perform my music. However, as is the case with many early works, it is now withdrawn. The presentation by the St. Olaf Band of the full band version of *Fanfare and Grand March* at the Baccalaureate service in May 1981 marks the first performance of one of my band works that I still keep in my catalog. This work was published in 1983 by the Neil A. Kjos Music Company within the same release as my *Fantasia in G*. I was fortunate to have both works selected to be performed at the Midwest International Band and Orchestra Clinic that December; it's been a wonderful ride ever since.

B. The Creative Process

One of the most common questions asked of a composer is "Where does all that music come from?" This is not an easy question to answer for me. I'm convinced the music is a divine gift from God, a blessing in my life (that at times feels like a curse)—some may refer to the muse, but I don't quite see if that way. Depending on the moment, I'm not always comfortable in citing this answer to the question posed, but it's what I feel in my heart and soul. For some reason, the ability to create music was given to me and I try to take the responsibility very seriously.

So for me the music comes from above...How? This is still a bit of a mystery as well. I combine the training I've had in composition and music theory with my experiences as a performer, conductor, and teacher to form a practical base from which to explore my imagination. I have difficulty getting started on the physical writing of a piece until I have a good sense of what the work is going to be or do. I need to know why the piece should exist—and this goes well beyond that fact that some party commissioned me to write it. I then try to sense the energy of the individual gesture, musical moment, or the entire work, and then search for the right music that will combine this sensation with its message to bring it all to life.

Composition is on the whole a balancing act between the exploration of the full potential contained in a musical idea and the need to make a decision about which particular potentiality is the best to follow at that moment. This is a search for that one idea among the many that is the "keeper," ultimately the only one to retain and the "right" one to chisel a particular musical moment into the granite of time. It was rather illuminating early in my education to review the facsimiles of Beethoven's sketch books and take note of how many of the explored possibilities didn't make it into the final composition.

I often improvise at the piano on the materials that are generating the work. At times I am deliberate in staying focused, directly relating the improvisations to the original motive or progression. At other times I will allow the music to travel wherever it wants to go. I typically record these sessions on cassette and in hindsight am always thankful that I do when a particular moment happens to go very well. A bit of quick transcription will help capture that idea in a usable manner. Additionally, I will gather up some of these tapes to play in the car if I have any extended driving ahead of me. I'm not necessarily scouring the tapes for usable music; rather, reviewing the previous few work sessions keeps the materials alive and growing within me.

I do a fair amount of composing while doing repetitive tasks, such as driving, showering, or mowing a lawn. These kinds of actions allow a drift in my thinking to the right side of the brain. Another means of allowing my sub-conscience to work on the material involves reviewing the piece as it stands that day just before going to sleep. The music engages my dream state and brings me face-to-face with those remaining challenges within the score. I also find it helpful late at night to listen to an audio playback (cassette or midi) and fall asleep while listening. These processes reveal a whole new world of connections and possibilities.

I find that I become steadily more absorbed in the work as it draws to conclusion. I would imagine I'm not that pleasant to be around, as I become too focused on the music at the expense of almost everything else going on in my life.

The best times of day for me to compose are early in the morning and late at night, both before and after the duties of parenting and teaching. It is impossible to compose during the day as other matters need my full attention (besides, there are too many interruptions).

I try to establish a thread of connective thought that holds the piece together from start until finish. I call it the skeleton. At first it might just be a verbal description of what the piece will be. Then it becomes a flow chart of sorts, with shapes, diagrams, musical sketching, and a cobweb of lines drawn to show relationships and order; this illustrates the pathway from one idea to the next. These lines are where the composing is quite interesting and rewarding, as I try to develop material from the first idea into an effective bridge to the next. I look for closely associated elements between the two ideas (intervals, rhythms, gestures, etc.) and build upon these. It's as if the ideas reach out to each other with hopeful tendrils looking for a meaningful, musical way to entwine.

Finally, specific music fleshes out the skeleton. It feels great when I can get this skeleton established—at that point, the piece is essentially finished in my mind. At this time, I will usually take a night off as a personal reward.

An analogy to the above process would be the architect who finally establishes the framework of the building; from that point on additional decision-making will complete the project but the structure itself is already firmly fixed.

I rarely start in measure one and go from there. As the materials develop, I order and reorder them to establish a meaningful pathway for the piece. My works typically have an organic, through-composed structure if I do not intend initially to follow an established form. The first ideas that come to me are hardly ever the first moments of the composition. I find it hardest to compose the beginning and ending of a work.

Lately I use the computer (Finale™ software) when composing as it is such a wonderful aid for part extraction. Having been a pencil pusher until just a few years ago, I began using the computer when my composition students started bringing their weekly work to me as midi files on discs. Although the computer figures heavily into my work process, I still do much sketching with pencil and paper. I admit I miss the physical action of turning a pencil over to erase a mistake and then brushing the paper clean with my little finger. I must have done that thousands and thousands of times during the first twenty years of my career. I also miss being able to see full score pages with a single glance; even though I use a large monitor I can't see the entire page without having to scroll up or down.

I would caution the composer who uses the computer to be aware of the seduction of the playback mode. It is wonderful to be able to hear almost immediately a realization of your decision-making. In the years before this capability was available one had to trust the inner ear or perhaps skills at the piano keyboard in order to hear the music. Now, an immediate performance of sorts is but a keystroke away. One can spend too much time listening over and over again, making small adjustments to the music, when before one would just trust the inner ear and keep going. Another warning: cut and paste capabilities are both a blessing and a curse. Use judiciously.

I am an observer of life just as much as a participant. There is music all around us, whether it be in the beauty of the natural world, the imposed order of the civilized world, or the interactions between people. I also draw and paint occasionally and recommend this to all composers. At least a few times every year, get the brushes and paints out and lose yourself for a time mixing, blending, and contrasting colors on a page or canvas while thinking about form, structure, gesture, and rhythm. Don't worry about having to show the result to anyone—paint for yourself. Let this process speak to you.

C. The Approach to Orchestration.

Orchestration—this is where much of the fun is!

Orchestration binds itself to the compositional process at various levels of certainty and commitment. At times specific instruments and combinations are associated by the composer with the development of certain musical materials, while at other points in the score the materials are heard in a more general sense, perhaps knowing they would be successful if orchestrated in any number of ways.

I enjoy playing little mental games with myself in whatever environment I might happen to be in at the time—when I hear an interesting sound or observe some sort of action, I try to figure out how I might translate it into a moment of music. First come the gestures implied by the physical actions of the observations; how can they be mimicked musically? Then come decisions about what instruments could bring those gestures to life. That's when I turn to that ever-expanding data bank in my mind that contains all of my memories of instrumental sounds in any combination.

I visualize the timbral potential of each instrument as a sphere that contains all the creative possibilities of the instrument. Within the sphere are considerations of tessitura, dynamics, and articulations, and their effect on the sound, as well as special effects, such as muting, alternate positions and fingerings, tremelos and trills, or the use of flutter tongue. One then considers where each instrument's sphere might overlap with another (instrumental sections have their spheres as well). This gives a sense for the potential of timbral modulation between the instruments and sections, as well as ideas for interesting combinations. For example, what are the crossover possibilities between the horn section and the clarinet section, or a solo oboe and the marimba? Where do they share common sonic ground? It's also engaging to conceive of the resultant sound from some type of instrumental combination as being a new singular timbre, rather than just the simultaneous sounding of individual contributions.

My work in the electronic music lab at St. Olaf College during my undergraduate years led to an interest in and concern for the morphology of a musical moment—its life, the envelope of its sound shape—and how the assignment of timbre (orchestration), dynamic, and articulation greatly affect the moment.

The percussion section is a world all its own. I tend to write percussion last when composing a band work. Certainly I make notes to myself during the initial sketching of the piece that outline what I want to have happen with the percussion; however, I find that it pays to wait until I finish the wind writing before fully composing the percussion parts. This way I can then concentrate on the unavoidable logistics one must consider, such as allowing the performer enough time to get to the next instrument, assignment of instruments to specific percussion parts, or creating reasonable timpani tuning changes. Often I use percussion to propel the music forward, especially when the wind writing suspends its forward motion for one reason or another.

Musical influences from beyond the normal world of the concert band (now there's an idea to explore—the "normal" world of the concert band!) have steadily made their way into the orchestration of many of today's band scores. One can trace the return of the soprano saxophone and flugelhorn to their resurgent popularity in jazz performance. Most high school programs can supply these instruments now days. Additionally, one certainly sees the influence of world music on the ever-expanding palette of percussion.

The piano appears in many band works of recent years both for its ability to add clarity to lines in the high register and immediacy of attack to bass lines, as well as its sustaining capabilities and extended range of pitch.

The young composer is encouraged to listen to as much music as possible; this is an experience greatly enhanced by following scores. Begin making those neural connections that are so important—to be able to see with one's ears and hear with one's eyes. Ask questions of performers to the point of being a pest about performance techniques and the idiosyncrasies of the instruments. Sit in on instrumentalists' practice sessions. Just as a young conductor starts filling a bag full of tricks of the trade in hopes of not fumbling around too much on the podium, so too should the young composer start creating an aural data bank supported by pertinent knowledge of the instruments.

D. Views from the composer to the conductor pertaining to score study and preparation

I'll begin the discussion here with a quotation from Paul Claudel (1868-1955), French poet, playwright, and diplomat:

> *"The poem is not made from these letters that I drive in like nails, but of the white which remains on the paper."*

The inexactness of music notation is frustrating. Even when the notation seems as though everything is clearly written and edited, it barely symbolizes all that is hoped will happen in a simple piece, let alone a complex score. Consequently, interpretation becomes one of the paramount responsibilities of the conductor when preparing the score.

Consider the following blatantly romanticized scenario: a composer toils and suffers to create a work in his or her mind and then wrestles it onto the page. When finished, the composer hands it off to the performers, offering the score from bended knee. The head bows in hopeful prayer that the conductor will invest much personal time to understand the score's intent and potential, and formulate an honest interpretation. The composer realizes that the work is now completely at the mercy of the conductor. The composer is worried. My commentary later in this chapter on the relationship between the composer and the commissioning party contains a listing of expectations each party should have of one another. One can modify this listing slightly to illustrate what a composer expects of a conductor and what a conductor should expect of a composer.

The potential for passion within a score lies waiting to be unlocked. Composers sense the passion in the moment they're creating and hope for its realization. However, this music lies in lifeless ink on paper until it's infused with passion from the conductor and performers alike. Composers hope conductors will internalize the music to the point that the very thought of one's band realizing the potential of the musical moment raises the hair on one's arm.

We are encouraged as conductors to get our musicians to perform with a strong sense of ownership, spirit, and conviction. What does technique have to do with these performance traits? To a point, everything. However, I would much rather have a band deliver one of my works with a great sense of ownership, spirit, and conviction, even if it is at the expense of performing with a lack of technical precision, than perform without a "heart." Certainly the message comes first, and the message can be blurred or miscommunicated if the technical preparation is lacking. When musicians are fearful of not being perfect, which results in an overriding focus on technical brilliance, much is lost, as they put little effort into the emotional shaping of the music.

A composer's reactions to a performance typically deal with the large issues first, before zeroing in on the particulars. Concerns about the overall pacing of the work or getting the message right far outweigh whether a certain note was chipped or a complex passage was not rhythmically precise.

Discerning the proper pacing of a composition is another important responsibility of the conductor. Score study warrants using a metronome for guidance and affirmation. The choice of tempi needs to take into account the level of performance preparation, the acoustic of the hall, the principles of note grouping, and the harmonic rhythm (the rate of change in the underlying harmonic progression). Take care to keep an ensemble from finding its comfortable groove at an unintended tempo; this can be a very difficult aspect of the performance to adjust later in the preparation phase.

The kind of language a conductor uses in rehearsal greatly affects the musical understanding conveyed to the performers. Eldon Obrecht, a music theory teacher at The University of Iowa, had a large influence on me during graduate school in that, for an entire semester in the Tonal Forms course, he made us talk about music with verbs. It wasn't an easy thing to do at first. He stressed that music-making is an active art form that lives in real time, and that we should both address the music and try to understand it with a vocabulary centered on action.

The rehearsal as an instructional vehicle is a fluid state. One can't predict what will be encountered during a given rehearsal, nor what will be done or said in response to what is heard and what is perceived as needing to be done next. Students need to hear, see with their mind's eye, and sense the journey of musical thought through the work. Consequently, things said by the conductor in rehearsal must have a grounding in a language of action to communicate what the music is asking of the musicians. Sometimes off-the-wall comments are used in hopes of capturing attention and making a point. Once a year the commentary may be rather eloquent; the performers should be encouraged to stay awake in rehearsal to not miss that one special moment!

Decisions, decisions, decisions.... The conductor is encouraged to base the interpretation and rehearsal strategies on those decisions already made by the composer. By asking the big "*Why*?" and the resultant "who?" "what?" "when?" "where?" and "how?" the conductor can peel back layers to reveal information that truly anchors the composition. For example, when studying a score, ask, "Why did the composer choose to take this particular musical moment in this direction when it very easily could have gone a number of other ways?" In other words, the conductor should attempt to discern the composer's intent by pondering these acts of decision-making (after all, that's all composition really is—decision-making).

I teach with the goal in mind of having performers understand the direction of thought in the music. It's important to understand how the music travels through time, from point A to B to Z—not only how it progresses but why it does so. This inevitably also calls forward questions involving "who, when, and where." So whether I speak of the creation of tension and its release, the withholding of arrival points to heighten impact, the agitation of a cadential extension, or the contrapuntal nightmare of a development section that entwines musical thoughts, I'm really just trying to have them sense the music the same way I do, so that we can be of the same mind as we try to recreate the composer's intentions.

Composers tend to have a much easier time creating principal thematic ideas than when they struggle with the challenge of piecing these ideas together into a complete musical structure. It's much like building a bridge: the lengthy, strong steel beams (the main themes) bolt together with various connecting devices and it's typically at these connections where the structure will break and/or fail if extreme care is not taken during construction. With this in mind, it is a prudent conductor who studies the score to locate these connections and understands what makes them work from a theoretical standpoint, and then follows up with rehearsal plans that ensure that these connections receive the attention they need. These connections most often involve change, whether in tempo, style or tonality, and most result in an increase of instability in the music. This instability is the challenge of musical transition and inherently requires greater attention. When made aware of the importance of these connections, performers will be more alert and confident as they negotiate transitive passages and will be more likely to firmly establish the structure of the work.

Musical moments contain implications for what might follow. Composers either realize these implications in the most predictable manner or they will allow some uncertainty and surprise into their scores by not succumbing to the obvious solutions contained in the implications. Understanding how these implications and their realizations propel the music forward in time is a crucial part of interpreting a score. I would recommend doing some reading about Implication-Realization Theory in the works of Leonard Meyer and Eugene Narmour.

What follows presents a simple illustration of this idea. The conductor can sound a second inversion dominant seventh chord and then ask the students what chord should follow next. Invariably they will choose the tonic chord, whether they know what to call it or not (if they've had some theory training they will be able to articulate their response; if they're young, sound three or four options including the tonic chord and ask them to choose). Next, sound the same dominant seventh chord followed by the submediant chord (e.g. D7 followed by the e minor chord in the key of G major). Students with knowledge of first year music theory will be able to name this as a deceptive cadence. The label, deceptive cadence, summarizes Implication-Realization Theory in a nutshell. The listener has been deceived. The expected realization of the harmonic implication did not occur; instead, the listener landed within a more unexpected harmonic moment with the second chord.

When performing a tonal piece governed by a key signature, consider the accidentals as red-flag indicators of something special happening in the music. The accidentals indicate that the composer has chosen to take the music outside the established tonality. The music can be viewed as traveling at these points. Often, these moments are merely "survived" by an ensemble when instead they should provide interest and impetus. There is an inherent need for eye contact and various levels of trust when dealing with music containing many accidentals. The performer needs to trust that he or she will not lose place or fall apart when taking the eyes away from the part.

Dissecting the principal themes into smaller components during the score study phase can lead to a deeper understanding of the relationship between parts within the composition. Search out thematic meaning in the background materials. Quite often a composer will develop a particular aspect of the principal material into material used in a secondary part. At times you will discover that the composer may have done just that, tearing a theme apart and using its elements earlier in the work, only to cleverly combine them at the end of the work in a long anticipated grand statement of the full theme.

Search out timbral connections between instruments in the score. Study the flow of orchestration within the score to locate moments where the tonal color of one instrument or section directly relates to those that immediately follow. There are times when the timbres meld with others when they transform seamlessly from one to the next. Bring these timbral relationships to life in the rehearsal. Composers seriously consider this subject! A fine conductor will recognize when and where the timbral connections are among the most important things happening in the score at that particular moment and bring this connection to the forefront.

More and more I'm sensing music as light. The sound glows with light, and often is colored many different hues due to a variety of instrumentation and dynamic. Light and sound have frequency of vibration at their core, so the connection I'm perceiving does not surprise me. An illustration of this might be the presence of a sheen of light arising from a crescendo. Certain articulation marks and dynamic shifts are concerned with light, as they invite alterations in the presence of the upper partials within an instrument's tone.

The following brief comments are additional thoughts on the preparation of musical scores and the musicians who bring them to life.

Warm up, then tune your band daily. It's very frustrating to find how common it is to *not* spend time on establishing a proper sense for intonation at the beginning of the rehearsal period. It's said that working on intonation is a lot like manure: the more you stir it up the more it stinks. The process may not be pleasant at times, but the effort fertilizes the growth of the ensemble.

Have the band sing, whether they want to or not. Develop within them a willingness to do it and a respect for how singing can benefit the ensemble. A conductor should take singing lessons if possible to increase vocal confidence when modeling.

Invest the time and effort to firmly establish basic musical concepts early on in the band year, such as proper breath support, tone production, interpretation of articulations and their consistent delivery, and matched release shapes.

Be concerned about fully establishing a resonant sustained quality of tone. In other words, get past the attack as quickly as possible to arrive at that vibrant resonance found in the sustained portion of the sound's sonic envelope.

Be reasonable in programming so that the challenge level of the repertoire is a proper match for the level of development across the ensemble. Composers are typically flattered that their work has been chosen for performance. A lot of the sparkle fades from the experience, however, if the composition is inappropriately programmed.

Share with your band how you feel about the music and help them discover means for getting in touch with their feelings about the work.

"Love your kids," as my mentor Miles Johnson would say. This pays a huge dividend in the quality of performance while it builds stronger relationships. There's an obvious price to pay for this dividend but it's certainly worth it.

There's certainly enough stress in a conductor's life—we're all experts at it—so plotting the dynamic course of tension and its release within a work being studied should be an easy, somewhat revelatory task.

Remember, *you* are a composer, too! Most people reading this text have had training in music theory and orchestration. By composing, you hone your skills at score preparation and study. Composing or arranging works for your ensemble is also an excellent way to connect with your band. If your work has any quality to it at all, the performers will be grateful that you believed in them so strongly that you gave willingly of your extra time to create a work just for them. Besides, few things beat the excitement and engagement of conducting your own work.

The best performance occurs when we don't perceive the performer(s)! I feel lucky to be at a performance when I can lose track of who is performing or conducting. When this happens, I interact directly with the composer; the music speaks intimately to my heart and mind, creating a transcendent experience. It's a high compliment to tell musicians that they weren't perceived during a performance because their connection with the music and their realization of the composer's intent was so strong.

E. The Relationship Between the Composer and the Commissioning Party

One might approach this subject by addressing the expectations the composer and the commissioning party bring to the process of premiering a new work.

What does the composer expect?

The composer should be able to expect an honest effort at the best performance possible, certainly one that has allowed for adequate rehearsal time (the composer meeting the deadline is part of this equation!). Recordings of recent performances by the commissioning ensemble will help communicate an understanding of the realistic expected strengths and non-strengths of the group. The premiere may not be for a few years, so as accurate an assessment as possible of the potential of the younger musicians should be made in an effort to predict the strength of the ensemble at the time of the premiere. One should be as honest and realistic as possible about this, so that the piece will indeed suit the ensemble and not be written at a level that is too difficult for them. Some form of informative correspondence during the rehearsal phase, such as tapes, letters, email messages, and phone calls that update how the piece is progressing keeps the composer in the loop and will help to fine tune the works as it heads to its premiere. Prompt payment of fees would certainly be expected.

What can the commissioning party expect?

It is realistic to expect some sort of interaction between the composer and the musicians, either live or through correspondence, especially if the commission is for a school group. Some school programs have had wonderful experiences setting up a conference call on a speaker phone with the composer, whereby the musicians can ask questions about the music, the composer, and the process—everyone gets to hear all of the questions and answers this way. Prompt delivery of a legible score and set of parts (black on white photocopy) is a minimum. The conductor should be able to obtain a copy of the score while parts are being extracted so that the score study process can begin as soon as possible, with the understanding that there might be some corrections made to this score as errors are detected while producing the parts. The music should meet the parameters of duration, level of difficulty, instrumentation, etc. that have been drawn up in the contract. Biographical information about the composer and a photo of the composer should be available for use in the printed program, posters, and press releases. Additionally, program notes and rehearsal suggestions contribute to a quality experience. Possible publication of the work if the composition is of a marketable nature is an added blessing, especially if the published edition contains a dedication to the commissioning party. Publication should not be expected, however, as this decision falls outside of the control of either party. Finally, the commissioning party should expect to have to wait for the "name" composer (get in line!)—one may get lucky, though, so it's always worth making the initial contact, even though it may seem unlikely that a particular popular composer will have time for your project.

Finally, a contract* (see page 274 for sample contract.) between the commissioning party and composer is crucial. It should outline the composer's fee and payment schedule, delivery date, and which party covers the expense of part extraction. One should not be surprised by a request for an advance payment—rather, it is the norm within professional circles. Set a delivery date that is weeks ahead of the first rehearsal. Manuscript and publishing rights remain with the composer. The composer's attendance at the premiere and its inherent expense reimbursement, the dedication wording to be included in the score, and the performance rights for the commissioning party should also be determined.

F. Views on the Teaching of Composition and How to Mentor the Young Composer

Recently one of my composition students said, "I guess this is all about getting outside of your comfort zone." I'm stimulated as a teacher of composition to find ways to unlock a student's imagination and to create that odd combination of courage and foolhardiness the student needs to finally put a mark on the page, a permanent act of notation that lays a composer's soul bare to the world.

I find that teaching composition is much more challenging than I had first thought. There are just so many things for the teacher to consider. Within the first few lessons, one hopes to assess not only the student's past work and present abilities, but also to catch a meaningful glimpse into his or her developing aesthetic soul. The ultimate goal is obvious—to help the student find and/or develop a personal compositional voice.

A weekly instructional schedule consisting of group lessons for the first semester students (three to four students within the hour lesson) coupled with a full class seminar seems to work well. The alert beginning student can pick up quite a bit from observing what happens with a classmate's composition and being asked to make insightful comments on what is heard. When it is the student's turn to have his or her work scrutinized, then commentary is received from two or three students as well as the instructor. The seminars allow for the hearing of student work as well as discussion of assigned works. Additionally, material pertinent to the kind of writing being addressed in the course at the time can be presented.

Presenting a student with projects aimed at limiting the number of decisions to be madc helps to focus efforts at building specific aspects of compositional technique. For example, a project that requires the student to only use four pitch classes eliminates the need to even consider the other eight; a work involving three performers all limited to the use of a single pitch (no octave transpositions) negates any real thinking about melody or harmony, concentrating efforts instead on rhythm and timbre.

Equally valuable are specific listening and score study assignments. For example, a student composing a work for solo flute would gain much from studying Debussy's *Syrinx*, Varése's *Density 21.5*, or Katherine Hoover's *Winter Spirits*.

The current times almost require the composition teacher to be well-versed in the computer software music notation programs in use by the majority of the students, as they are bringing their work to lessons in electronic formats with increasing frequency.

A comment my students hear with regularity is, "Make decisions. Act." Now if I could only heed my own advice....

There is a great temptation to "fix" a student's music, as well as explore its options for development from within your personal aesthetic. Frankly, I find some of my student's music very engaging and I would enjoy the opportunity to work with it, getting my hands dirty with the creative process as borne from within that particular excerpt. The easier challenge is to help the students see possibilities for refinement and development of their music as it stands at each lesson. The more difficult one is to help students realize that their music is not living up to its potential, or that it just doesn't work.

G. Individuals Who Have Been Especially Influential in My Development and Career

My musical life began the moment I was aware of my mother, Jeneane; she was and still is a piano teacher and church choir director and was the person who opened the world of music to me. She gave me my first piano lessons and then was smart enough to farm me off after a bit of time to another teacher. I stayed with the lessons until those difficult junior high years when it just wasn't cool to take piano lessons anymore. In hindsight, stopping my lessons was one of the costliest decisions in my life. I did start them up again in college to meet basic requirements, but I had already missed some valuable time for growth.

My father, Donald, would be the last to claim any personal musicianship and to this day, I think that what I do as a composer remains a bit of a mystery to him. However, as I was growing up, some of my favorite things to do were to listen to my dad whistle tunes through his teeth while he worked around the house or to hear him sing the hymns at church with great conviction but little regard to proper pitch. He showed me early on that music lives strongly in the hearts of those who may not have any musical training. He was also the founding scoutmaster of Troop 17 and my time as a Boy Scout was full of important opportunities for personal growth and maturation as well as great fun.

Both of my parents sacrificed much to bring up five hungry boys, gave of themselves to others in our community and were strong leaders within organizations. They were and still are amazing.

My older brother, Tom, was two years ahead of me. His experiences as a performer on trumpet, music arranger, and student leader were all wonderful models for me.

William Baker, my high school band director, and the choir director, Henry Aronson, were consummate musicians and pedagogues. Early on I felt a strong urge to emulate them. Mr. Baker provided me with opportunities to conduct the band in my junior and senior years, as well as arrange works for our stage band and chart halftime shows for the marching band. Mr. Aronson had us performing double motets by Bach and works by Vaughan Williams and Grieg. His standards were very high and we all worked like crazy just to get that heartfelt smile of acknowledgment that he would share. These two teachers were also about the classiest men I knew at the time. I also knew they respected and cared for me.

Over the course of my four years as a student at St. Olaf College, I studied with teachers who pushed and prodded me to give my best efforts, all the while sharing their expertise. My trombone professor, Derald DeYoung, impressed me greatly with his artistry, level of commitment, and caring nature. I studied composition with Arthur Campbell, whose interest in electronic music was infectious and who searched long and hard to find his own compositional voice. My time in the electronic music lab, getting my hands dirty with sound while patching together the modules of a Moog synthesizer, proved to be some of the most valuable time I've ever spent doing anything in life.

Miles "Mity" Johnson is my musical father. My time under his baton in the St. Olaf Band was instrumental (no pun intended) to the development of my whole being, not just to my growth as a musician. We in the band thought he was a conductor who taught us music; he knew he was at the center of a great musical experience through which he could teach the course "Life 101."

Not surprisingly, most of the lessons were grounded in the music we were creating. While under Mr. Johnson, I discovered the beauty in the band sound, whereas before I primarily found excitement. He showed us that an excellent ensemble will respond to the slightest opening of a hand or the softening of the look in the eyes. From Mity I learned of the quiet strength of expression found in a full concert band performing at a pianissimo dynamic level. He shared the when, where, why, and how of turning a phrase. He reaffirmed my sense of working hard to attain the best results possible and that the reward was in the effort made. He proved that love and what one feels inside are at the center of the musical experience. And I will never forget the simple eloquence of his advice to all of the future teachers in our band: "Love your kids."

During my graduate work at The University of Iowa my trombone teacher was the late John Hill, a master pedagogue and superb musician. He was known for putting you in your place at the beginning of a lesson and then building you back up during the next hour so that you left his studio brimming with the bravado it takes to make it through the trials of the practice room during the coming week. I performed in the UI Symphony Band under Dr. Myron Welch, the UI Orchestra and Sinfonietta under the baton of James Dixon, and the Center for New Music with William Hibbard. All of these men were exacting in their demands and backed their interpretations with scholarly preparation and inspired conducting. I tried to take composition lessons with Richard Hervig but had to drop them after about four weeks as I couldn't keep up with the expected writing pace on top of my trombone work. I was there as a trombonist and conductor, not a composer. I regret not having more time to compose at that point in my education.

Dr. Frank Comella was the Department Head at the University of Minnesota, Duluth, and was the mentor who took a chance at hiring a 27 year old graduate student as the next Assistant Professor of Music and Director of Bands at UMD. He shepherded my attempts, shared his expertise willingly and openly, and inspired me to take chances.

When people ask me with whom have I studied composition, I acknowledge Arthur Campbell at St. Olaf College, and then typically say, "I study composition with the composer of each work I conduct."

H. Ten Works I Believe All Band Conductors at All Levels Should Study

My first response to this question was that it was too hard of a question and that I didn't want to answer it. It's a lot like asking a parent to name a favorite child from among the many in the family. I will fudge a bit on the answer and list a few collections among the single works. The listing is not in any particular order.

1. Any of the Mahler symphonies (although *Symphony No. 1 in D major* is a good starting point)—as Mahler himself supposedly said, each of these symphonies is "a world unto itself." They plumb the depths of human experience and are models of the highest level of human achievement.

2. The *Six Suites for Unaccompanied Violoncello* of J.S. Bach—to see their elegant simplicity in the printed score and then to experience their performance by any number of great artists is a lesson of highest magnitude about the delivery of an expressive line.

3. The three Mozart serenades for winds—this isn't your ordinary table music. If there is any doubt as to the expressive power of this music, screen the opening of Milos Forman's 1984 film, *Amadeus,* and listen to F. Murray Abraham as Antonio Salieri describe moments of the *Gran*

Partita. Personally, I'm especially taken by the simple eloquence of the Adagio movement of *Serenade No. 11.*

4. The Holst suites for military band—not listed here simply because they are considered cornerstone works in the band repertory, (which would be reason enough for their inclusion) but because they are works that, when performed well, tell the world who we are as an artistic medium.

5. "Una Furtiva Lacrima" from Donizetti's *Elisir D' Amore*—don't we all want to be able to sing this?

6. Richard Strauss' *Ein Heldenleben*—this monumental work is anchored (I believe) on incredible wind writing. One of the most invigorating "band" rehearsals I ever experienced as a trombonist was a winds and percussion orchestra sectional on this piece. Who needs the strings?

7. Joseph Schwantner's *and the mountains rising nowhere...*—a stunning example of music conceived for the modern wind ensemble, marked by brilliant orchestration and evocative music that suspends one's normal sense of the passing of time.

8. Egil Hovland's "Stay With Us" from the opera *Captive and Free*—this very recent choral work is sublime music-making at its best.

9. Percy Grainger's *Lincolnshire Posy*—for exposure to a courageous and daring mind as perceived in a work for band, as well as consideration of the score's inherent conducting challenges, innovative writing, and masterful scoring. This is music that reaches in and stretches out.

10. Gyorgy Ligeti's *Sechs Bagatellen für Blaserquintett*—his expert knowledge of these wind instruments shines in these clever bagatelles, and combined with innovative musical thought, creates a stunning display of wind music. We need a band work from him!

11. One could include in this listing any work that simply amazes oneself beyond belief, reaffirms one's reasons for being a musician, and when heard, makes one realize each and every time that the act and art of making music is a divine gift.

I. Ten Composers Whose Music Overall Speaks to Me in Especially Meaningful Ways

I'm going to fudge again on this answer, in that as I started making the list, the composers began to group themselves as to when I first encountered them. All of them spoke to me with heartfelt clarity through their music at a time in my life when their message was needed and welcomed. Their music touched my soul then and it still does today. And there's more than ten of them!

Composers who got into my blood during my formative teenage years:

Johann Sebastian Bach
Ludwig van Beethoven
Edward Elgar
Gustav Holst
Leos Janáček
Richard Strauss
Peter Tchaikowsky

Composers confronted and imitated during those impressionable college years:

George Crumb	Percy Grainger
Gustav Mahler	Wolfgang Mozart
Joseph Schwantner	Igor Stravinsky
Ralph Vaughan Williams	William Walton
John Williams	Paul Winter

Composers who are my musical heroes during the skeptical years of middle age:

Stephen Albert	John Corigliano
Donald Grantham	Michael Kamen
Libby Larsen	Zdeněk Lukáš
David Maslanka	Stephen Paulus
Maria Schneider	Daniel Welcher
Ellen Taaffe Zwillich	

J. The Future of the Wind Band

I am very optimistic about the future of the wind band and look forward to meeting the many challenges to be faced in the years ahead. Undoubtedly the future of the wind band is tied to the freedoms and constraints of budget, time, and technological advancement, as it has always been. It is also linked obviously and inexorably to the future of music education within our schools. We should take comfort and strength in knowing that we've survived rough times in the past, and that these struggles have prepared us for the battles yet to come.

We need to remain open to innovation and new ideas. I recently had the opportunity to attend *Blast!*, the Broadway show that features an exciting blend of complex brass and percussion music with elaborate choreography and staging. It was an exhilarating show and a bit of a revelation. *Blast!* is a direct descendant of the drum corps world. I was a member of the La Crosse Blue Stars Drum and Bugle Corps (a Division I Corps at the time) for two seasons in the early 1970's and have marveled at the development of the corps movement over the last 30 years. It was unimaginable when I was marching that this activity would evolve over a few decades into an artistically respected new form of expression that would be (and this is even more impressive!) financially viable. With the benefit of hindsight, it's easy to see why this transformation has been so successful. I came away from the *Blast!* performance wondering what the band world might learn from this evolution and what we might assimilate from it in the years ahead. I am in no way saying we should duplicate what they have done, per se; rather, we should note that they built upon what they did the best with a sense of urgency and conviction, while staying true to their heritage.

The value and merit of the band experience have not faltered; if anything, they have deepened over the years, turning the experience into a much more artistic undertaking. It has been argued for some time now that the future of our medium lies in the hands of the composers. We should celebrate the situation we find ourselves in at the moment—some of the finest composers of our time are excited about writing for bands and wind ensembles. Educational band repertoire, while still swamped with works of lesser value, has increasingly improved in quality and substance as well. Now is such a great time to be involved with the wind band, due in large part to the exciting new repertoire that is building upon the masterworks of our past. We should not rest on our laurels in this important area, however, and commissioning efforts launched at those exceptionally fine composers that have yet to contribute to our medium should be increased and fully supported.

I certainly believe in music and the value of performing, creating, studying, absorbing, and relishing it. I believe in the need for the arts, and music specifically, within the lives of all, especially our young. I believe in the communicative power of band music, both sublime and grandiose. I believe the band experience will remain a pillar of the music education curriculum in our elementary and secondary schools. I believe in the ability of band music and its performance to meet the artistic needs of all people, at all ages. I'm excited by and involved in the growing community band movement and see this as an area of increased support for what we do in the schools.

Finally, I believe we should be what we are and who we are and not try to become anything else. This has been a hard lesson for me to learn and I'm still just in the beginning throes of changing my perspective to examine and embrace this notion. Certainly we should aspire to improve our standing within professional circles, but more and more, I think we should bring the critical public to us on our terms, rather than trying to become what we might feel they want us to be. We're bands and we give band concerts. These performances are hopefully a wonderful combination of artistic exploration and expression, and a genuine ability to uplift and inspire the audience and performers alike. We are steadily distancing ourselves from that part of our heritage mired in mockery (and I speak here of the unfortunate image of the bands person that is still so prevalent in popular media)—a perception which stunts the growth of most people's expectations of who we are and what we're about. We're not orchestras. We're not choirs. We are the band. Our repertoire and programming are unique and our heritage is our own.

K. Other Facets of My Everyday Life

My wife, Jill, and I center our lives around the raising of our two daughters, Jenna, 9, and Hannah, 4, and we take great pleasure in doing so. It never ceases to astonish me how the love within a family for one another can be the most sustaining, relaxing, stabilizing thing in a person's life, even though at the time life seems as frantic as one could imagine. To get a wondrous, unsolicited hug at the start and end of a day from someone close to you is an absolute blessing. They put bookends of love on the day—they figuratively wrap their arms around the day in a hug all their own.

And then there's having a dog as one of your best friends....

I'm an avid movie fan and enjoy them for many reasons beyond the sheer entertainment of the story being told. One can hear excellent music lurking in the background that features the latest compositional techniques from some of our finest composers of the day. I'm also intrigued by the work of the cinematographers and film editors as it relates to the effective propulsion of the plot line and the transitive emotional states in the characters.

I collect coins as a hobby (and for mental health reasons!), finding them also to be a pretty decent investment. I love holding an old coin in my hand and letting its well-worn beauty speak to me of its history. I used to try to fill all of the holes in the collection books, but am now much more interested in acquiring individual coins representing a variety of types and periods. If I had a lot of disposable cash, I would expand on my very small collection of hand-hammered European coins from the 17th century. They are truly unique works of art.

I dabble with painting and find it to be complementary to my music-making. On a recent sabbatical, I tried daily to read about painters and take slow, thoughtful looks at their works, as well as occasionally paint on my own. I'm not about to mount a show yet, but I do have a few paintings that are pretty dear to me for what I thought about and learned while creating them and for what they share. I'm floored by the risks taken by the great artists. Their use of light, color, hue, form, balance, and rhythm, all speak to me on a musical level. Nothing beats spending leisurely quiet time in a good art museum.

If I could start all over I would be a painter, or perhaps an architect. I've spent many an hour reading about the great buildings and structures built throughout the ages. Once again, the parallel to my attempts as a composer seem obvious.

I believe strongly in the power of visualization, both for its role in the creative process and its ability to aid a person in achieving a higher level of performance.

I'm a diehard Green Bay Packer fan, having grown up in Wisconsin during the Lombardi era.

I love getting out into nature and being quiet within it—with my eyes, ears, and heart wide open.

The older I get the more I'm convinced of the hand of the Lord in my life.

L. Comprehensive List of Works for Band

Academic Flourish from ***Festivals*** (1991)

c. 4:00. Grade 5, Manuscript*

Commissioned by the St. Olaf Band, Miles Johnson, conductor. Premiered April 21, 1991 (20th Annual Cathedral Concert), Wooddale Baptist Church, Eden Prairie, Minnesota.

And, Behold, There Was a Great Earthquake Version I (1983)

c. 3:20, Grade 4-, Manuscript* Version II (1988) Duration: c. 4:30, Grade 4, Manuscript*

Version II commissioned by the Nebraska Wind Symphony, Tony Snyder, conductor. Premiered April, 1988, Nebraska Wind Symphony, Timothy Mahr, conductor, University of Nebraska, Omaha.

Argentum: An Overture for Band (1986)

c. 7:30, Grade 4+, Neil A. Kjos Music Co.

Commissioned by the Nebraska Bandmasters Association for the 25th Anniversary of their association. Premiered March 8, 1986, Nebraska Intercollegiate Band, Timothy Mahr, conductor, Hastings College, Hastings, Nebraska.

Christmas Adoration from ***Festivals*** (1994)

c. 6:00, Grade 5, Manuscript*

Commissioned by the St. Olaf Band, Miles Johnson, conductor. Premiered December 4, 1994, St. Olaf Band, Timothy Mahr, conductor, Boe Memorial Chapel, St. Olaf College, Northfield, Minnesota.

Daydream (1989)

c. 4:15, Grade 3, Neil A. Kjos Music Co.

Commissioned by the St. Olaf Band, Miles Johnson, conductor. Premiered November 11, 1989 (St. Olaf Festival of Bands), Festival Band, Timothy Mahr, conductor, Skoglund Center Auditorium, St. Olaf College, Northfield, Minnesota.

Endurance (1991)

c. 10:30, Grade 5, Neil A. Kjos Music Co.

Commissioned by the American Bandmasters Association as the inaugural work in their commissioning series. Premiered March 7, 1992 (58th Annual Convention of the American Bandmasters Association), United States Interservice Band, Ed Lisk, conductor, DAR Constitution Hall, Washington, D.C.

Everyday Hero (2000)

c. 6:30, Grade 4+, Neil A. Kjos Music Co. [spring, 2003]

Commissioned by the Middle Tennessee School Band and Orchestra Association. Premiered January 20, 2001, All Middle-Tennessee First Senior High Band, Timothy Mahr, conductor, Middle Tennessee State University, Murfreesboro, Tennessee.

Fanfare and Grand March (1980)

c. 2:00, Grade 4, Neil A. Kjos Music Co.

Commissioned by the New Limitations Corporation, originally for brass choir, organ and percussion. Premiere of full band version May 24, 1981, St. Olaf Band, Miles Johnson, conductor, Skoglund Center Auditorium, St. Olaf College, Northfield, Minnesota.

Fantasia in G (193)

c. 5:00, Grade 5, Neil A. Kjos Music Co.

Premiered January 25, 1983, St. Olaf Band, Timothy Mahr, conductor, Boe Memorial Chapel, St. Olaf College, Northfield, Minnesota.

Festivals (1991-94)

c. 4:00; 5:45; 6:00; 7:00; 8:00, Grade 5, Manuscript*

Mvt. 1 Academic Flourish

Mvt. 2 Thanksgiving Meditation

Mvt. 3 Christmas Adoration

Mvt. 4 Lenten Reflection

Mvt. 5 Easter Celebration (still in progress)

Commissioned by the St. Olaf Band, Miles Johnson, conductor, to celebrate the centennial anniversary of the founding of the band. See separate citations for premiere information.

Flourish (1996)

c. 2:00, Grade 4, Neil A. Kjos Music Co.

Commissioned by the University of Wisconsin-Green Bay to celebrate the 30th Anniversary of the UWGB Junior and Senior Summer Music Camps. Premiered August 3, 1996, UWGB Honors Band, Timothy Mahr, conductor, Weidner Center for the Performing Arts, UWGB.

Hey! (2001)

c. 2:30, Grade 4, Manuscript*

Commissioned by the Anoka High School Concert Band, Anoka, Minnesota, John Lace, conductor. Premiered June 11, 2001, Hornindahl, Norway.

Hymn and Celebration (1990)

c. 5:00, Grade 4, Neil A. Kjos Music Co.

Commissioned by the Tipton High School Concert Band, Tipton, Iowa, David Haaverson, conductor. Premiered June, 1990, Tipton High School Auditorium.

Immigrant Dreams (1986)

c. 8:00, Grade 5+, Neil A. Kjos Music Co.

Commissioned by the Anoka High School Concert Band, Anoka, Minnesota, Michael Hiatt, conductor. Premiered June 20, 1986, Anoka High School Concert Band, Timothy Mahr, conductor, Anoka High School Auditorium.

Imprints (1989)

c. 8:00, Grade 5, Neil A. Kjos Music Co.

Commissioned by the Milwaukee Knightwind Ensemble, Jon Steinke, conductor, in memory of Dr. Frank Comella. Premiered October 28, 1989, Milwaukee, Wisconsin.

In Circles (2002)

c. 7:00, Grade 4+, Manuscript*

Commissioned by the Robert Shirek Family in memory of Susan Shirek and in recognition of the newly-constructed Fond du Lac High School, Fond du Lac, Wisconsin. Premiered April 23, 2002,

Fond du Lac Symphonic Winds and Percussion, Symphonic Orchestra and A Capella Choir, Timothy Mahr, conductor, Fond du Lac Performing Arts Center.

In mind, in spirit (1996)

c. 7:30, Grade 4+, Manuscript*

Commissioned by the Bowling Green High School Symphonic Band, Bowling Green, Ohio, Thom Headley, conductor. Premiered April 27, 1996, Bowling Green High School Symphonic Band, Timothy Mahr, conductor, Kobacker Hall, Bowling Green State University.

Into the Air! (1998)

c. 10:00, Grade 6, Neil A. Kjos Music Co.

Commissioned by the United State Air Force Band, Col. Lowell E. Graham, conductor. Premiered July 11, 1999 (Ninth International Conference of the World Association for Symphonic Bands and Ensembles), Harmon Hall, California State University-San Luis Obispo.

Lenten Reflection from ***Festivals*** (1993)

c. 7:00, Grade 5, Manuscript*

Commissioned by the St. Olaf Band, Miles Johnson, conductor. Premiered March 20, 1994, Wooddale Baptist Church, Eden Prairie, Minnesota.

Lines from Lanier (2000)

c. 7:30, Manuscript*

Commissioned by Woodward Academy Wind Ensemble, College Park, Georgia, Charles Brodie, conductor, for the Woodward Academy Centennial Celebration. Premiered April 14, 2000 (Centennial Concert), Woodward Academy Wind Ensemble and Choirs, Timothy Mahr, conductor, Richardson Hall Theatre, Woodward Academy.

The Mankato March (2002)

c. 3:20, Grade 3+, Manuscript*

Commissioned by the Mankato Municipal Concert Band, Ed Stock, conductor. Premiered June 11, 2002, Mankato Municipal Concert Band, Timothy Mahr, conductor, Mankato, Minnesota.

A Mighty March (1999)

c. 2:15, Grade 5-, Neil A. Kjos Music Co. [fall, 2002]

Commissioned by the Minnesota Symphonic Winds, Miles Johnson and Timothy Mahr, conductors, in recognition of Miles Johnson's 20th and final season as the conductor of this community ensemble. Premiered May 8, 1999, Minnesota Symphonic Winds, Timothy Mahr, conductor, Central Lutheran Church, Minneapolis, Minnesota.

Mourning Dances (2001)

c. 13:00, Grade 6-, Manuscript*

Commissioned by Kappa Kappa Psi/Tau Beta Sigma, National Band Fraternity and Sorority. Premiered by the KKP/TBS National Intercollegiate Band, Timothy Mahr, conductor, at the 2001 National Convention on July 24, 2001 in the Omni Bayfront Hotel Ballroom, Corpus Christi, Texas.

Noble Element (2002)

c. 7:15, Grade 5, Manuscript*

Commissoned by The American School Band Directors Association Foundation in observance of the 50th anniversary of The American School Band Directors Association, with generous additional support from the Minnesota Music Educators Association and The Wenger Foundation. Dedicated to the 2002-2003 MMEA All-State Symphonic Band. Premiered August 3, 2002, Duluth Entertainment Convention Center Auditorium, Timothy Mahr, conductor.

Nightdream (1998)

c. 6:45, Grade 4, Manuscript*

Commissioned by the Lancaster High School Symphonic Band, Lancaster, Ohio, Christopher Heidenreich, conductor. Premiered May 28, 1998, Lancaster High School Symphonic Band, Timothy Mahr, conductor, Lancaster High School Auditorium.

O Brother Man (1987)

c. 10:30, Grade 5+, Manuscript*

Commissioned by Hastings College Wind Ensemble, Thomas O'Neal, conductor, in conjunction with the college's Artists Lecture Series theme for 1987–88: "Peace, Security and Defense." Premiered May 12, 1987, Hastings College Wind Ensemble, Timothy Mahr, conductor, Hastings College, Hastings, Nebraska.

Passages (1984)

c.17:30, Grade 6-, Manuscript*

Commissioned by the St. Olaf Band, Miles Johnson, conductor, in memory of Marc Francis Priest, former member of the band. Premiered November 10, 1984, St. Olaf Band, Timothy Mahr, conductor, Skoglund Center Auditorium, St. Olaf College, Northfield, Minnesota.

A Quiet Place to Think (1999)

c. 7:00, Grade 4+, Neil A. Kjos Music Co.

Commissioned by the Michigan State University Bands Alumni Association celebrating their 25th anniversary and dedicated to the memory of Leonard Falcone, Director of Bands at MSU from 1927–1967 on the occasion of the 100th anniversary of his birth in 1899. Premiered April 18, 1999, MSU Alumni Band, Kenneth Bloomquist, conductor, Wharton Center for the Performing Arts, Michigan State University.

Rollick (2002)

c. 6:30, Grade 4+, Manuscript*

Commissioned by the University of Missouri—Rolla to celebrate the 75th Anniversary of the UMR Bands. Premiered May 5, 2002, University of Missouri—Rolla Symphony Band, Timothy Mahr, conductor, Castleman Hall.

The Soaring Hawk (1990)

c. 9:30, Grade 5+, Hal Leonard/Jenson Composer's Editions

Commissioned by the University of Iowa Symphony Band, Dr. Myron Welch, conductor, for their appearance at the American Bandmasters Association National Convention. Premiered March 3, 1990, Krannert Center for the Performing Arts, University of Illinois.

sol solator (1998)

c. 8:00, Grade 5, Neil A. Kjos Music Co.

Commissioned by the New Trier High School Symphonic Wind Ensemble, Winnetka, Illinois, John Thomson, conductor. Premiered May 5, 1998, New Trier High School Symphonic Wind Ensemble, Timothy Mahr, conductor, Pick-Staiger Auditorium, Northwestern University.

Spring Divertimento (1992)

c. 13:00, Grade 5-, Neil A. Kjos Music Co.

Commissioned by the La Crosse Central High School Wind Ensemble, La Crosse, Wisconsin, Alex Vaver, conductor. Premiered May 31, 1992, La Crosse Central High School Wind Ensemble, Timothy Mahr, conductor. La Crosse Central High School Auditorium.

Thanksgiving Meditation from ***Festivals*** (1992)

c. 5:45, Grade 5, Manuscript*

Commissioned by the St. Olaf College Band, Miles Johnson, conductor. Premiered April 14, 1996, St. Olaf College Band, Timothy Mahr, conductor, Central Lutheran Church, Minneapolis, Minnesota.

The View from the Mountaintop (1994)

c. 5:30, Grade 4, Neil A. Kjos Music Co.

Commissioned by the Music Educators National Association to celebrate the adoption of the National Standards in the Arts. Premiered, April 8, 1994 (54th National Biennial In-Service Conference of the Music Educators National Conference), Park Hill High School Symphonic Band [Kansas City, Missouri], John D. Bell, conductor, Cincinnati, Ohio.

They Sing of Love (1997)

c. 15:00, Grade 5, Manuscript*

Commissioned by Morehead State University Symphony Band (Kentucky), Richard Miles, conductor, to celebrate the 75th Anniversary of the founding of the university. Premiered February 13, 1998 (40th Annual Concert Band Clinic), Button Auditorium, Morehead State University.

Variations on "All Hail the Power of Jesus' Name" (2001)

c. 2:30 (mvt. 2) Grade 4, C. Alan Publications [fall, 2002]

Fanfare	Jack Stamp
Retreat	Timothy Mahr
Dance	Andrew Boysen, Jr.
Fantasia	Joseph Pappas
Finale	David Gillingham

Composed as a gift to honor James Cochran of Shattinger Music. Premiered October 20, 2001, Concordia University Wind Symphony, Richard Fischer, conductor, St. Louis, Missouri

When I Close My Eyes, I See Dancers (1992)

c. 7:00, Grade 5, Neil A. Kjos Music Co.

Commissioned by the Indiana Bandmasters Association. Premiered March 15, 1992, Indiana All-State Honors Band, Timothy Mahr, conductor, Clowes Memorial Hall, Butler University, Indianapolis.

* All manuscript works available on rental from the composer c/o Music Department, St. Olaf College, Northfield, MN 55057

Grading scale for level of difficulty is the standard grade 1 to grade 6.

Sample Contract for the Commission of a Musical Work

It is agreed that ____________ (composer) will compose a musical work expressly for the ______________ (commissioning party). The commissioned work is to be about ________ minutes in duration, and of a grade ________ level of difficulty (1-6 scale). The work will be written utilizing the instrumentation of the ______________.

The commission fee shall be $__________ (fee written out). An advance of $__________ will be paid for the musical work upon the signing of the contract by both parties. The remaining $__________ will be paid upon the delivery of the musical work. The copyist's fee for part extraction (if needed, estimated to be $___________) will be paid by the commissioning party. Black on white photocopies of the score and each part will be delivered to the commissioning party as soon as possible, and no later than __________. Duplications of the parts will be the responsibility of the commissioning party.

The commissioning party will have the sole right to the first performance and shall retain a copy of both the full score and the one set of parts. The original manuscript score and set of parts will remain the sole property of the composer. The composer will retain all publishing rights.

The composer ____________ (will/will not) be in attendance for the final rehearsals and premiere of this work, tentatively scheduled for ____________. The composer is willing to conduct these rehearsals and premiere if desired. The commissioning party will pay an honorarium of $________/day and will cover the composer's expenses (travel, lodge, meals) for this appearance.

A dedication to the commissioning party shall appear on the title page of the printed score, the wording of which will be agreed upon at a later date.

This contract will be declared null and void if the above specifications are not met.

________________________	________________________
composer	commissioning party
________________________	________________________
witness	witness
________________________	________________________
date	date

chapter **8**

w. francis **McBeth**

A. Biography

William Francis McBeth was born March 9, 1933, in Lubbock, Texas, to parents Dr. Joseph Phinis McBeth and Lillie May Carpenter McBeth. His father was a college Greek professor and his mother a musician. Dr. Francis McBeth was named after the chairman of his father's department, Dr. William Francis Fry.

He started his music study in piano with his mother at age 5 and his father taught him to play the trumpet before he started to school. McBeth was playing in the church orchestra before he ever started in band.

McBeth's public school education was all in Texas and he graduated from high school at Irving, Texas. His high school band director was Hal J. Gibson, who later became the director at West Point, the United States Army Field Band in Washington and the director of the military's Bicentennial Band in 1976.

McBeth's higher education was at Hardin-Simmons University where he studied composition with Macon Sumerlin, the University of Texas, where he studied with Kent Kennan and James Clifton Williams, and the Eastman School of

Music where he studied with Bernard Rogers and Howard Hanson.

While fulfilling his military obligation, he played in the 101st Airborne Division Band at Ft. Jackson in Columbia, South Carolina, and in the 98th Army Band at Ft. Rucker, Alabama.

Dr. McBeth was Professor of Music, Resident Composer and Chairman of the Theory-Composition Department at Ouachita University in Arkadelphia, Arkansas. He held this position from 1957 until his retirement in 1996. Upon his retirement he was appointed Trustee's Distinguished University Professor.

He was conductor of the Arkansas Symphony Orchestra in Little Rock for many years until his retirement in 1972, whereupon he was elected Conductor Emeritus.

The most outstanding of his awards have been the Presley Award for outstanding bandsman at Hardin-Simmons University in 1954, the Howard Hanson Prize at the Eastman School of Music for his Third Symphony in 1963, recipient of an ASCAP Special Award each consecutive year from 1965 to present, the American School Band Directors Association's Edwin Franko Goldman Award in 1983, elected Fellow of the American Wind and Percussion Artists by the National Band Association in 1984, National Citation from Phi Mu Alpha Sinfonia fraternity in 1985, Phi Mu Alpha Sinfonia's American Man of Music in 1988, Kappa Kappa Psi's National Service to Music Award in 1989, Mid-West International Band and Orchestra Clinic's Medal of Honor in 1993, John Philip Sousa Foundation's Sudler Medal of Honor in 1999 and Past President of the American Bandmasters Association. In 1975 McBeth was appointed Composer Laureate of the State of Arkansas by the Governor.

He is a member of the American Bandmasters Association, Past President, American Bandmasters Association, 1993-94, National Band Association, Phi Beta Mu, Kappa Kappa Psi, Phi Mu Alpha, Tri-M Honorary Music Society, contributing editor of the Instrumentalist Magazine and American Society of Composers, Authors and Publishers. The majority of his published catalog (music and books) is published by Southern Music Company of San Antonio, Texas. His publications include works for all media, choral, chamber, orchestral and band. His intense interest in the wind symphony has been a shaping force in its literature, and his style is much reflected in young composers.

As a player, McBeth has performed in Germany, France, Italy, England, Scotland and Iceland. As a composer, he has consistently been in the top group of the most performed American symphonic wind composers the past thirty years, and as a conductor and lecturer, he travels nine months of the year and has conducted in 48 of the 50 states, Australia, Canada, Europe and Japan.

B. The Creative Process

To describe the creative process is both easy and difficult. The easy part is to state that creativity comes directly from imagination. The difficult part is to explain where the precise ideas come from. I have been asked many times about where my ideas come from and the only answer that I have is that they come from imagination. When I imagine something I then must think of ideas that will enable me to bring about what I have imagined. A person cannot explain where imagination comes from, but it must be called up. Imagination rarely shows up on its own. It is called up by thinking about a specific project.

Student composers tend to approach composition by adding measures as they go. This is rarely a workable approach. A composer must have a general sketch of the entire piece before proceeding. Without the overall structure in your head the work will just wander with a lack of direction. I must know how a work is going to end before I start it. A blueprint must be there before notes are added.

Amateur composers write when they feel like it, whereas professional composers work most every day. A disciplined schedule for working is imperative. A person cannot wait for time, they must make time. When this time is set aside it is usually in the morning or at night. I have noticed that composers who work in the mornings tend to write clever music, where composers who work at night seem to write more dramatic music. I do think that when you work does influence the work. I do think our emotions run more deeply at night. Most babies are born at night, and when we are sick we are always sicker at night than in the mornings.

With the advent of the computer, a great misunderstanding has come about, and that is that one can compose on the computer. This is not possible, the computer can only copy and play back. Composition is only possible to do in the brain. If a composer wishes to store his work in a computer, then that is fine. I find it much faster to do it with pencil and paper. I do all my scores and parts by hand before entering them into my computer for a print quality copy. By doing it first by hand it gives me an opportunity to make adjustments in scoring and articulation and find errors.

Working at the piano or away from it makes no difference. It is what is produced that counts. I have found that the younger composers tend to work always at a keyboard and the older they get the less they need to use it. When composers use sonorities that they know how they sound, there is no need to check them, but when they use a sonority that they have never used before, it is imperative to check it. The best use of a keyboard is after a piece is finished, and that is to conduct through it while someone else plays it. I prefer the organ.

C. The Approach to Orchestration

When it comes to the matter of orchestration, most university students are misled because they must use piano music and other sources to learn to orchestrate. This causes students not to realize that composers do not orchestrate in this manner. Composers compose the music already orchestrated. I have never written a note that I didn't know what instrument was to play it. To compose music and then decide who to give it to is backwards and will completely destroy good voice leading.

There are some differences in orchestration between the band and the orchestra, but not many. The most obvious is in the French horn's stack. In the orchestra it is 1,3,2,4 and in the band it is 1,2,3,4. I do something with French horns that Clifton Williams taught me, and that is to combine the 3rd and 4th horns into one voice. This is especially important in music for the high school level for better section balance. In most high schools the 3rd and 4th horns are so weak that to combine them gives them more volume and courage.

I approach the clarinets a bit differently. Fifty years ago I fell in love with the sound of the chalumeau register of the clarinet. I have always used the low register of the clarinets a great deal. I like to double the chalumeau of the clarinet with the French horns or the euphonium.

Another important technique that affects balance is the matter of divisi. The divisi is used so much because our three part sections must be able to play four and five notes since the chord cannot always be just three notes.

I always divisi from the top down because the higher the tessitura, the less volume is needed. With four notes for trumpets, I divisi the first, never the thirds. With five notes for trumpets, I divisi the first and seconds. The only problem is the conductor seldom assigns the divisi but leaves it up to the players. When left to the players, they will invariably go heavy on the top divisi note and light on the bottom note. If there are three first trumpets, always go one and two, if five first trumpets, go two and three. The same for all sections.

In my grade 3 music I don't just orchestrate anything that I wish to write. Fingerings and slide positions are a major concern while composing for Grade 3 music. I alter much of my composing to stay away from awkward fingerings. Any good orchestrater knows the fingerings and slide positions of all the instruments. Most composers worry about rhythms and registers when writing grade 3. I don't, I worry about fingerings.

As a string and brass player, I knew the problems in these, so to learn the wood-winds I took private lessons on each woodwind, one per semester, from the best teachers at the Eastman School. I talked to each teacher and told them I was taking the lessons for orchestrational reasons. They all understood that I was wanting to learn the problems that are characteristic with each instrument.

I don't know how anyone could score well without this knowledge because awkward fingering and slide positions can really affect the overall pitch and sound. You can really tell the difference in the orchestration of Tschaikowsky, who really knew the instruments, and the orchestration of Prokofiev, who didn't.

D. Views from the Composer to the Conductor Pertaining to Score Study and Preparation

Volumes of articles have been written about score study, and as a young conductor I learned little from any of them. They always start with the least important to me, and that is form and harmonic usage.

How do you actually learn a score, a poem or a role in a play? The first step always must be memorization, but that's just the first step. If the word *memory* bothers you, please note the great book by Elizabeth Green, *The Modern Conductor,* one of the few books that discusses score study in depth, and does not use the heading of score study or preparation. The chapter is entitled "Memorizing the Score." It does not say studying or learning the score. It speaks only of memorizing the score and gives excellent information in Chapter 17 about how memory works.

The first step in score study is to memorize the score, and the second is to decipher the composer's intent. The third step is to determine your concept of what you want to hear, and the fourth step involves the technical approaches, such as form and harmonic usage.

When I became the conductor of the Arkansas Symphony in Little Rock, I was faced with learning a huge amount of music in a short amount of time. I searched for short cuts in the process, but never found any. It just took time. I did learn the way memory was achieved, and it comes about from repetition. There is no way to avoid repetition in the act of learning anything. The words "repetition" and "drill" are hated by modern educators, but they are the only paths to remembering something. If you can't remember it, then you don't know it, and it's that simple. Knowledge is memory, wisdom is not.

When using the word memory, I do not mean that you should know specific notes that an instrument has in measure 126 or even rehearsal letters. I mean that knowing by memory the sequence of events of a work and being able to sing it from beginning to end. I also don't mean that you must conduct without a score, but have it memorized to the point that if it falls off the stand, you will be no worse off. Sometimes I use a score on the concert when I didn't in rehearsals. This is always when I feel the group is a bit shaky. I will often put a paper clip in a score so I can flip to a specific page that I have memory problems on, usually concerning multiple meter changes. Again, I am not saying that you should conduct without a score. I'm saying use it for reference now and then but don't follow it page after page.

Composers have a problem that other conductors don't. I usually use a score when conducting my own music. Some think it odd that I won't use a score on several pieces on the concert and then always use a score on what I wrote. The reason for this is that when you have composed for fifty years, you have done many things that are similar and it is easy for your brain to go into another of your pieces. I don't conduct from the score, but use it to remind myself as to which piece I am conducting.

In marking a score, I know that I am in the minority. I truly believe that a marked score is an unlearned score. I don't mean you can't use some markings. Enlarging the numerals in multiple meter changes and reminders every now and then are alright and necessary, but the articles and chapters I have read on marking the score are unbelievable, especially the ones suggesting the use of various colors. When you turn a page in a score to markings, your eyes and ears go straight to the markings. When you turn a page to an unmarked page, your eyes and ears stay with the music.

I have seen scores so marked up with colors that it looked like the score was shut on a butterfly. I can't imagine how the brain can stay with the music with all those distractions.

I would like to say again that, with a few exceptions, a marked score is an unlearned score.

Understanding the composer's intent is much more difficult to explain how it is done. It is difficult to explain because so much comes from one's personal understanding of music and composition. Wilhelm Furtwangler said, "Everything purely mechanistic is a matter of training. But that understanding from which the word art derives has nothing whatever to do with training." To understand music and what it is trying to do is a lifetime personal experience that cannot be taught, but a lot about re-creation is on the score. Why do half of the timpanists in America play *mf* when *ff*'s are written? So much in the score never gets done, especially volume variants.

The third step is to arrive at what you want to hear as to interpretation, balance, tone, etc. Young conductors accept what comes out of the band. Experienced conductors change the sound to comply with their preconceived decision as to what they want to hear. This preconceived idea comes from your complete familiarity with that score, but each score is not a complete re-start. Composers fall into schools, and if you understand the school, it brings several composers under the umbrella. If you understand Howard Hanson, you automatically will understand Clifton Williams, John Barnes Chance, and myself.

The fourth step involves form and harmonic usage. Once you have memorized the piece, the form is obvious. Knowing the form is not necessary in step one. I have never learned a poem by starting with the knowledge of its form, but knowing the form after memorization pulls it all together in the brain.

Understanding the harmonic usage is very important in your work with balance. For instance, the more dissonant the piece the fatter the balance pyramid must be, or when working 18th century common practice, the outer voices must be emphasized to achieve what they called the polarity of the outer voices.

To return to step one, conducting from memory always produces the most musical performance. Herbert von Karajan, who loved to drive fast cars, said that conducting from memory is like driving a fast car on a road course that you know from memory. You will brake and accelerate at exactly the correct instant.

When driving a course that you don't know, you will brake early and accelerate late. It is the same for conducting: without having to watch for road signs, a smoother and more musical product results.

E. The Relationship Between the Composer and the Commissioning Party

Many have asked me how a person goes about commissioning a composition. It is very simple, just a telephone call to the composer is sufficient. Be prepared to find out that it usually won't be possible in the next year because composers usually have several commissions in the works. Just plan ahead. In this call you will decide deadline and price. Be sure to check with the composer if your agreement entails parts. Some composers furnish parts and others send only a score and you must extract the parts. This can be time consuming and expensive, so understand everything up front.

The commissioning party will be guaranteed to receive the premier performance, with its name and information on the title page of the printed score. Remember that your commission is not a guarantee of publication, but if the composer is regularly published, it probably will be.

If possible, it is good to have the composer conduct the premier, because he or she knows the work better than anyone at that time. Also, the composer might want to make a change here and there, especially on the tempo.

F. Views on the Teaching of Composition and How to Mentor the Young Composer

The teaching of composition can be frustrating because it is probably not possible to teach a person to imagine in sound. Ron Nelson once said that you could not teach a student to be a composer, only to be composer-like.

It is true that a teacher cannot teach imagination, but a teacher can teach composition devices that can save the student years of self-searching. A student with talent can take these devices of composition and orchestration and advance rapidly.

When I was a student, most instruction in composition was only a critique of the student's work with very little or no instruction. It was what not to do and almost nothing of what to do. A teacher must give the students information from his own experience and work. Many teachers do not do this, and I have always wondered why not. Could it be that they don't want to share their personal inventions? I don't know. I was fortunate to have several teachers who shared with me their personal devices and others that did not. Later I discovered many from their music and wondered why they didn't tell me about them.

The value in studying from any composer is that just from the association you will gain much of that teacher's musical taste and learn to critique your own work.

The teaching of composition is a heavy responsibility. The teacher needs to encourage as much as possible and also discourage in some cases. Can a teacher teach a person to be a composer? No, but a teacher can save students from years of trial and error.

G. Individuals Who Have Been Especially Influential in My Development and Career

The most influential two people in my career were my mother, a pianist and singer, and my father, a French horn player. Our home always had good music, and my taste was set at an early age. Most fathers are not happy when their sons decide to major in music. My father was thrilled. He was aware of the finer things in life.

My first influence to become a professional musician came from Hal Gibson, my high school band director. I was so impressed with him as a player of the French horn and musician. He opened my world to the possibilities of a life in music.

Of course, all of my composition teachers were a great influence on me. My undergraduate teacher, Macon Sumerlin, is one of the only geniuses that I have known. He had more original ideas in composition and theory than anyone I have worked with. Other major influences were Clifton Williams, Kent Kennan, Bernard Rogers, Thomas Canning, and Howard Hanson. Most of my work before meeting Williams was for orchestra. He convinced me and John Barnes Chance that the band avenue was the way to go if we wanted to hear our music, and he was correct.

Of all my teachers, Macon Sumerlin and Kent Kennan are the only ones still alive, and I have stayed very close to both of them.

H. Ten Works I Believe All Band Conductors at All Levels Should Study

To list ten works that band directors should study is really difficult. I would prefer to list ten works that I think all musicians should know. I could list fifty, but to reduce it to ten, I will list works that have had the greatest influence on me.

They include Beethoven's *Seventh Symphony,* Brahms' *Second Symphony,* Shostakovich's *Tenth* and *Fifth Symphonies,* Strauss' *Don Quixote,* Honegger's *King David,* Stravinsky's *Rite of Spring,* and Howard Hanson's *Lament for Beowulf.* In the band area, I would include Persichetti's *Masquerade,* Thomas

Cousins' *Moses Symphony,* Clifton Williams' *Pastoral,* John Barnes Chance's *Capriccio for 24 Wind Instruments and Piano,* and if I may, my own *Through Countless Halls of Air.*

There are hundreds of others, but I wanted to list those that I am personally drawn to and think of their lasting merit.

I. Ten Composers Whose Music Overall Speaks to Me in Especially Meaningful Ways

Of all composers, Beethoven and Shostakovich speak to me the most. Shostakovich is in an unusual position. He is like the nursery rhyme, "There was a girl who had a little curl right in the middle of her forehead. When she was good she was very, very good, but when she was bad she was horrid." I say this because Shostakovitch was forced to write so much theater and film music that falls short of his symphonies and other works. Beethoven speaks to me so much because he was the first to combine direction with the catastrophic.

J. The Future of the Wind Band

I think that the wind band has one of the brightest futures of any medium because of several reasons. There are now thousands of quality wind players in America and this number is growing each year. The American concert band concept is spreading all over the world, especially in Asia, Australia, and Europe.

Recently the community band programs have escalated over the country and are doing very well in providing a performance area to post graduate musicians.

Finally and most importantly, the winds have attracted so many composers now with high artistic merit. It is the literature that determines the status of all musical mediums, and good literature is being added rapidly to the band repertoire. When I started there were just a handful of serious concert composers, and now there are hundreds.

I think the wind band as an artistic medium has a very promising future.

L. Comprehensive List of Works for Band

Second Suite for Band, opus 20 (1960)
5 min. 25 sec.; Grade 3; Written for the Camden High School Band, Camden, AR; Bonner Ruff, conductor; Publisher: Southern Music Company

Chant and Jubilo, opus 25 (1961)
6 min. 50 sec.; Grade 3; Commissioned by the Four States Bandmasters Association, Texarkana, TX; Publisher: Southern Music Company

Mosaic, opus 29a (1963)
8 min. 40 sec.; Grade 5; Commissioned by the Fayetteville High School Band, Fayetteville, AR; Don Wright, conductor; Publisher: Southern Music Company

Reflections Past, opus 30 (1964)
5 min. 20 sec.; Grade 3; Commissioned by the Camden High School Band, Camden, AR; Bonner Ruff, conductor Publisher: Southern Music Company

Joyant Narrative, opus 34 (1964)
7 min.; Grade 3; Written for Col. Harold B. Bachman Publisher: Southern Music Company

Battaglia, opus 36 (1965)

7 min.; Grade 2+; Commissioned by Madison Junior High School Band, Abilene, TX; Warren Thaxton, conductor; Publisher: Southern Music Company

Cantique and Faranade, opus 39 (1966)

7 min. 30 sec.; Grade 3; Commissioned by the Arkansas State Band and Orchestra Association; Publisher: Southern Music Company

Masque, opus 44 (1967)

7 min. 15 sec.; Grade 3+; Commissioned by the State College of Arkansas, Conway, AR; Homer Brown, conductor; Publisher: Southern Music Company

Drammitico, opus 48 (1969)

7 min. 40 sec.; Grade 4; Commissioned by Monahans High School Band, Monahans, TX; Dan Gibbs, conductor; Publisher: Southern Music Company

Divergents, opus 49 (1969)

13 min. 30 sec.; Grade 5; Commissioned by the Kappa Kappa Psi and Tau Beta Sigma chapters of the University of Arkansas, Fayetteville, AR; Publisher: Southern Music Company

The Seventh Seal, opus 50 (1971)

13 min. 25 sec.; Grade 5; Commissioned by National Intercollegiate Band of Kappa Kappa Psi/Tau Beta Sigma convention; Publisher: Southern Music Company

Festive Centennial, opus 51 (1973)

3 min. 20 sec.; Grade 4; Commissioned by Christian Brothers High School Band, Memphis, TN; Ralph Hale, conductor; Publisher: Southern Music Company

To Be Fed by Ravens, opus 52 (1973)

11 min. 35 sec.; Grade 5; Commissioned by Texas Music Educators Association for their 50th anniversary; Publisher:Southern Music Company

Capriccio Concerant, opus 54 (1974)
10 min. 50 sec.; Grade 3+; Commissioned by South Dakota All-state Band and the South Dakota Bicentennial Commission; Publisher: Southern Music Company

Kaddish, opus 57 (1975)
7 min.; Grade 3+; Commissioned by Richardson High School Band, Richardson, TX; Howard Dunn, conductor; Publisher: Southern Music Company

New Canaan, opus 58 (1976)
12 min.; Grade 3+; Commissioned by the Clark County Bicentennial Committee, Clark County, AR; Work remains unpublished

Canto, opus 61 (1977)
4 min. 30 sec.; Grade 2; Commissioned by the All-Japan Band Association; Publisher: Southern Music Company

Caccia, opus 62 (1979)
4 min. 45 sec.; Grade 4; Commissioned by Kappa Kappa Psi Chapter, Stephen F. Austin Univ. Nacogdoches, TX; Publisher: Southern Music Company

Cavata, opus 63 (1979)
5 min.; Grade 2; Commissioned by Burns Junior High School Band, Lawndale, NC; Dawn Taylor and Carl Rohleder, conductors; Publisher: Southern Music Company

Feast of Trumpets, opus 64 (1981)
5 min. 15 sec.; Grade 4; Commissioned by Phi Mu Alpha Sinfonia Chapter, University of Texas, Austin, TX; Publisher: Southern Music Company

Grace Praeludium, opus 65 (1981)
5 min. 40 sec.; Grade 3+; Commissioned by the Arkansas Bandmasters Association; Publisher: Southern Music Company

Flourishes, opus 66 (1982)

7 min. 15 sec.; Grade 4; Commissioned by Clawson High School Band, Clawson, MI; Jack Foster, conductor; Publisher: Southern Music Company

Variations on a Theme of Youth, opus 68 (1982)

8 min.; Grade 3; Commissioned by the Southern Baptist Convention; Publisher: Broadman Press

Praises, opus 70 (1983)

5 min.; Grade 2; Commissioned by Trinity Lutheran School Band, Utica, MI; Dennis Schmidt, conductor; Publisher: Southern Music Company

Beowulf - An Heroic Trilogy, opus 71 (1984)

9 min. 30 sec.; Grade 5; Commissioned by Avon Lake High School Band, Avon Lake, OH; Harry Pfingsten, conductor; Publisher: Southern Music Company

To The Unknowns, opus 73 (1986)

4 min. 30 sec.; Grade 3; Commissioned by Connecticut Valley Youth Wind Ensemble, Hartford, CT; Peter Boonshaft, conductor; Publisher: Southern Music Company

With Sounding Trumpets, opus 74 (1986)

3 min.; Grade 4; Written for the 100th anniversary of Ouachita Baptist University; Publisher:Southern Music Company

The Fifth Trumpeter, opus 75 (1987)

7 min. 30 sec. ; Grade 3+; Commissioned by the Montana Music Educators Association; Publisher: Southern Music Company

They Hung Their Harps in the Willows, opus 77 (1988)

8 min. 25 sec.; Grade 4; Commissioned by Plano East Senior High School Band, Plano, TX; Larry Tucker, conductor; Publisher: Southern Music Company

Of Sailers and Whales -
Five Scenes From Melville, opus 78 (1990)
14 min. 20 sec.; Grade 6; Commissioned by the California Band Directors Association; Publisher: Southern Music Company

Drayton Hall Esprit, opus 79 (1991)
7 min.; Grade 2; Commissioned by Drayton Hall Middle School, Charleston, SC; Debbie Oxner, conductor; Publisher: Southern Music Company

Daniel in the Lion's Den, opus 80 (1992)
7 min.; Grade 6; Written for Daniel Perantoni and the International Tuba Congress; Publisher: Delta Publications

This Land of El Dorado, opus 81 (1992)
7 min.; Grade 4; Commissioned by Phi Mu Alpha, Tau Beta Sigma chapters of University of California at Fullerton; Publisher: Southern Music Company

Wine from these Grapes, opus 83 (1993)
9 min. 30 sec.; Grade 4; Commissioned by the Dallas Wind Symphony, Dallas, TX in memory of Howard Dunn; Publisher: Southern Music Company

Through Countless Halls of Air, opus 84 (1993)
12 min.; Grade 6; Commissioned by the United States Air Force Band, Washington, DC, ; Lt. Col. Alan Bonner, conductor; Publisher: Southern Music Company

The Sea Treaders, opus 85 (1995)
10 min.; Grade 5; Commissioned by the U. S. Naval Academy, Annapolis, MD; Commander Tom Metcalf, conductor, for the 150th anniversary of the Academy; Publisher: Southern Music Company

The Dream Catcher, opus 86 (1995)

4 min. 30 sec.; Grade 3; Commissioned by Renbrook School Concert Band, West Hartford, CT; Gary L. Partridge, conductor; Publisher: Southern Music Company

Lauds and Tropes, opus 87 (1996)

14 min.; Grade 6; Commissioned by the Gamma Eta Chapter, Phi Mu Alpha Sinfonia, Furman Univ. in celebration of Dan Ellis, Furman University, Columbia, SC; Les Hicken, conductor; Publisher: Southern Music Company

24th Lancers Afoot, opus 88 (1997)

5 min.; Grade 4; A march published under the pseudonym "Col. William F. Manchester"; Publisher: Southern Music Company

When Honor Whispers and Shouts, opus 90 (1997)

7 min.; Grade 6; Commissioned by the U. S. Marine Band for their 200th anniversary; Lt. Col. Tim Foley, conductor; Publisher, Southern Music Company

Estampie, opus 92 (1998)

7 min. 30 sec.; Grade 3; Commissioned by Deer Path Junior High School Band, Lake Forest, IL; Heather Pettit, conductor; Publisher: Southern Music Company

The Lions of North Bridge, opus 93 (1999)

9 min.; Grade 5; Commissioned by the United States Army Band, Washington, D.C.; Col. Bryan Shelburne, conductor; Publisher: Southern Music Company

The Sacred Flame, opus 94 (2000)

11 min.; Grade 4; Commissioned by the Tennessee Bandmasters Association, Phi Beta Mu Chapter; Publisher: Southern Music Company

Scaramouche, opus 95 (2000)

6 min.; Grade 3+; Commissioned by Woodward Academy Band, Atlanta, GA; Charles Brodie, conductor; Publisher: Southern Music Company

chapter 9

robert Sheldon

A. Biography

My first attempts at writing music began while attending Manatee High School in Bradenton, Florida. Most of the pieces I wrote at this time were for the high school jazz band, although my first piece for concert band, written during my junior year in high school (*Divertimento*) later resulted in winning the American School Band Directors Association "Volkwein Award" for composition, which included publication, a cash prize, and a performance by the United States Army Band at the ASBDA National Conference in Columbus, Ohio in 1975.

I attended the University of Miami in 1972, graduating in three years (Bachelor of Music Education, Magna Cum Laude, 1975). During this time I worked professionally as a free-lance musician in the Miami area, and studied Composition with Clifton Williams, Theory with Alfred Reed, Jazz with Jerry Coker, Instrumental Techniques with John Kinyon, and Conducting with Frederick Fennell. Following graduation I became Director of Instrumental Music at North Shore High School in West Palm Beach, conducting the band and orchestra programs, a position I held for 4 years. In 1979 I began coursework at the University of Florida, completing my degree in one year (M.F.A. in Conducting, Magna Cum Laude, 1980). During this time I studied Conducting with Frank Wickes and Composition with Richard Bowles. I also became Conductor of the Alachua County Youth Orchestra, and was announcer for several classical music programs on the National Public Radio affiliate, WUFT-FM.

Upon completion of my Masters Degree, I became Director of Bands at P. K. Yonge Laboratory School in 1980. During my tenure, the band achieved numerous top division ratings at the state level and was invited to perform for the State Convention. It was at this time that I began to be invited to conduct various honor bands across the state of Florida, and I began publishing with the C. L. Barnhouse Company, starting with *Fall River Overture* in 1980. After three years I returned to Bradenton to become Director of Instrumental Music at Southeast High School, conducting the band and orchestra programs. During my six years at Southeast, the program tripled in size to 330 students, and the band achieved top ratings at the state level. My conducting schedule increased in frequency and range of travel, and I began conducting All-State and Regional Honor Bands throughout the southeast United States.

In 1989 I was invited to become Assistant Director of Bands at the Florida State University in Tallahassee. My position included conducting the university bands, teaching Conducting and Music Education classes, and being Director of the 430-member FSU Marching Chiefs. I was also Program Director for the FSU Summer Music Camps, advisor to several student music organizations, and had several private composition and arranging students. After two years, I decided to dedicate more of my time to composition, and left FSU to move to Normal,

Illinois, where my wife had accepted a university teaching position. I also accepted a position as Director of Instrumental Music at East Peoria Community High School in 1991, directing the high school band and orchestra programs. During this time my commission schedule increased dramatically, and my conducting schedule began to include numerous invitations to conduct All-State and Regional Honor Bands across the country and in Canada, Japan, and the Republic of China, as well as appearances as clinician and speaker for numerous universities and state Music Educator associations. I began an affiliation with Alfred Music Company, beginning with *A Longford Legend* in 1997, and with FJH Music Publishers in 2002.

B. The Creative Process

Since most of the pieces I write are commissioned works, I necessarily begin the process of writing a new piece by determining the purpose and intent of the commission. It is essential that I consider the difficulty level, length, instrumentation, and type of piece I have been asked to write. The next part of the process requires a specific creative impetus. This can be a suggestion by the commissioning party or something that I find particularly attractive to me, such as poem, story, title, historical or geographical feature, or just a musical thought. Once this has been decided, I begin sketching musical ideas, and these ideas often grow into a series of melodic and harmonic cells that will be used to create the entire piece.

The process of actually crafting the piece is somewhat of an intellectual game for me. I often discover or create musical "puzzles" during the writing process that tend to entertain me as I orchestrate and develop the composition. These diversions could include using and re-using motivic devices in various voices in ways that are somewhat hidden, but subconsciously provide a musical link to previous material. This is done by reinstating material using different color combinations or countermelodic lines, and developing a motive until it has traveled far from "home," and then finding the most interesting way to get back! Other examples are writing a piece without using any minor chords (*Sorry, No Minors* for jazz band, 1973), and using a recurring rhythmic ostinato on the same note throughout the piece (3rd movement of *West Highlands Sojourn*, C. L. Barnhouse Co., 1993).

Each piece tends to evolve in a different fashion—some develop from melodies, others from a rhythmic "catch" or a tonal base, or cluster of sounds. Some just seem to be drawn from a color or mood. I usually determine the general form of the piece after I have selected the principal musical ideas I want to employ. Once I can establish which primary themes I am going to use and commit to a format, I feel as though the piece is done—and this usually happens before I have even written one note on the score! As I see it, the bulk of the creative process is now complete. I already know the message and the meaning behind the piece, and I have determined the principal musical language I intend to use to communicate them. The rest is just...*notes*—and *that* is where I like to really be creative with the scoring and motivic development because it keeps me interested, engaged, and will hopefully bring about a more substantive final product. It may also be important to note that not all pieces are written from beginning to end—sometimes I write the ending first, or start with a theme that I may use in the middle of the piece.

Since composing began as a form of entertainment for me, I still approach it as more a hobby than as a job. Consequently I tend to write only after I complete all of my other obligations as a parent, teacher, homeowner, etc. Therefore I don't write on a specific schedule, but more as I find the time and the mental energy. This could be late at night, after dinner, or immediately after school in my Music Technology Lab, but it could also be in the middle of the night, or on a flight to a conducting engagement.

When I first began writing, I felt a great need to sit at the piano. I used the piano to check pitches, voicings, and even to ramble around the keyboard allowing my fingers to do some "stream-of-consciousness" (or unconsciousness?) composing. As time progressed I used the piano less, and now I use it very little.

Until 1999, I wrote all of my music using manuscript paper and a mechanical pencil. I had tried "Finale" when it first was available, but I never really felt comfortable using it. For some reason the end result didn't ever feel or look like it was "mine" unless it was in my handwritten manuscript, and I enjoyed the look and feel of my handwritten scores. But as the number of commissions increased to 6-8 pieces per year, I couldn't find the time to hand extract parts, and I found "Sibelius" very easy to use. I like the look and feel of the final product, and I appreciated being able to check errors by listening to a playback, and extract parts by pushing a button. Of course, "Finale" can do this also, but my initial experience with "Sibelius" was such a positive one that I have stayed with it ever since. The ability to cut, paste, transpose, insert measures, and otherwise edit a score in progress is such a wonderful time saver. My move to "Sibelius" from handwritten manuscript has had the greatest impact on my increase in productivity.

C. The Approach to Orchestration

Each instrument has a specific variety of colors that are very important in the expression of the message behind the music. These colors are altered by changing range, the number of players on the part, and using different combinations of instruments. From a practical standpoint, the difficulty level of the piece will often dictate doubling requirements as younger ensembles require a higher degree of "safety" scoring, but I firmly believe that regardless of any perceived orchestration restrictions or requirements, it is essential that the color of the piece engage the listener and communicate the message. In order to do this, instrument combinations and voicings must be creative and dynamic to achieve a fresh and energized representation of the music. Solo passages, vocalization, brass mutes, and the wealth of colors accessible in the percussion section can be easily used to alter timbre and mood, along with other changes in texture and context. Perhaps more than any other compositional element, orchestration is the most obvious window to the composer's heart.

As I begin the writing process, I select the instruments I intend to use very carefully depending on the message, the mood, and the key. As I move through the piece, I attempt to alter the combinations of instruments that are used for melodic and accompaniment purposes so as to provide greater interest, a more colorful presentation, and specific characterization to each segment of the piece. Creative scoring can make a good composition an unforgettable one, as it does so much to enhance the expression of the real meaning behind the music.

D. Views from the Composer to the Conductor Pertaining to Score Study and Preparation

Since I do as much conducting as I do composing, it may be best for me to address this process from the standpoint of the conductor. Most composers I know that also conduct a great deal tend to look at the piece from the inside out. I probably do this as well.

Suggestions for the Overall Study and Preparation of the Score:

A good piece of music has something happening at every moment to interest me as a conductor. This could be the energy in a phrase, the development of tension in the line, the exact point of release of that tension, the entrance of a new voice or the release of others, a color that needs to be emphasized, an articulation that must be heard, or a musical dialogue that needs direction. These are elements of the score that I try to analyze along with the obvious mechanics of feeling comfortable with the tempo, meter, and dynamics that I need to address before stepping in front of the ensemble.

After becoming completely familiar with these individual elements of expression, I then try to look at the total piece to determine how the work develops, where it is headed, what the overall purpose and feeling is behind the piece, and what I hope to achieve by programming this composition. At this point I may also want to listen to several recordings of the piece by different conductors and various ensembles.

How to Attain a Better Sense of Proportion (macro) of the Work:

The entirety of the piece has to be considered when determining the composer's intent. What is the real meaning behind the piece? What is the message? What do I want to say to the audience through my interpretation of this piece? To determine this, I try to understand how all of the various parts of the piece are connected. I attempt to follow the thought process behind the development of the composition and decide how to best convey the music through my conducting. There will certainly be a few *very* special moments in every piece that will become my main focus, and I feel that I *must* get the ensemble to successfully negotiate these points in the music for me to have a satisfying experience on the podium.

Within the entirety of the piece there will be several obvious demarcated sections. By looking at these individual sections and determining the real purpose of each of them in the overall expression of the piece, it is then critical to prioritize them in order of importance in the piece. As the message travels through each of these venues on its way to the final destination, it will encounter these sections that will shape and transform the music in order to get the listener to the desired logical conclusion. Just as it is when you are traveling, there are significant elements of each experience that lend color and meaning to your journey. It is up to the conductor to make each of these "places" a special experience for the performer and the listener.

How to Achieve a Better Sense of Pacing (micro) in the Work:

It is the music leading up to and out of those "special moments" that guide my pacing. How to set the "stage," tell the story clearly, and create the right mood are the focuses of my attention, but usually my concern at this point will be the phrase and the color. I must determine the best phrase length, the location of the peak of the phrase, the tension point, the point of repose, and the strongest beat in each measure. The greatest challenge then is to find ways to make the music come alive, and this is often achieved through color changes, tempo and dynamic fluctuations, and manipulation of the intensity in the phrase. Of course a good piece has those things already *there*! But sometimes these clues are not as evident, and it is the conductor's job to figure it out and make it happen by whatever means necessary (within reason!). To me, this is what rehearsal is all about, and is the key to unlocking the expressive elements in the piece. Once the ensemble understands these inherent elements and knows how to communicate them musically, the process becomes one of the most rewarding experiences one can have as a conductor or performer.

Thoughts on How to Discover and Better Convey Passion in the Music:

The ability to convey passion is a real gift. Perhaps the most difficult part of conducting is allowing yourself (forcing yourself?) to *be* the music. In order to really get to this point, a conductor must not only have the technical means through which to successfully express the music, but also the wherewithal and self-confidence to do and say *whatever* is necessary to get the ensemble to *respond*. Each member of the ensemble is like an actor in a stage play. It is their presence of sound and their delivery of their part that will provide a convincing rendition of the piece. The conductor therefore must be able to define each player's role at any point in time, and be able to demonstrate the expression of their part by some means—visually, through gesture, facial expression, body language, vocal modeling, verbal discourse, allegory, etc. It is only then that the true message behind the music can have unity of expression, and be understood and appreciated by the listener and the performers.

E. The Relationship Between the Composer and the Commissioning Party

In my experience, the relationship between the commissioning party and myself has been as varied as the pieces I have written. After agreeing to accept a commission, I will have discussions about the length, difficulty, genre, and intent behind the commission with the commissioning party. At that point I am usually left on my own until the piece is delivered. I often ask for suggestions as to title or an extra-musical idea that may help me in the creative process. Since my commission schedule is usually booked 3–4 years in advance, I will re-visit these thoughts with the commissioning party before I begin the initial sketches on the piece. I am often asked to conduct the premiere performance of the piece, and have enjoyed meeting the directors and ensembles that have asked me to write for them. I have been thrilled to be a part of making the initial performances convincing and expressive.

The commissioning process is a real joy for me since it often includes others in the creative process. When an ensemble is responsible for commissioning a work, I have found that the experience of premiering a piece and bringing a new composition to life can be extremely rewarding to the members of the ensemble. It is an honor for me to be a part of that experience.

F. Views on the Teaching of Composition and How to Mentor the Young Composer

My composition students often approach the process in very different ways than I do. It is sometimes difficult for me to keep from intervening, but I also feel it is important for them to find their own voice, method and procedure. Therefore I try to focus on the process, and that often involves keeping the student organized. I explain that the creation of a new composition is somewhat like taking a journey. It is usually helpful to know where you are starting, where you want to go, how long of a trip you want to take, and how you want to travel—otherwise you may end up somewhere you don't want to be! Surprises can be fun, and sometimes can take you on to experiences that can be meaningful and significant, but being the type of person (and composer) I am, I prefer to *plan* my "unplanned" journeys so they stay within the parameters of my own comfort zone, musically speaking. Once I am able to focus my students' thoughts, they are usually able to complete their projects more quickly and with a more satisfying result.

It is very important for composition students to experience a wide range of music, and that they be permitted to experiment often outside the realm of what my own personal prejudices would allow. Each student needs to find his or her own identity. When it comes to live performance however, it is also critical that the composer understand and recognize certain facts of life: 1) Few ensembles can play your music *exactly* as you imagined it; 2) There is *never* enough rehearsal time; and 3) Few people care as much about your piece as you do! Realization of these facts can possibly help shape the final product but should never shape the real intent of the music. In other words, if there is a way to say it in a more playable way, it will take less time to achieve your desired effect. This is not to say that a composer shouldn't write difficult music, but rather that the accessibility of the piece will largely determine the ease with which the piece will be first played, and the number of ensembles that can play it. Also, the more enjoyable the individual parts are to play, the more motivated the musicians will be to play the piece, and the more energy the performance will have when brought to an audience. If the composition *must* be in Db minor for a reason, that is fine...but if D minor will work just as well, why not use that key instead?

Students wishing to have their music published will encounter many additional concerns as they attempt to locate a publisher who will agree to accept a piece by an "unknown" entity. Assuming the finished product is of high quality, publishers may still be hesitant to publish works that are too lengthy, too difficult, too "different," or just don't seem to fit in the company's catalog. And there we find the real "balancing act"—to produce works that are meaningful, quality music that the composer can release with pride, but also music that a publisher feels will produce enough sales to warrant their financial support. That is not to say that publishers don't want quality works! But it sometimes can be difficult to get a publisher to accept a quality piece that may push the parameters of what they feel can be sellable and playable.

G. Individuals Who Have Been Especially Influential in My Development and Career

My mother and father were entertainers and vaudeville performers. Dad was a comedian and Mom was a songwriter and singer. She later taught dancing, so my childhood was always full of music of all kinds, from classical to Broadway to jazz. After moving from Philadelphia to the Florida West Coast, they purchased a restaurant/night club and performed floor-shows on weekend nights. From the time I was in 7th grade I performed in the band at the nightclub as well as in my school band. My band director, Robert Greatwood, provided me with a wealth of musical experiences throughout high school, and allowed me to try a variety of instruments. During my senior year in high school, I was playing trombone in the Symphonic Band, tenor saxophone in Jazz Band, flute in Orchestra, oboe and clarinet in Concert Band, bassoon and horn in chamber ensembles, conducting the band, and playing in the pit orchestra for various musicals. These early experiences with my parents and my high school program helped to give me a great deal of perspective as a performer and composer by exposing me to so many types of music.

My Bachelor Degree in Music Education at the University of Miami was a wonderful writing time for me as I studied composition with Clifton Williams, and theory with Alfred Reed. Williams was continually pushing me to expand my technique and think "outside the box," while Reed showed me so many practical and sensible approaches to writing. My Master of Fine Arts at the University of Florida in Wind Conducting was a time of great growth for me as a musician, conductor, and composer. Frank Wickes was my conducting teacher, and he exposed me to wonderful literature while pushing me to be as expressive as possible in my approach to conducting. Richard Bowles became my composition teacher. His primary goal was for me to learn to focus my creativity in ways that would result in the most people being able to play my music. He wanted me to be published, and his approach to writing music was so well thought out, sensible, and musical that rarely a day goes by that I don't recall his advice from those lessons over twenty years ago.

Chuck Barnhouse had a profound affect on my career when I began having my music published at C. L. Barnhouse in 1980. His willingness to take a chance on me and his continued friendship and support allowed me to have dozens of my pieces published, and therefore provided me with wonderful conducting and writing opportunities around the world for which I will always be grateful. John O'Reilly has more recently allowed me to have a wide range of my music published with Alfred Music— especially some works of greater difficulty and scope. Additionally, I have now begun working on some projects with Frank Hackenson at FJH Publications. I feel so fortunate to be affiliated with these three fine individuals and outstanding publishing companies. They have had and continue to have great influence on my life and my writing.

H. Ten Works I Believe All Band Conductors at All Levels Should Study

Adagio for Strings–Barber

Appalachian Spring–Copland

The Chichester Psalms–Bernstein

Daphnis and Chloe–Ravel

Don Juan–Strauss

Irish Tune from County Derry–Grainger

The Rite of Spring–Stravinsky

Suite in E-flat–Holst

Symphony No.1–Brahms

Symphony in B-flat–Hindemith

In my opinion, the most important single thing a musician must be able to do is to understand and express a melody. All of these pieces have melodic moments of great simplicity and beauty. The scoring, points of tension and release, and pacing of the climax of the phrase are of ultimate importance in these pieces. Each of these works is so beautifully and intelligently crafted that they have become essential pieces for me to study. Although most of them are very difficult to perform, they are particularly rewarding for the conductor, as they require a total understanding of the construction of the piece, and a very musical touch to bring off a convincing performance. Since I am particularly attracted to a variety of musical styles as well as to the colors behind the orchestration, I find each of these works to really stretch my musical imagination as well as the technique behind my conducting gestures.

I. Ten Composers Whose Music Overall Speaks to Me in Especially Meaningful Ways

Perhaps it makes sense that most of the pieces listed previously were written by composers whose music significantly affects me.

Samuel Barber	Leonard Bernstein
Aaron Copland	John Corigliano
Percy Grainger	Gustav Holst
Maurice Ravel	Richard Strauss
Igor Stravinsky	Richard Wagner

Although each of the composers I include here have quite different approaches to composition, they all have some common elements in their music that attracts me and speaks to me in very special ways. My reaction to the music of Wagner and Barber has always intrigued me, because although I feel a great connection, there is an intellectualism that allows me to view it more as a spectator than a participant. I have similar feelings about Stravinsky, but I am more emotionally drawn into his music. I am always affected by the energy of Bernstein. Copland and Corigliano seem to touch me deeply; although they use different musical vocabulary, I am always very moved by their compositions. Although most of the music Grainger wrote was based on previously existing themes, his incredible inventiveness has provided many stunning moments in his works. Since I am always attracted to color in orchestration, I find I often turn to the music of Ravel, Holst, Strauss, and Stravinsky. All of these composers are masters at achieving great impact with the way they create tension and release.

J. The Future of the Wind Band

Will the "wind band" actually have a future? I am concerned about this for several reasons. Without successful school band programs, we cannot be assured of a future for wind bands at all. Although many school band programs continue to thrive, I have detected a change in attitude toward school bands among school students in general. It is human nature to want immediate results and instant gratification. That runs contrary to the process of learning to perform in an ensemble. Additionally, since only rock stars can rival all of the attention and money that sports figures get, younger musicians may not see the point of putting in all the time and energy it takes to succeed in formal music studies. Young musicians often do not get the recognition they deserve from those outside their program. The work ethic and philosophy that create a positive environment for band programs to grow are not behaviors that many young adults see as worth emulating. When this problem is coupled with a lack of support from the school administration or community, an atmosphere can develop that may bring about the demise of a music program. Therefore it is essential that musicians become effective ambassadors for their art. Not only must we find ways to encourage students to take part in school music programs, but also we must convince school boards and administrations to support these activities in their schools.

As musicians, we must work to promote concert attendance, and we must become the best musicians we can be. As conductors, we must carefully select music that will speak to the performers and the audience, and we have to be certain that performances are special and meaningful events. Music educators must have a clear understanding of how to teach expression, because it is the aesthetic experience brought about by the understanding of musical expression and the creation of expressive performances that will be the reason students will want to continue to play their instruments and support music throughout their lives. As students become more isolated from others in this computer age, musical ensembles are more important than ever as an activity that can provide meaningful and substantive social, expressive, and humanizing experiences.

K. Other Facets of My Everyday Life

I doubt anyone would find my everyday life to be particularly interesting, but I find life to be fascinating! I teach high school band and therefore am at work by 7:30 every weekday morning. Afternoons and evenings are spent with my nine-year old daughter Marie when possible. I enjoy traveling, cooking, attending concerts, stage plays and musicals, eating in wonderful restaurants, and going to art, history, and science museums.

My first wife Marilyn was my high school sweetheart. Following my graduation from college, we were married for 13 years until her death from Cystic Fibrosis at the age of 34. She taught me so much about life, death, and what is *really* important, and I am so grateful for the time we shared. I am still very close to her family. My own mother and father are now deceased, Dad in 1972 at the age of 62, and Mom in 1999 at the age of 85.

Although my second wife Deborah and I ended our marriage after eleven years, we remain very close and enjoy working together on writing and conducting projects as well as parenting. She has been continually supportive of my writing and has been responsible for giving many of my pieces their titles! Deb is an amazing individual, wonderful mother, master teacher, and prolific researcher, and I am very proud of her.

My time spent writing music is what I consider my hobby time. Since I enjoy my guest conducting experiences so much, I tend to think of them as my leisure time. I am writing this chapter while on a flight to Honolulu to conduct an honor band. Now *that* is what I call *fun*! I feel so very fortunate to able to live my life surrounded by music, and to know so many wonderful people who are involved in music-making activities.

L. Comprehensive List of Works for Band

Published/Commissioned works of Robert Sheldon

Appalachian Legacy, op. 46
C. L. Barnhouse Co; 1995; Grade 4; 6:50; Northwest Dist. All-State Band, Boone, NC; Dr. William Gora, Chairman

Barrier Reef, op. 81
C. L. Barnhouse Co; 2002; Grade 2; 3:55; Roosevelt Middle School, River Forest, IL; Brek Hufnus, Director

A Bayside Portrait, op. 21
C. L. Barnhouse Co; 1984; Grade 3; 5:00; Citrus County High School Band, Inverness, FL; Kathleen Thompson, Director

Beyond the Higher Skies, op. 62
C. L. Barnhouse Co; 1999; Grade 4; 7:00; Tenafly Middle School Band, Tenafly, NJ; Walter C. Schneider, Director

Bristol Bay Legend, op. 29
C. L. Barnhouse Co; 1988; Grade 2; 3:45; Long Beach Middle School Band, Long Island, NY, Richard Hornung, Director

Brule River Celebration, op. 77

C. L. Barnhouse Co; 2002; Grade 4; 5:00; Michigan Upper Peninsula Band Directors Association, Norway, MI

Cape Fear Chronicles, op. 54

C. L. Barnhouse Co; 1997; Grade 4; 7:30; Southeastern District Honor Band, Wilmington, NC; Chuck Allen, Chairman

Century Point, op. 61

C. L. Barnhouse Co; 1998; Grade 4; 6:25; East Mecklenburg High School Band, Charlotte, NC; Scott Clowes, Director

Chanteys, op. 70

Alfred Music; 2000; Grade 4; 6:00; Louisiana Dist V Band Directors Assn "Contraband" Festival, Lake Charles, LA

Chiaroscuro: Symphonic Dances in Shades of Darkness and Light, op. 79

Alfred Music; 2002; Grade 5; 9:00; Tara Winds, Atlanta, GA; Dr. David Gregory, Director

Coldwater Creek, op. 56

C. L. Barnhouse Co; 1996; Grade 1+; 3:00; Robein Grade School Band, East Peoria, IL; Dr. Ted Bradshaw, Superintendent

The Corsairs Landing, op. 26

C. L. Barnhouse Co; 1991; Grade 4; 6:10; Boca Ciega High School Band, Gulfport, FL; Frank Williams, Director

Crest of Nobility, op. 31

C. L. Barnhouse Co; 1989; Grade 2; 4:40; Osceola Middle School Band, Seminole, FL; Michael Vail, Director

The Crossings, op. 64

C. L. Barnhouse Co; 1999; Grade 1; 3:45; Conway Schools Elementary Bands, St. Louis, MO; Rick Dammers, Director

Danse Celestiale, op. 28

C. L. Barnhouse Co; 1989; Grade 5; 7:35; Univ of Florida Band, Gainesville, FL; Tau Beta Sigma & Kappa Kappa Psi

Eagle Mountain Overture, op. 34

C. L. Barnhouse Co; 1990; Grade 2; 5:00; Mt. Dora Middle School, Mt. Dora, FL; Tina Laferriere, Director

Fanfare and Intermezzo, op. 24

C. L. Barnhouse Co; 1988; Grade 4; 5:45; Palm Beach Gardens HS Band, Palm Bch Gardens, FL; Wayne Miller, Director

Four Winds, op. 43

C. L. Barnhouse Co; 1993; Grade 4; 6:20; LaBelle Middle School Band, LaBelle, FL; Jeff Moore, Director

Garden of the Black Rose, op. 72

Alfred Music; 2002; Grade 2; 5:10; Edward A. Fulton Junior High School Band, O'Fallon, IL; Dan Christ, Director

Ghost Fleet, op. 71

Alfred Music; 2001; Grade 3; 5:00; Virginia Eastern District Junior High School Honor Band, Newport News, VA

Hill Country Holiday, op. 76

C. L. Barnhouse Co; 2001; Grade 4; 6:00; Association of Texas Small School Bands, San Antonio, TX

Images, op. 45

C. L. Barnhouse Co; 1994; Grade 4+; 6:00; Louisiana Music Educators Assn District VII Honor Band, Thibodaux, LA

Infinite Horizons, op. 73

C. L. Barnhouse Co; 2001; Grade 2; 4:30; Glenview Middle School Band, East Moline, IL; James Weir, Director

In the Shining of the Stars, op.57

C. L. Barnhouse Co; 1996; Grade 2; 3:30; Woodward Academy Band, College Park, GA; Charlie Brodie and Marguerite Wilder, Directors

A Lantern in the Window, op. 59

C. L. Barnhouse Co; 1998; Grade 2; 4:00; Lake Villa Intermediate School Band, Lake Villa, IL; Matthew Kastor, Director

Legend of Starved Rock, op. 53

C. L. Barnhouse Co; 1996; Grade 3; 5:20; Illinois Valley Band Festival, Ottawa, IL; Karen Bartholemew, Donna Martin and Tom Rice, Directors

Let Evening Come, op. 68

C. L. Barnhouse Co; 2000; Grade 2; 4:00; New Hampshire Band Directors Association, Plymouth, NH

Lindbergh Variations, op. 36

C. L. Barnhouse Co; 1991; Grade 3; 4:55; Fletcher Jr. High School Band, Jacksonville Bch, FL; William Holman, Director

A Longford Legend, op. 58

Alfred Music Publishers; 1998; Grade 4+; 6:20; Normal Community West HS Band, Normal, IL; Lisa Preston, Director

Lost Colony, op. 41

C. L. Barnhouse Co; 1994; Grade 4; 6:45; Eastern District All-State Band, Greenville, NC; John Davis, Chairman

Manatee Lyric Overture, op. 23

C. L. Barnhouse Co; 1986; Grade 4; 5:40; Manatee County HS Honor Band, Bradenton, FL; Gene Witt, Superintendent

Mark of Triumph, op. 22

C. L. Barnhouse Co; 1985; Grade 4; 6:25; P. K. Yonge Laboratory School Band, Gainesville, FL; Robb Hyatt, Director

Northwest Rising, op. 50

Alfred Music Publishers; 1999; Grade 4; 6:20; North Carolina Central Dist Band Directors Assn, Raleigh, NC; Ruth Mock, President

Ocean Ridge Rhapsody, op. 32

C. L. Barnhouse Co; 1989; Grade 3; 7:10; Boca Raton Middle School Band, Boca Raton, FL; Matt James, Director

Of Kindred Spirit, op. 60

C. L. Barnhouse Co; 1997; Grade 2; 4:45; Illinois Music Educators Association, Jim Rimington, President, Peoria, IL

The Pioneer's Passage, op. 69

C. L. Barnhouse Co; 2000; Grade 2; 4:20; Herrick Middle School Band, Downers Grove, IL; Jonathan Ball, Director

Prairiescape, op. 55

C. L. Barnhouse Co; 1996; Grade 4; 5:00; Regina Catholic Schools Honors Wind Ensemble, Regina, Saskatchewan, Chuck Hendrickson, Director

Prelude on an Old English Hymn, op. 67

C. L. Barnhouse Co; 2000; Grade 4; 4:45; Shenandoah Valley Academy Band, New Market, VA; Robert Anderson, Director

Quixotic Episode, op. 80

Alfred Music Publishers; 2002, Grade 3; 5:25; Eureka High School Band, Eureka, IL; Todd Stalter, Director

Red Rock Canyon, op. 48

C. L. Barnhouse Co; 1994; Grade 2; 5:00; Lake Butler Middle School Band, Lake Butler, FL; Neil Brooks, Director

Ritmico!, op 75

Alfred Music Publishers; 2001; Grade 1+; 4:00; Robein Grade School Band, East Peoria, IL; Dr. Ted Bradshaw, Superintendent

Rock Island Trail, op. 82

Alfred Music Publishers; 2002; Grade 1.5; 3:00; Central Jr HS 6th Grade Band, East Peoria, IL; Adam Schneblin, Director

Sandcastle Sketches, op. 27

C. L. Barnhouse Co; 1987; Grade 2; 5:20; Long Beach Middle School Band, Long Island, NY; Richard Hornung, Director

Silver Spring Soliloquy, op. 37

C. L. Barnhouse Co; 1992; Grade 3; 5:05; Bradford Middle School Band, Starke, FL; James Brownlee, Director

A Simple Celebration, op. 49

Alfred Music Publishers; 2001; Grade 4; 6:00; Bath High School Band, Lima, OH; Dale Laukauf, Director

Southwest Saga, op. 25

C. L. Barnhouse Co; 1987; Grade 4; 6:55; Southwest Junior High School Band, Lakeland, FL; Frank Howes, Director

Spirit Lake Overture, op. 35

C. L. Barnhouse Co; 1991; Grade 2; 5:05; Iowa Middle School All-State Band, Des Moines, IA; Iowa Bandmasters Association

Storybrook Mountain, op. 63

C. L. Barnhouse Co; 1998; Grade 2; 4:10; Pembroke Intermediate School, Corfu, NY; Skip Taylor, Director

A Symphonic Narrative, op. 38

C. L. Barnhouse Co; 1992; Grade 4; 6:35; Venice High School Band, Venice, FL; Skip Williams, Director

Visions of Flight, op. 30

C. L. Barnhouse Co; 1990; Grade 4; 7:00; Homestead High School Band, Homestead, FL; Rodester Brandon, Director

Voices from the Battlefield, op. 52

C. L. Barnhouse Co; 1995; Grade 2; 5:00; Laing Middle School Band, Mt. Pleasant, SC; Miller Asbill, Director

West Highlands Sojourn, op. 39

C. L. Barnhouse Co; 1993; Grade 3; 6:20; Cobb Middle School Band, Tallahassee, FL; J. William Miller, Director

Winds of Morocco, op. 78

C. L. Barnhouse Co; Grade 2; 3:50; Abraham Lincoln Elementary School, Chicago, IL; Martin Kalas, Director

Other Published Compositions by Robert Sheldon

Christmastimes Three

Alfred Music; 2002; Grade 2; 2:40

Divertimento, op. 9

Volkwein Bros; 1976; Grade 5; 5:20; Winner of the 1975 ASBDA/Volkwein Composition Award

Fall River Overture, op. 18

C. L. Barnhouse Co; 1981; Grade 3; 5:00

Gently Touch the Sky, op. 74

Alfred Music; 2001; Grade 2; 4:00

Intrada for Winds, op. 20

C. L. Barnhouse Co; 1983; Grade 4; 5:20

A Joyful Journey, op. 83

Alfred Music; 2002; Grade 1 1/2; 3:15

Pevensey Castle, op. 44

C. L. Barnhouse Co; 1993; Grade 2 1/2; 4:50

Spoon River

C. L. Barnhouse Co; 1999; Grade 2 1/2; 4:50; A setting of a fiddle tune by Percy Grainger

Willow Grove, op. 40

C. L. Barnhouse Co; 1992; Grade 2; 5:05

Additional Compositions and Commissioned Works

Golden Panther March, op. 42

Grade 3; 3:00; Eustis High School Band, Eustis, FL; Tina Laferriere, Director

In Every Age, op. 65

Grade 3; 5:00; Ottawa Elementary and High School Music Department, Ottawa, IL

Maqamat, op. 13

Grade 6; 6:00

Once the Man, op. 66

Grade 4; 6:00; Lincoln Park Academy Band and Chorus, Ft. Pierce, FL; Mary Lou Goldberg, Principal, Karen Crocco, Rolanda Jones and Howard Lerner, Directors

Paragon, op. 51

Grade 4; 6:00; Monett High School Band, Monett, MO; Randy Mealer, Director

Storm Chaser March, op. 47

Grade 3; 3:20; Dixon Community Band, Dixon, IL; Kent Nightlinger, Director

Variants on a Union Hymn, op. 33

Grade 4; 6:05; Union County High School, Lake Butler, FL; Dean Cassells, Director

Additional compositions and commissioned works soon to be published by Alfred Music, the C. L. Barnhouse Company and FJH Music

The Final Voyage, op. 85

Grade 3; 5:00; Illinois Music Educators Association District I Junior High School Honor Band, New Lenox, Illinois

Golden Panther March, op. 42

Grade 3; 3:00; Eustis High School Band, Eustis, FL; Tina Laferriere, Director

In Every Age, op. 65

Grade 3; 5:00; Ottawa Elementary and High School Music Department, Ottawa, Illinois, for Band and Chorus

Maqamat, op. 13

Grade 6; 6:00; A multi-meter fantasy based on an Arabian maqam

Once the Man, op. 66

Grade 4; 6:00; Lincoln Park Academy Band and Chorus, Ft. Pierce, FL; Mary Lou Goldberg, Principal, Karen Crocco, Rolanda Jones and Howard Lerner, Directors

Paragon, op. 51

Grade 4; 6:00; Monett High School Band, Monett, MO; Randy Mealer, Director

Storm Chaser March, op. 47

Grade 3; 3:20; Dixon Community Band, Dixon, IL; Kent Nightlinger, Director

Variants on a Union Hymn, op. 33

Grade 4; 6:05; Union County High School, Lake Butler, FL; Dean Cassells, Director

Welsh Ayres and Dances, op. 84

Grade 4; 6:05; Union County High School, Lake Butler, FL; Dean Cassells, Director

chapter **10**

jack Stamp

A. Biography

I was born in 1954 in Washington, DC, since Columbia Women's Hospital was the closest hospital to the suburban Maryland area. My mom was a housewife and my dad worked for the telephone company. Though neither of my parents are particularly musical, they always encouraged my musical pursuits, from tolerating my vibrating pictures off the wall with my teenage drum set playing to driving hundreds of miles to attend a concert where I was guest conducting. However, my grandfather and uncle were quite proficient at the piano. My grandfather was also an accomplished vocalist, serving as a "paid tenor" in a Washington area church as a young man. I can remember quite vividly his teaching me *Chopsticks* at the piano as we shared the bench, as he playing a harmonized accompaniment to my melody. Eventually, I inherited my grandfather's piano after he purchased a Wurlitzer electronic organ. At that old Lester piano, I would compose tunes; mostly rock 'n roll songs. I began to teach myself chords by reading the guitar chord symbols on "lead sheets" of pop music and show tunes. Soon I could play out of a "fake book," learning several jazz tunes and teaching myself about harmony in the process.

I began my formal study of music in the seventh grade as a percussionist in the "Beginning Band". That summer I started private percussion lessons that continued through my senior year in high school. While in high school, our Symphonic Band played great literature including *Lincolnshire Posy*, Persichetti's *Symphony for Band, Fanfare and Allegro, Toccata Marziale,* and *Fiesta del Pacifico*, to name a few. My exposure to these superb works trained my ear to a higher level of listening, though mostly I was enchanted with the percussion parts.

In retrospect, what may have influenced me most as a budding composer was the interaction I had with Robert Washburn. After performing his *Symphony for Band* while in high school, I wrote to him expressing my appreciation for his coloristic percussion writing. Much to my surprise, he wrote back to me! I still have that letter. This initial interaction was to come to fruition three years later. Upon graduation from high school, I pursued a music education degree with a percussion major from Indiana University of Pennsylvania. It was during this time that I became increasingly interested in the formal study of composition. My theory teachers were very influential in my interest in theory and composition. In my sophomore year, I decided to write to Robert Washburn again, this time requesting summer study in composition. Though he was not assigned to teach composition that term, he arranged for me to study with him for six weeks during the summer of 1974. In fact, the assistant dean was so impressed with my relentless pursuit of Dr. Washburn that she arranged for me to have in-state tuition! That summer was a revelation for me! Though the work I wrote for band that summer was not very good, it did teach me a lot about composing and scoring for band.

However, my eyes were also opened to 20th Century American music, a passion that I continue to pursue to this day. The following summer I returned to Potsdam, NY to study again with Dr. Washburn and that summer I produced a work that I am still very proud of: *Three Turns for Brass Quintet.*

Following graduation from IUP, I pursued a Master of Music degree in percussion performance from East Carolina University, all the time studying composition as a minor area. Again, I took advantage of composer correspondences by writing to Fisher Tull, expressing my affinity for his works and sending him a recording of a performance of his *Toccata* that I conducted with the East Carolina Concert Band.

Upon graduation from ECU, I began teaching at John T. Hoggard High School in Wilmington, NC. It was there that I began the practical implementation of my compositional skills. I was constantly writing for the school ensembles, including the marching band and jazz ensembles. I even won second place in a national contest to set the Libby's Company signature tune for concert band! However, it wasn't until I left high school teaching in 1982 and began teaching at a small private university that I began composing seriously. The two earliest works, *Canticle* and *Past the Equinox,* were written for friends. During the pursuit of my doctorate in conducting, my first piece for band, *Antithigram,* was published. But, it was my *Gavorkna Fanfare* written for Eugene Corporon and the Cincinnati Conservatory Wind Symphony for a performance at the National CBDNA Conference in Kansas City in 1991 that launched my compositional career. This was the first work written after I assumed my current position at Indiana University of PA. Needless to say, the "Gavorkna factor" changed my life as a musician; particularly as a composer.

B. The Creative Process

I believe every composer's approach to the creative process is different. Yet, I think one will probably find a common thread through all of the composers' approaches in this book. I actually spend a lot of time thinking about a work; formulating it in my mind. I think about form, structure, style, energy level, scoring, and the overall impression of the work well before I write any notes down. Once I am comfortable with this somewhat vague conceptualization of the work, the hardest part begins: starting with the first notes. Based upon my "pre-thinking" of the work, I might try to come up with a theme, motive, or harmonic progression to anchor the work. Once I can compose this initial idea, the work takes shape quickly because I have already "frameworked" its design. However, much like the composer Carl Ruggles, who said that he would play a chord 100 times and if he wasn't tired of it, he'd use it, I have to let my initial ideas ferment. Many times, what I come up with first is not the material I end up using in the work. However, it does create a path of discovery for me.

I prefer working early in the morning, at least during the initial creative process. Once the instrumentation has been decided, the actual scoring of the work can occur whenever I have the time to devote to it. Currently, I both sketch and compose at the computer. Rarely do I play anything "into the computer," but work it out and enter it via the computer keyboard and mouse so that I have contact with each note entered. I do use a musical keyboard and have found that the computer frees up my process and allows me to move quickly between the creative and evaluative processes that occur during composing.

I am constantly trying to refine and expand my skills and vocabulary as a composer. In many ways, my style is a synthesis of all of those styles past and present that I particularly enjoy. A wonderful quote several years ago in *USA Today* stated: "The art of originality is the ability to hide your sources." I would like to think that my style has become a homogenous grouping of various voices of 20th Century composition, compiling a fresher look (and listen) to various approaches to composing.

The wonderful band pedagogue Francis McBeth (also included in this book), once said to me, "Jack, you are a harmonic composer, aren't you?" I believe he was right in that the core of much of my music is its harmony, even if it occurs in highly contrapuntal sections.

C. The Approach to Orchestration

Every composer's approach to orchestration and scoring differs. Many composers' unique orchestration is their signature and the core of their identifiable style. I marvel at those composers whose subtle shifts and carefully structured combinations of timbres create an atmosphere unique to their music. I believe my approach to scoring comes from a natural outgrowth of the work itself. My main aim when scoring a work is to create variety as well as similarity with subtle changes. Variety in orchestration allows the work to evolve; move forward. Similarity gives the listener something to "hang their hat on" and usually is restricted to some type of recapitulation. A subtle change to this "recap" allows the work to continue to evolve while giving the listener something recognizable. I also work with the idea of textures rather than particular instruments. Two and three voice combinations create a stark hollow sound, which can be followed with richer chordal statements. Within those shifts I try to create timbral contrasts. We all have our favorite solo instruments; certainly Aaron Copland and William Schuman exhibited a preference for solo flute and solo trumpet. I particularly enjoy solo English horn and bassoon. I personally think that the English horn is one of the most expressive timbres there is. For me it is much like the sound of a solo cello; impossible to replicate.

As I compose, I am always thinking about orchestration while I am creating the work. However, in many cases the pitch center may dictate which group of instruments might be playing at a given time. For instance, if I am working on a contrapuntal section that has four voices, certain ranges within this section may require a particular group of instruments. On the other hand, if I have pre-determined an instrument or group of instruments for a particular section, I may have to alter the pitch center to accommodate the ranges of my selected instruments. This may require an insert of a modulation or a reworking of the entire section of music.

Since I am a percussionist, I tend to "color" my score with percussion sounds. Many times while composing, I will add the percussion parts last in particular sections to highlight or accentuate different sections of a work. In this vein, I think of the timpani as both a solo instrument and as an extra "tuba." Many timpanists have accused me of requiring more pitch changes than actual played notes!

Earlier, I referred to my preference for two and three voice combinations. I believe it is within these chamber-like sections of my music that I experiment with instrumental combinations the most.

Again, my main aim in orchestration is contrast and variety based on textural manipulation.

D. Views from the Composer to the Conductor Pertaining to Score Study and Preparation

In discussing the areas of **preparation**, **proportion**, **pacing**, and **passion**, the key to being a successful "re-creator" of my music lies in one's analysis of the work being performed. In most of my music, I am obsessed with form. I am not necessarily concerned about traditional forms, but that there is a tight unity to the work. I try to use an economy of thematic material that I begin to manipulate. Much of this compositional technique is not obvious to the listener, especially on a first hearing. However, such manipulation provides an organic unity or a "rightness" to the work, perhaps not heard, but felt in its presentation. So, a key to the preparation of one of my scores is an analysis of this thematic manipulation. Through this analysis, one will get a sense of the **proportion** of the work. In a majority of my works, the manipulation that I refer to in the previous paragraph leads to some culmination of the materials used. Once the conductor finds that area of culmination, he/she needs to retrace steps and ascertain how the music got there. Not only will the conductor have a sense of the overall development of the work, but he/she will have achieved an idea of the **pacing** of the work as well. If we know where we are going, it is easier to pave the path to get there. Though I work very hard creating seamless transitions, many of my works have contrasting sections. Therefore, rehearsing the work is not difficult as these individual sections lend themselves to logical rehearsal. Many times I will rehearse a work backwards, starting with the climatic section so that everyone experiences the arrival first, without spending an entire rehearsal in search of that moment.

There are few composers who can separate the role of creator from the responsibility of re-creator. Baton and rehearsal technique aside, an independent voice can bring energy and new perspective to a work. Most conductors are intuitively drawn to a work before they are intellectually stimulated by it. This lends itself to a reactionary interpretation; motivated by the very elements the composer hopes will stimulate the listener. Though there is **passion** in my work, I believe passion is an individual trait and, conductors bring their own passion to a work. The great composer and friend of bands, Vincent Persichetti, concurs:

> "One of the things I encounter very often that really bothers me is a false respect for the composer's intentions. They (conductors) try to be slaves to what the composer has written. There are some things that can be written; we can write ritards and accelerandos. But there are times when we cannot write accelerandos and ritards, but we mean them, when a phrase has to shape itself, and you must give and take. There has to be flexibility. Too many conductors are almost too afraid to show a disrespect for the composer."

Therefore, composers expect and request interpretation of their music. The conductor should be, in Erich Leinsdorf's terms, "the composer's advocate." He/she should be subservient to the music. Much as the same clothes look different on different individuals, performances of the same work by different conductors sound different, but are welcomed by most composers as long as they are rooted in careful study, thorough preparation, and honest feelings.

E. The Relationship Between the Composer and the Commissioning Party

Since my "day job" is that of a college band director, I have had the opportunity to be on both sides of a commissioning project. I always consider a commission an intimate connection between the ensemble one is writing for and the composer. I want to know everything I can about the group, their strengths, weaknesses, background, and musical desires. As a commissioned composer, I am writing a work for the group that commissions it, never with the idea of mass appeal or publication. My commissions have varied from works written in memory of individuals for groups with limited abilities and instrumentation, to the "write anything you want" approach for a professional ensemble.

Depending upon who the commissioning body is determines my interaction with them. If I am asked to write a work for the US Air Force Band, I rarely interact with them, as they are so used to the process that they don't need any interaction to create a deeper understanding of the process and the work being created. However, if a middle school band in Waukesha, WI commissions me, I will try to initiate a variety of interactions including videotaping, conference calls, and progress reports. For ensembles associated with educational institutions, the process of a commission is every bit as important as the work being created. I enjoy these interactions immensely. Most students marvel at the opportunity to talk to a living, breathing composer.

I believe that any commissioning body, whether an individual or consortium, has the right to dictate the exact type of work that they would like written. I also believe the composer has the right to turn down such an offer if it does not fit in to what he/she would like to write at that particular time in his/her schedule.

As a commissioned composer, I don't mind parameters (restrictions) when I compose. These limitations help me to better focus on the direction the work will take. I just include these during that mental formulation period prior to writing the work. I like to ask about the strong players in an ensemble so that I might feature them in a solo capacity. I also ask about the ensemble weaknesses, whether instrumentation or technical abilities, so that my work does not expose difficult moments that will certainly be unsatisfying to the players as well as the composer.

It is my belief that the commissioning process is one of the most important aspects in the creation of quality works for band. I particularly believe that this activity is crucial at the school band level and should be encouraged and supported. Consortium commissions are an inexpensive way to be involved in this process. As recently as twenty years ago, the idea of school bands commissioning a new work was an isolated event. The concept to most teachers seemed unattainable. It was a project only for the exceptionally gifted and financially-endowed ensemble. This misconception was mostly based on a lack of understanding of the commissioning process. Thankfully, in more recent years the commissioning of new works has become a regular activity of many school band programs. Through commissioning, the ensemble has the opportunity to contribute quality literature to the existing repertoire while having an individual interaction with a living composer. The process benefits the medium as well as the individuals of the ensemble. Therefore, a careful and responsible commissioning project will provide years of benefits not only to the commissioning party, but also to all those ensembles that eventually perform the work.

F. Views on the Teaching of Composition and How to Mentor the Young Composer

At my current institution I do not teach composition, though I have had a variety of private students as well as the opportunity to work with the wonderful NBA Young Composer Mentor Project. I believe the real skill of a composition teacher lies in their ability to teach students the important tools of composition without making them sound like "compositional clones."

The level and background of the student determines the approach that I take in the teaching/mentoring process. Composition study is highly individualized. It is common for young composition students to have much creative ability; actually writing very advanced music. However, many of them have no idea of the "how" and "why" it sounds that way. Most of the time, one has to teach on two levels with these young composers: a continuation of the high level of creativity and some remedial work to raise the student's knowledge of the compositional process. Therefore, I believe it is important that all students acquire the basic tools of composition including melody, harmony, form, counterpoint, orchestration, etc. If an abstract artist does not have the ability to paint a "still life" of a bowl of fruit, I have less respect for their innovations and abstract works. Look at the early works (sketches) of Picasso and Dali. These men had great technique in the area of realism, but chose another path. I believe that is why their most contemporary creations are masterpieces. The root of their initial training was in the basic techniques of art. Arnold Schoenberg is a perfect example in the musical world. Though many of us would not sit down and "curl up" while listening to one of his 12-tone works, it is obvious that he was a great musical mind and had the ability to write in any style or level of complexity. That is why, for me, Schoenberg's works seem very musical even in the harshness created by the 12-tone manipulations. Therefore, I require my students to work out of textbooks, all the time still composing original music. The two outstanding books that I still use are Vincent Persichetti's *Twentieth Century Harmony: Aspects and Practices* (W.W. Norton), and Leon Dallin's *Techniques of 20th Century Composition* (Prentice-Hall). I also require students to do contrapuntal exercises, whether from Kent Kennan's or Walter Piston's book on counterpoint.

I always encourage young composers to write for their own instrument first. I remember that my first original work, called *Daybreak,* was for marimba ensemble. In the early stages, it is important for the young composer to write works for instruments that they know they will be able to hear performed. The discovery process of hearing early works is as educational as taking a composition lesson. Over the years, I have found that the success of a composition student lies in the ability to receive criticism. Many students come to study with the idea of showing their work and receiving praise only. Those students are rarely successful. All great composers have developed throughout their compositional career. One only needs to look at the music of Beethoven to realize this. The truly successful composition student is one who wants to develop their talents at a high level of creativity and productivity. I also feel it is my duty as a conductor/composer to champion the music of young band composers. I am indebted to those composers who supported me and I feel I must give back by supporting the music of the younger generation of band composers.

G. Individuals Who Have Been Especially Influential in My Development and Career

As was stated earlier in my biography, though I didn't grow up in a uniquely musical family, my musical pursuits were nurtured and encouraged. My grandfather had an earlier influence on me. I marveled when he would play the piano for me and always ask him to play a work he had written, *The Woodmen of the World March.*

My mother and father are possibly the most supportive parents that one could have. They never questioned my pursuit and love of music, or my quest to make it my profession. There is a great quote that states:

Teachers Affect Eternity; They Never Know Where Their Influence Stops.

I have been blessed by great teachers; not just those who taught me composition, but all those who taught me how to be a musician! Certainly the strong foundation I received from Don Smith and Ramsey Meredith in high school prepared me to pursue music in college. My theory teachers in college, particularly Charles Davis, instilled a love of writing music in me. My percussion teacher Gary Olmstead taught me self-discipline and the pursuit of personal excellence. My great teachers at East Carolina University including Herbert Carter, Harold Jones, and Otto Henry all influenced who I am as a musician.

In composition, I am most indebted to Robert Washburn, who took me as a composition student when I hadn't written any original music! There is hardly a day that goes by that I am not thankful for his incredible influence on my life. The wonderful composer Fisher Tull had a great effect on my work; he took me as a student when I had just begun to compose original music again. He led me to look at harmony in a different way. Throughout my music you can here the influence of Fisher Tull.

However, the greatest influence on my musical life was and still is Eugene Corporon, Director of Wind Studies at the University of North Texas. Any success that I might have had in the past twelve years as a musician can be directly attributed to this master teacher's influence. The story is too long to tell here, but it is safe to say that if I had not met Eugene Corporon, there would have been no need or opportunity for me to be writing these words for you to read!

Composers like Aaron Copland and William Schuman were very influential on me though I never had the opportunity to study with them. I still study their music! My great fortune to have composition sessions with David Diamond, Joan Tower, and Richard Danielpour continues to enrich my musical life. Then, there are those musicians who believe in me as a composer and continue to promote my music. Colonel Lowell E. Graham, Commander and Conductor of the United States Air Force Band, has commissioned five different works from me and recorded six of my compositions. This world-class musician is a dear friend and one to whom I will always be grateful.

H. Ten Works I Believe All Band Conductors at All Levels Should Study

I am purposefully listing non-band music in this section:

J. S. Bach—any of the unaccompanied cello suites

This is truly remarkable music; the idea of harmony and melody having to be combined in a single line is masterful; we are not worthy!

Ludwig van Beethoven—any late string quartet

His effect on the 19th century is staggering. It can be heard in these quartets.

Johannes Brahms—A German Requiem

It would be best to hear a live performance of this work. It truly is a masterpiece in the combining of vocal and instrumental forces.

Richard Strauss—Four Last Songs

Some of the most beautiful music ever written! There are lots of fine recordings; Jessye Norman, Debra Voight, Renée Fleming, and Elisabeth Schwarzkopf to name a few.

Maurice Ravel—String Quartet in F

There are not enough superlatives to describe this masterpiece. Form, modes, melody, and texture all in a semi-impressionist wrapper.

Aaron Copland—Appalachian Spring (original 13 instrument version)

Some think it is the best we have! The original version is masterfully scored and really brings the work to life. There are several fine recordings of this version.

Charles Ives—Three Places in New England

Some feel that he is the only true "American" composer. This has always been a fascinating work to me.

Arnold Schoenberg—A Survivor from Warsaw

Schoenberg's influence on the music of the Twentieth and Twenty-first centuries is staggering. It's not just because of his 12-tone concepts, but the reaction it caused in the entire world of music. Everyone must learn to marvel at this great master!

David Diamond or Walter Piston—Second Symphony

These are two of the finest symphonic works ever produced by an American. Both are neo-romantic as well as neo-classical in style. They represent the mainstream of American classical music thought in the mid 1930's and 1940's.

Richard Danielpour—Concerto for Orchestra

Truly an exceptional work! This will give you a taste of what is happening right now in the world of classical American music.

I. Ten Composers Whose Music Overall Speaks to Me in Especially Meaningful Ways

I'm not sure that I can only list ten composers, since there are many whose music speaks to me. However, I will narrow the list to those composers/works that influenced me and to which I continue to return for inspiration and pleasure.

Ralph Vaughan Williams

I dearly love his music, particularly his symphonic music;

the third movement of his *Fifth Symphony* may be the most beautiful slow movement in any symphony of the 20th century. The folk elements and harmony in his music were very influential on the development of an "American Sound" in classical music.

Aaron Copland

He is truly the "Dean of American Composers." One needs to learn all of the style periods in Copland's music. Though I have my personal favorites, I believe his music is always fresh and always sounds like "Copland" from *Music for the Theatre* to *Connotations.*

William Schuman

I call myself a "Schumaniac." Much of my harmonic language has been influenced by his music. His *Third Symphony* is one of the great symphonic works by an American.

David Diamond

Mr. Diamond is probably the greatest American symphonic composer. Now almost 87-years old, his music of the 1990's is perhaps the summation of the 20th century American composer and the "American sound." The "Adagio" from his *Eleventh Symphony* is **the** second movement of 20th Century American symphonic music!

E. J. Morean

A little known British composer, Morean's music is fresh, lyric, and British, "with a twist" of Stravinsky.

Joan Tower

Joan's music is exciting, rhythmically vital, and very organized. Her use of rhythm is fascinating. Her composition, *Silver Ladders* is an outstanding example of her style.

Richard Danielpour

What appeals to me about Richard's music is his ability to combine aspects of popular music, but fit them in the framework of the classical idiom. He is very careful to filter these "pop" ideas into a very fresh and appealing musical voice.

Michael Torke

I've always enjoyed Michael's music since I first heard his *Adjustable Wrench* in the 1980's. Torke's music also combines aspects of "pop" music but into a quasi-minimalist framework. His music is always very colorful.

J. The Future of the Wind Band

The future of the wind band lies in the hands of five main constituents: school band directors, college band directors, military bands, composers, and community bands. First, the band world must continue to strive to get the very best composers in the world to write for the band. Most recently, the results have been impressive. Works by John Harbison, Joan Tower, George Walker, and William Bolcom, as well as new commitments from Michael Torke, Andre Previn, and Richard Danielpour have increased the wealth of quality works of art for band. Within the last seven years, several of our military bands have assumed a leadership role in the development of the band. Through their commissions and convention performances, they have increased both composer and public awareness of the expressive and artistic foundation of the band. Since these military groups are our professional models, they must continue to lead the profession in their commitment to the advancement of this art form while maintaining their rigorous duties as a military organization. Colleges and universities must exist at a dual level. They have a responsibility to their players and to the medium. Being an integral part of the college music curriculum, the band serves as the major performing ensemble of most wind and percussion players. Therefore, a primary function of the ensemble is to educate the students to a variety of quality wind literature that gives them both a historical perspective and allows for the exploration of current trends in composition. Few musical venues provide the opportunity to both preserve the old and blaze a path for the new. Though other media have richer heritages, the wind band far excels in the commissioning of new works and supporting the efforts of current composers. Therefore, the opportunity to examine the history of our "instrument" as well as interact with those individuals creating the musical art of our time is an opportunity that should be a mandate for every college band program. Through the repertoire, we also hope that our music education students will gain the ability to recognize the characteristics of quality literature and, in turn, make informed and musical choices when selecting works for their school ensembles.

The second purpose, that of responsibility to the medium, is a somewhat vague notion, but critically important to the advancement of the art form. The situation is simple. The wind band really only exists in academia. Though there are a few "professional bands" in the country, the responsibility for the advancement of the art form remains in educational institutions, particularly those of higher learning. We don't have models; *we are the model!*

If we are to preserve compositions of the past (Harmonie, and music of the French Revolution), revere the cornerstones of the modern wind band (works by Holst, Vaughan Williams, and Grainger), pay homage to the great American composers who wrote band works (Persichetti, Schuman, Gould, Mennin, and Piston) and champion the music of our time (Harbison, Torke, Gregson, Maw, Larsen, Ticheli), we must actively promote the genre.

The orchestra, choir, and string quartet of the university, because of their professional counterparts and rich history, can limit themselves to providing quality performance experiences via repertoire to their students. The advancement of the medium will take place on the professional level. The college wind band cannot afford this luxury. If it indulges in such a practice, the genre will die and the medium will become a museum—colorful but lifeless!

It is the co-existence of these two responsibilities that challenges every college band conductor's teaching ability. We must convince our students of the importance of their role in the advancement of the art form while nurturing their music education needs. Convention performances, active participation in our national organizations, commissioning and recording projects, consortium memberships, and workshop presentations all serve to further the cause! We must feel responsibility to our students and our medium and be dedicated to the advancement of the "band movement" as well as our students' educational needs. Finally, school band directors must instill in their students a "love of music"—not just a love of "band." This is achieved by focusing on those elements vital to music and not concentrating on the superfluous "activities" that band can create.

I have most recently come to the realization that the community band will play an important role in the future of the band movement. I do not believe that this is the community band's responsibility to advance the band movement artistically, though many have added much to the repertoire through commissions. It is my belief that music education, particularly band education, comes to fruition in the community band. I recently had the opportunity to work with the Casco Bay Band from Portland, Maine. I was not only impressed with their musicianship, but I was given a sense of true value of the community band. The bass clarinet player in the ensemble was 84 years old. One of the euphonium players, a woman in her late sixties, had only been a member of the band for a couple of years. She joined after her husband passed away. Concerned about a life without her spouse, she took insurance money and bought a new instrument and began playing again. Somewhere out there, her high school band director is smiling. Remember...a teacher affects eternity. This is never more realized than in the community band. Ordinary people, with a love of music, sharing that love with their communities. Isn't that why we do what we do? Creating lovers of music and the means by which to experience it for a lifetime should be the goal of music education and band.

K. Other Facets of My Everyday Life

As you can probably tell from my work "Pastime," I really love baseball. Every spring break for the past five years I have traveled to Florida to watch exhibition baseball. With the new PNC Park in Pittsburgh, it is a real treat to attend a game, even if my team doesn't win! I also love to play racquetball! I'm not fond of running or "working out." As a friend says, "I don't mind exercising as long as we keep score!" I would rather play two hours of racquetball than exercise for 15 minutes!

I have been married for 21 years to Dr. Laurie Nicholson Stamp, who is a fine musician and early childhood education authority! Laurie is my biggest fan and toughest critic. Most importantly, she is my best friend and none of my musical accomplishments could have occurred without her support.

L. Comprehensive List of Works for Band

Escapade+, **

2001; commissioned by the United States Air Force Band, Col. Lowell E. Graham, conductor; premiere 2/01 CBDNA National Conference; dur. 8 min.

Three Places in England

2000; Neil Kjos Music; commissioned for the Region I Band Festival, Oil City, PA; premiered 2/01; dur. 9 min.

Treasure Us Even More (chorus and band)

2000; commissioned by the Highlands Ranch High School (CO) Music Department; premiered 5/00; dur. 11 min.

Ricercare (formerly Partita)

1999; Neil Kjos Music; commissioned by the North Carolina Central District Band Directors Association, premiere 2/01; dur. 6'30"

Cloudsplitter *, **

1999; Neil Kjos Music; commissioned by the United States Air Force Band, Col. Lowell E. Graham, conductor, premiere WASBE Conference, San Luis Obispo, CA 8/99; dur. 2 min

Pastime *, +

1999; Neil Kjos Music; commissioned by the Santa Clara County Band Directors Association; dur. 4'30"

Fanfare Sinfonia *

1998; Neil Kjos Music; commissioned by the Phi Mu Alpha chapter at California State University-Stanislaus, Dr. Edward Harris, conductor; dur. 2 min.

Held Still in Quick of Grace *

1998; Neil Kjos Music; Commissioned by the Eastern Division of the N.C. Bandmasters Association; dur. 4'15"

Aloft! *, #

1997; Neil Kjos Music; commissioned by the ACC Heritage of America Band, Capt. Larry Lang, conductor; dur. 1'50"

'Ere the World Began to Be *, %

1996; Daehn Publications; commissioned by Central Middle School, Waukesha, WI; Laura Kautz Sindberg, conductor; dur. 4'40"

Fanfare for a New Era **

1995; Neil Kjos Music; commissioned by and written for Lt. Col. Lowell E. Graham and the United States Air Force Band; dur. 2'25"

Variations on a Bach Chorale *, %

1995; Neil Kjos Music; commissioned by the Maine Band Director's Association for the Maine All-State Band; dur. 9'20"

Four Maryland Songs for Soprano and Band +

1995; C. Alan Publications; commissioned by the Beta Eta chapter of Tau Beta Sigma and the Gamma Xi chapter of Kappa Kappa Psi, in commemoration of John Wakefield's 30 years as University of Maryland Director of Bands.

Aubrey Fanfare +

1995; Neil Kjos Music; written for Eugene Corporon and the University of North Texas Wind Symphony; dur. 2'15"

Cheers! *, #

1995; Neil Kjos Music; commissioned by the ACC Heritage of America Band, Lt. Col. Lowell Graham, conductor; dur. 1'55"

In Final Obedience for Narrator and Band *

1994; Neil Kjos Music; commissioned by the Florida Southern Symphonic Band, Dr. Don McLaurin, conductor; dur. 9'30"

Be Thou My Vision ^

1994; Neil Kjos Music; written for the Arkansas State University Wind Ensemble, Dr. Thomas O'Neal, conductor and Ms. Pat Ellison and the Springdale H. S. Band (Arkansas); dur. 3'55"

Celebration Fanfare *

1994, published 1996 by G. Schirmer; transcription of the final movement of Joan Tower's ballet; dur. 4'50"

As If Morning Might Arrive *, ^^

1994; Neil Kjos Music; commissioned by Bands of America for their 1994 Honors Band; dur. 4'10"

With Trump and Wing *, #

1994; Neil Kjos Music; commissioned by the Air Combat Command Heritage of America Band, Lt. Col. Lowell Graham, conductor; dur. 7'30"

Divertimento in "F" *

1993; Neil Kjos Music; commissioned by the Louisiana State University Bands, Frank Wickes, conductor; dur. 15'45"

Prayer & Jubilation *, ^, ##

1993; Neil Kjos Music; commissioned by Wright-Patterson Air Force Band; dur. 6'55"

Jigsaw for Tenor Saxophone and Band *

1992; Volkwein Brothers Music, Pittsburgh, PA; dur. 8'50"

Fanfare for the Great Hall *

1992; Neil Kjos Music; written for Kenneth G. Bloomquist in honor of the Michigan State faculty; dur. 1'32"

The Melting of the Winter's Snow *

1992; C. Alan Publ.; commissioned by the Waukesha (WI) Area Symphony Band, Dr. Larry Harper, conductor; dur. 7'50"

Chorale & Toccata *

1993; Neil Kjos Music; commissioned by the OPCICA; dur. 5'30"

Cenotaph (Fanfare for Band) *

1992; Neil Kjos Music; commissioned by the California State University; Fullerton Bands, Dr. Mitchell Fennell, conducting; dur. 1'50"

Elegy & Affirmation *

1991; Neil Kjos Music; commissioned by the Croswell-Lexington (MI) High School Band, Jeffery Ehardt, conductor; dur. 5'30"

Gavorkna Fanfare ++

1991; Neil Kjos Music; written for Eugene Corporon and the Cincinnati College/Conservatory of Music Wind Symphony; dur. 1'30"

Remembrance of Things to Come *

1990; published 1991 by Neil Kjos Music; commissioned by the Enloe High School Symphonic Wind Ensemble, David Rockefeller, conductor; dur. 5 min.

Past the Equinox %

1988; published 1989 by Neil Kjos Music; co-commissioned by the Carroll College Wind Ensemble and the Concordia College Wind Symphony; dur. 5 min.

Antithigram *

1977; published 1988 by Manhattan Beach Music; dur. 5 min

Elegy for English Horn and Wind Ensemble *, #

1988; C. Alan Publications; dur. 6'10"

Canticle *

1984; published 1994 by Daehn Publications; written for the Enloe High School Symphonic Wind Ensemble, David Rockefeller, conductor; dur. 4'50"

Five Contrasts

1981; 1995 published by Counterpoint Publ.; commissioned by the Southport Jr. High Band (NC), Steve Skillman, conductor; dur. 6'30"

Harnett County Celebration

1984; 1995 published Counterpoint Publ.; dur. 3 min.

Available Recordings:

* Recorded by the Keystone Winds with the composer conducting

\+ Recorded by the University of North Texas Wind Symphony

\# Recorded by the ACC Heritage of America Band

^ Recorded by the Arkansas State University Wind Ensemble

++ Recorded by the CCM Wind Symphony

% Recorded by the Concordia University Wind Symphony

** Recorded by the United States Air Force Band

^^ Recorded by the DePauw University Wind Ensemble

\## Recorded by the Wright-Patterson Air Force Band of Flight

chapter 11

frank Ticheli

A. Biography

Frank Ticheli (born 1958 in Monroe, Louisiana) joined the faculty of the University of Southern California's Thornton School of Music in 1991, where he is Professor of Composition. From 1991 to 1998 he was also Composer in Residence of the Pacific Symphony Orchestra in Orange County, California.

Ticheli is well known for his works for concert band, many of which have become standards in the repertoire. He has also gained considerable recognition for his orchestral works, with performances by the Philadelphia Orchestra, Atlanta Symphony, Detroit Symphony, Dallas Symphony, American Composers Orchestra, Austrian Radio Orchestra, Frankfurt Opera Orchestra, Frankfurt, Stuttgart, and Saarbrücken Radio Orchestras, Pacific Symphony Orchestra, Chicago Youth Symphony, and the orchestras of Austin, Colorado, Harrisburg, Hong Kong, Jacksonville, Long Island, Louisville, Lubbock, Macon, Memphis, Nashville, Phoenix, Portland, Richmond, San Antonio, San Jose, and others.

Awards for his music include the Charles Ives Scholarship and Goddard Lieberson Fellowship, both from the American

Academy of Arts and Letters, the Walter Beeler Memorial Prize, the Francis and William Schuman Award, and First Prize awards in the Britten-on-the-Bay Choral Composition Contest, Texas Sesquicentennial Orchestral Composition Competition, and the eleventh annual Virginia CBDNA Symposium for New Music.

Commissions and grants have come from Chamber Music America, the American Music Center, the Revelli Foundation, the Pacific Symphony Orchestra, the Pacific Chorale, Worldwide Concurrent Premieres, Inc., Prince George's Philharmonic Orchestra, the Adrian Symphony, the City of San Antonio, the Indiana Bandmasters Association, and numerous universities.

Frank Ticheli received his doctoral and masters degrees in composition from The University of Michigan where he studied with William Albright, Leslie Bassett, William Bolcom, and George Wilson. His works are published by Manhattan Beach Music, Helicon Music (of European American, Inc.), Hinshaw Music, and Encore Music Publishers, and are recorded on the labels of Koch International Classics, Klavier, Albany, and Mark Records.

In addition to his work as a composer, Frank Ticheli appears often as a guest conductor at universities and music festivals in the United States and abroad. For more information, please visit his website at www.frankticheli.com.

B. The Creative Process

It is difficult to write about composing. It's such an elusive process in which the brain and the heart are always keeping each other in check. No two pieces are composed in the same way, and with every new piece I must learn the creative process all over again. Sometimes I am able to begin at the beginning, but more often I begin all over a piece, sketching little moments that don't go anywhere in particular. Sometimes a theme or harmonic progression comes first. Other times it's not a musical idea, but a visual image that ignites the spark. Some pieces come easily, such as *An American Elegy*, but most of the time I cannot escape a tedious and often painful embryonic phase. *Blue Shades* was one such work. It took months of sketching, writing, destroying, and re-writing before it finally revealed itself to me, and then the final decisions seemed so obvious. It was like making a long, tortuous journey to find what was right under my nose.

It's a myth that inspiration comes from sitting under trees, at least in my experience. It comes from patience and a lot of hard work. You simply have to put in the hours. Those who tend to make up all kinds of excuses for a piece that isn't going well are often denying the single fact that they aren't putting in the time. I love American composer John Adams' comparison of the creative artist to that of an athlete. You stay in shape through discipline and regular activity, and if you get out of shape, it takes time and patience to get back in. This happened to me recently with a work in progress. It had been going very smoothly before I temporarily left it to do a series of guest conducting engagements. When I finally picked it up again, it took a couple of weeks to get back in the flow. And even then I think I lost something of the work's inner self that I can never get back.

On an ideal workday, I rise shortly before sunrise, have a light breakfast, and make a hasty escape out to my backyard studio before the daily concerns of normal life have a chance to overtake me. I usually produce my best work before lunchtime, and I rarely compose at night. I find that my mental energy is insufficient for creative thought after about 4 pm. Fortunately, I am able to consolidate my teaching responsibilities into two days per week, allowing me three full weekdays to compose, plus time during the weekend. Some composers need distractions, even noise. Not me. I need complete silence and solitude. I suppose this is why artist colonies like MacDowell and Yaddo work so well for me.

I generally do not use the computer for composing. I tried sequencer programs back in the early 1990's and found them useful for improvisation. But eventually it became apparent that I was not that kind of composer. I prefer pencil and paper, with my piano nearby. I don't even use notation software, preferring instead to submit the pencil score to my publisher for engraving. I use the piano quite a lot to check out the harmonies and voice-leading. I believe that no matter how good your aural imagination is, there is a difference between imagined and real sound. I have to find a balance between the two, going back and forth between playing real sounds at the piano, and dreaming sounds while taking walks, sitting at my desk, or lying down on my studio couch.

I also spend a lot of time singing through my music and playing it on my trumpet, not so much to hear it but to *feel* it. I need that visceral connection, and I have never fully understood those who don't. I am especially leery of those who are not able to play or sing—even badly—their own music. It suggests to me that something is missing in the ear-brain connection, but this could be arrogance on my part. Everybody is different.

I am much tougher on myself than I used to be. I agonize over issues that I never even considered in my younger days. Is there a sense of urgency behind the notes, or do they seem unmotivated? Are arrival points well paced, or does the piece cry wolf too often? Is there a genuine sense of development? Most importantly, is there a sense of inevitability—a sense that every note *had* to be there? For example, what makes the opening movement of *Holst's Suite in Eb* so powerful is not so much its melody or harmony. They are both wonderful, to be sure. But what really drives it is the sense of inevitability—the sense that each variation motivates the next one, that the climax occurs precisely when it must, that anything other than its final major triad, scored exactly as it is, would have been a letdown.

I don't think I accomplish such perfection very often, but I aspire to it. Part of the creative process involves striving for goals that are not always within our grasp. But another goal is to prevent perfectionism from interfering with a sense of wildness. (This is equally true for conductors and performers!) I think I used to take more risks in my student days, partly because there was relatively less pressure back then, and I felt freer to try anything, even if it failed. I certainly take risks now—every composer must—but I've grown much more picky. Without sacrificing my higher standards, I am seeking ways to recapture the sense of adventure that I had in my younger days—to ask the question, "What if?" more often.

For the last ten or fifteen years I have been trying to find connections between my own musical voice and that of my culture, especially that of American folk music. Growing up near New Orleans, I was surrounded by a thick gumbo of musical styles: Cajun, Creole, Southern Folk music, and New Orleans jazz. I avoided those influences in my student days, but I've come back around to them with a vengeance.

I used to get so worked up when a piece wasn't coming easily. Things got really out of hand in the early 1990's as my music began to receive more recognition, and the demands and responsibilities increased. That was a period when I became almost paralyzed by anxiety, and I very nearly gave up composing. It took time, a lot of soul searching, the birth of a daughter, and the wise advice of some very supportive friends for me to begin to learn that the bad days are a necessary part of the creative process. Indeed, they may be the most important part of the process, because the sense of crisis triggers the subconscious mind into action. It takes over the job of working out musical problems in ways that the conscious mind cannot.

It is important to remember this, especially at the beginning of a work when things come very slowly. I am about to begin a large work for concert band, and I am dreading it right now, because I know it will be tough going at first. I will have to swim in this dark sea of uncertainty for quite awhile, to patiently create a whole sound world, a personality— something tangible that I can love or hate. Only then can I react to it and determine the next move. It takes a lot of faith—faith in my own abilities to nurture it wisely and carefully, and faith in the likelihood that the piece will have dignity and lasting value.

C. The Approach to Orchestration

Like many composers, I am inspired by color—by the instruments themselves. I love the pure, direct quality of a solo instrument. I also get excited by the huge expressive range inherent in a large ensemble. It can be just as subtle, just as light on its feet as a small chamber group, and yet you've got all those huge forces when you need them.

I feel fortunate to be a beneficiary of orchestration's extraordinary evolution. As each generation of masters informed the next, instrumental color was gradually elevated to a status equal with that of all the other parameters of music. And the stratospheric rise of the percussion family has completely revolutionized the way we think about instrumental color.

I am intrigued by the way in which composers develop their own personal orchestration style. Debussy's heavy reliance upon solo woodwinds to carry the melody, Mahler's magical way of transferring a single pitch from one color to another, Grainger's use of the low reeds to enrich the harmonic texture—all of these are orchestrational "thumbprints" that inform conductors about the composers' musical personalities, and enable them to make all kinds of important interpretive decisions.

I've certainly developed my own set of orchestrational thumbprints over time. I love reinforcing accents by doubling the attack point with a string pizzicato or a muted trumpet bite, then removing the doubling during the sustained portion of the note. This keeps the texture translucent and light, while zinging life into the accents. I also love exploiting how an instrument's personality can change with its register—the sensuality of the flute in its lower octave, the bravado of the trumpet in its upper octave, the feisty intensity of the violin on its G string. My thumbprints may not be terribly unique, but I've found that those who are aware of them tend to give more powerful performances of my music.

I sometimes enjoy superimposing several layers of activity to make a complex texture (e.g., the beginning of *Gaian Visions*, or mm. 31-45 of *Postcard*). The trick is to strive for maximum activity without sacrificing transparency. If things get too complex, the individual layers combine to form one amalgam, and then I've defeated my purpose. I liken it to good food. The great chefs always talk about the importance of maintaining individual flavors, even in their most complex dishes. The secret, for me, is to keep airspace within and between the actual layers. I use rests within each layer so that a brief window is opened for another layer to come through. Also, I tend to assign each layer its own register and rhythmic identity to maintain its individuality. Sometimes I miscalculate, but the process is always fascinating for me.

I have never been able to compose directly onto the orchestrated page, or even onto a detailed short score. It's not that the orchestration is a totally separate phase in my creative process. My sketches are fairly complete in terms of the harmony and voice-leading, and they contain quite a few general indications about the instruments. Often my musical ideas grow directly out of a particular instrument's strengths (e.g., the long clarinet solo in *Blue Shades*, or the offstage trumpet solo in *An American Elegy*). But only after I have completed the more tedious task of getting the notes down on paper can I then focus exclusively on orchestration to elevate what I already have—to enhance the surface details, clarify the harmonic structure, heighten the expression, articulate the form.

Whether I am composing for a small chamber group, a concert band, or a large orchestra, I am drawn to the expressive power of pure colors and transparent textures. *Tutti* scoring is, of course, more effective when used sparingly. I try to hold onto this principle, even when I compose for young musicians. To be certain, carefully written color combinations can produce unique and beautiful results, and well-mixed colors are usually a necessity during a strong climax. But *constant* doubling weighs down a piece and reduces its expressive potential. Unfortunately, this sound is so prevalent in band music that many listeners accept it as "the band sound." I certainly understand one reason for the practice. Music educators, seeking ways to encourage greater confidence in their students, have been drawn to thick doublings as a kind of musical insurance policy. But ironically, this leads to a dependency-based relationship that ultimately keeps students down. I try to provide an alternative for young musicians by writing somewhat leaner, more transparent textures. When students are expected to carry the ball from time to time, they ultimately become more confident, more self-aware, and more sensitive.

D. Views from the Composer to the Conductor Pertaining to Score Study and Preparation

I don't know where I'd be without conductors. They have been the most powerful champions of my music, and a constant source of encouragement. Most of my commissions have come from them, and much of my growth as a composer is owed to them. The best ones have elevated my music beyond anything I ever imagined. When this happens, there is no greater thrill for me, and no greater honor.

It takes a lot to be an effective conductor—a lot of talent, knowledge, patience, and love. It also requires good instincts, diplomacy, communication skills, and, just as importantly, a constant awareness that music making is supposed to be *fun*. The ones I admire most have a genuine passion for music. It drives them to invest whatever time and effort is required for them to internalize a work. The process, when carried out thoroughly, engenders far more than a mere surface-level understanding. It enables them to peel back the layers of a work, and find its deeper self. In so doing, they can begin to discover: 1) the relationship between the details and the whole; 2) the composer's expressive intentions; and 3) how successful the composer was in realizing those intentions.

These discoveries help to liberate the conductor from the notated page. They give him or her the freedom to make enlightened interpretative decisions, and to form a personal vision of the work. All that remains is for the conductor to plan effective ways to convey his or her vision to the performers, and to convince them to follow that vision. It's a tall order, but those who achieve it pay the highest respect to the composer and inspire the performers to play beyond their capabilities.

There is no one magical way to internalize a score. Each conductor is different and, over time, develops ever more highly refined and personalized techniques. Many prefer to learn a piece from the general to the specific. Robert Reynolds, for example, first scans through a new piece several times, as one might flip through a magazine. In so doing, he tries to get an overall sense of the big picture before going back to look for large sectional divisions. The process continues as he discovers ever smaller sections, always with an eye on the goal of each section.

Others prefer to move from the specific to the general. I heard Sir Georg Solti say in a television interview that he studies a new score one page at a time. He may devote hours internalizing page one before moving on to page two, then he repeats the process. Carl St. Clair takes this approach to an even greater degree, learning *measure* one thoroughly before moving on to *measure* two. Only then does he look at the first two measures as a single entity. He doesn't even consider the phrase as a unit until after he has learned each of its individual measures.

Regardless of how a conductor internalizes a score, he should, at some point, begin to hear not just *what* is there, but *why* it is there. Small things begin to add up to something bigger, and some details reveal themselves as being more important than others. Everything has to be contextualized. Those who overlook this law often fail to see the forest through the trees. As Chopin said, "They will find that the thread holding the whole thing together will break." For example, think about how awkward it would be to caress every note, milk every *ritardando,* play every *sforzando* marking with equal emphasis. As a composer and a listener, I prefer those conductors who don't ignore the details, but who use them to enhance the bigger picture.

Another part of the conductor's job is to be discerning. Before venturing to conduct a work, he must first find meaning in it, and believe passionately in that meaning. If he doesn't, he should not waste time trying to convince others of it. The conductor is the mouthpiece for the composer. If he stands before an ensemble with a work that doesn't speak to him, everyone picks up on it, and everyone suffers—the performers, the composer, the audience, and the conductor himself.

Assuming a conductor has internalized a score and is convinced by its meaning, he can then get beyond it! Mahler said that what is best in music is not to be found in the notes. There is a lot of truth to that. I once played in a band under a conductor whose body language never changed. He would say things like, "install a crescendo here," or "please observe the rhythmic accuracy there," and in a tone of voice that suggested he was at a business meeting. It very nearly drove us all crazy! Our concerts, while technically accurate, seldom revealed the passion in the music. The world doesn't need any more conductors who follow blindly every detail of the score at the expense of passion.

There are occasions in which an interpreter can go beyond the notated page to more clearly reveal the composer's *intended* meaning. I love it when a gifted conductor is able to show me another "correct" point of view. Such occasions are often the most fruitful and exciting for me, for they reveal aspects about my music that I didn't even know existed! It's funny how we, as musicians, develop an almost religious attitude to the notated score, in which every staccato, every tempo marking, every *mezzo forte* is held as sacred. Years of conditioning solidifies this attitude in our psyche so that by the time we are adults, we accept the illusion that the composer is some kind of omnipotent figure who should not be questioned.

I'm not saying that the score is only a suggestion! Those conductors who assume the role of the composer do not impress me, nor do the flashy Romantic types who seek to "wow" an audience at all costs. I enjoy fresh takes on my music, but within *my* intended frame of reference. The further a conductor strays from the page, the more profound and enlightened his reasons must be for doing so.

It all comes down to trust. Composing a piece is a bit like raising a child. After investing a lot of time and effort creating, nurturing, and worrying about it, the composer must let it go. If it survives and enters the repertoire, it becomes a living thing—something which evolves—and its evolution is shaped not by the composer, but by the interpreters. That's an important responsibility, and a privilege.

E. The Relationship Between the Composer and the Commissioning Party

Without commissions, there would be less great music, period. The unique needs and qualities surrounding a commission can inspire the composer to find sounds that she might not otherwise hear. Even when no specific demands are made on the composer, a commission, by its very nature, influences the outcome of a work, and in the larger sense it helps shape the evolution of the repertoire. Commissions keep music alive and breathing!

In the ideal situation, a commission joins the composer and performer at the hip, making them two halves—one creative, the other "re-creative"—of a single entity. Both parties assume a kind of spiritual ownership of the piece, playing equally unique roles in its refinement. The premiere is such a delicate time, like a birth. The infant work is fragile and needs to be nurtured carefully. Both parties share in the pain and joy of it, and both are forever linked to it.

Most of my music has been commissioned, and I am grateful for that. I've enjoyed the collaborations, and I need the deadlines (although I have a real love/hate relationship with them). I need to be given a few guidelines from the commissioning party: the approximate length desired, the nature of the premiere event, the unique strengths (and weaknesses, if any) of the premiering ensemble. With the exception of these guidelines, I prefer to be left alone during the creation of the work. Too many specific demands can inhibit the process.

I often seek ways to individualize a piece by incorporating something personal about the commissioning party. *Postcard,* commissioned by Robert Reynolds in memory of his mother, derives one of its motives from the letters of her name, and makes use of a palindromic theme as a tribute to the Reynolds family tradition of giving palindromic names to their children. These ideas were not just used as gimmicks, because I took them to an extreme degree, informing the piece at every structural level. Indeed, it remains one of my tightest, most unified pieces. Before composing *An American Elegy* for the Columbine High School Band, I considered ways to link the students directly to the piece. When I found out they didn't have an *Alma Mater,* I composed one for them (words and music!). Fortunately for me, they adapted it as their school song, and I was able to quote a fragment from it at the elegy's climax. It is a dramatic moment, and the piece would not be as powerful without it.

Some of my most memorable commissions have been inspired by the musicians themselves. During my years as Composer in Residence with the Pacific Symphony, I became more and more attuned to the orchestra's sound and the unique qualities of each player. Over time I developed a strangely wonderful symbiotic relationship with their conductor, Carl St. Clair. It reached a point where we almost never needed to speak to one another in rehearsals. It was scary and wonderful at the same time. I literally grew up as a composer while working with him and his orchestra.

My trumpet concerto, composed for the late, great Armando Ghitalla, was deeply inspired by his uniquely lyrical sound. There are flashier, more technically impressive players today, but nobody has ever been able to sound quite like Armando. He had a way of making the trumpet sound like it was crying, and that quality directly inspired much of the concerto, especially the slow movement. (I also got a lot of mileage out of his initials!) Before the premiere, he took a very active role in the refinement of the piece, suggesting ways to stretch a phrase or color a note. He played some passages that far exceeded in expression what I had written on the page. It was a very satisfying experience.

There are some things to watch out for when commissioning a piece. First, it is a good idea to plan at least three years ahead of your target date, if not longer. Most composers worth their salt are going to be backed up, and I think it is better to wait for the right composer rather than settle for the wrong composer who can do it right now. Secondly, it is wise to include enough money in the commissioning budget to support the composer's attendance to final rehearsals and the premiere. I have heard of composers who have had to pay their own way to their premieres. It insults the whole experience. Finally, it is crucial to give the new piece the time it deserves. So often, especially in professional situations, neither the conductor nor the ensemble have sufficient time to prepare a new piece properly. This is unfortunate, because they miss the chance to experience one of the most exciting aspects of music making—the completion of the creative process.

I have great admiration for the many public school ensembles that commission music. What better way is there to allow students to work closely with a living, breathing composer? Sometimes I get just as excited about composing for a young group as for a professional group. Students have an enthusiasm that is rarely seen among professional players, and the commissioning experience can really change their lives in a positive way. I hope I can always make time for that.

F. Views on the Teaching of Composition and How to Mentor the Young Composer

There is so much about composition that cannot be taught. Students first have to have a certain amount of natural talent, imagination, and desire. You can teach students an extraordinary range of skills—harmony, counterpoint, orchestration, an understanding of musical forms, and an awareness of musical styles—but none of these skills can replace the value of listening. Student composers have to hear their music in live performances. They learn more from that experience than anything a teacher can say. I believe it is also very helpful for composers to continue performing at some level, and to study conducting. Both of these activities help composers to maintain a visceral connection to music-making.

At USC, we place a lot of emphasis on traditional craft courses. Our undergraduate composers complete a sequence of eight semesters of composition, three semesters of counterpoint, and four semesters of orchestration; far more than is required at most other universities. And yet it is also important to work *with* students, not just *on* them. Students must be empowered by their own creative thoughts and convictions. I try to challenge students to rely on their own judgement and not only that of their teacher.

Because it takes so long to develop their craft, many young composers lose patience along the way, or they become paralyzed by negative self-talk. Every year, I hear statements such as these:

"I compose much more slowly than others."
"My musical ideas never seem to flow."

"I always hit a brick wall somewhere in the middle of a piece."
"I am terrible at developing my ideas."
"I am worried that I will never find my own personal voice."
"I just don't have the chops."

Constant negative messages will trigger a self-fulfilling prophecy. They will come true! I like to remind students of this fact, and I try to show them alternative ways of thinking. I am not suggesting that they can solve all their problems by adhering to some simplistic notion, such as "mind over matter." But I do believe that positive self-talk can slowly nurture the kind of self-respect that is essential for any composer. And in the process, one can begin to confront the saboteur in his head—the judge, the inner critic, the voice that is often that of a well-meaning parent, teacher, or older sibling.

Not only are composers self-critical by nature, but they can also be obsessed about how much work remains to be done. I urge students to think about how destructive that obsession can be over time. More than anything else, it saps the joy out of composing and leads to creative burnout. When my students are in the middle of a work in progress, I urge them to look over the parts of their piece that they love, to devote more time appreciating what they have completed, and less time lamenting what remains to be done.

Encouragement and understanding are important, but I also try to challenge students with tough questions about musical integrity and inevitability, especially the graduate students who have more experience. A typical student, lacking sufficient skill to maximize a single idea, will often compensate by forcing too many ideas into one piece. I call it the door-to-door salesman approach: "Here, I have this gadget, and this one, and if you don't like this, I have *that* one." I try to encourage students to have faith in one idea, to let it cook, to give the listener an opportunity to fall in love (or hate) with it. It can be compared to writing a novel. The better a character is developed, the more we care about whether that character lives or dies.

The American composer, George Rochberg, addressed this problem in a slightly different way. He once said to me, "In a piece of music, there are only two things: there's 'A' and there's 'not A'." I was still in my twenties at the time, and these words didn't mean as much to me then as they do now. "A" refers to the main idea, the backbone of the piece. Everything else is secondary. If we neglect "A," we lose sight of what the piece is about. We drop the ball. I constantly challenge students to explain what their piece is about, what is important, and what is just decoration.

I used to try to demystify composing with my students, to give them hope by persuading them that it really isn't all that difficult and elusive. I've since come to realize this was a mistake. It *is* difficult and elusive. It is, as Leslie Bassett describes it, a house of mirrors. And that is partly what draws us to it.

G. Individuals Who Have Been Especially Influential in My Development and Career

The first major influence on my musical development was my father. When I was a young boy growing up near New Orleans, he would take me to hear all kinds of live traditional jazz, and he was always playing old LP recordings of Pete Fountain and Louis Armstrong. When I was nine-years old, he took me to a pawn shop in the French Quarter to buy my first instrument. In the shop window were an old silver clarinet and a badly dented copper-belled trumpet. I was attracted to the shinier clarinet, but it was $80, and the trumpet was only $45. He said, "Son, you're going to play the trumpet."

When I was thirteen, we moved to a suburb of Dallas where I was introduced to a whole new musical world: the Texas public school band scene. I had no idea that bands could sound so good. It was an ear opener for me, and really lit a fire in my adolescent belly. The man who fueled that fire was Robert Floyd, my high school band director. His passion for music was inspiring, and he expected more from me than anyone ever had. I was a pretty good player, but, as many teenagers can be, an occasional pain in the neck. Still, he never gave up on me, and I've never forgotten that. He is the main reason why I continue to compose educational music. Every piece I write for young musicians serves as a kind of token of thanks to him.

My time in graduate school at the University of Michigan was certainly the most crucial to my development as a composer. I was pretty unseasoned when I first arrived there, and I'll never forget the day I showed up for my first lesson, under William Bolcom, with what I thought was an impressive week's worth of work. He quickly, flawlessly, read through it at the piano, and said, "Nice little sequence, but what else do you have today?" At that moment, I learned that if I was going to call myself a composer, I'd better start composing! Bill also taught me a lot about musical pacing, and how to keep a certain amount of unpredictability in my music, but mostly he woke me up. Leslie Bassett was an extraordinary teacher of fine details, and he had a fabulous ear for color and balance. He also taught me a lot about being a human being. William Albright stressed beauty of sound, freedom, and wildness. He used to say, "If you are going to be a composer, you have to jump off cliffs." George Wilson helped me to focus on the musical line and direction. He challenged me to find ways for one phrase to motivate the next—to keep a sense of urgency in the music.

Many conductors have had an impact on my life and career, but two in particular stand out. Robert Reynolds was a supportive mentor, and encouraged my wind music very early on, before anybody else cared about it. Watching him conduct was always inspiring. He had a way of making music I'd known all my life seem new again. He continues to be a true friend, and one of the most powerful interpreters of my music. Another conductor I first met at Michigan, Carl St.Clair, has been a source of inspiration, and a great champion of my orchestral music for many years. He handed me one of the most important gifts of my career when he appointed me Composer in Residence of the Pacific Symphony Orchestra. My eight years with him and his orchestra showed me what it means to be a professional composer, and caused me to grow in ways I could not have otherwise imagined. We are very close friends, and I feel ten feet tall every time he conducts my music.

H. Ten Works I Believe All Band Conductors at All Levels Should Study

Of all the topics I've been asked to address in my chapter, this one has caused me the most discomfort. Most band directors know their repertoire better than I ever will. Furthermore, band masterworks such as Hindemith's *Symphony in Bb* and

Grainger's *Lincolnshire Posy* are assumed to be obvious, and need no further recommendation from me. What I *can* offer is a list of non-band works that I believe every band director (indeed, every *musician*) should study. This, too, is a difficult task. The act of selecting only ten essential works from the mountain of great music is at best, approximate, and at worst, artificial. In the end, the only solution I could conjure up—and it is a woefully inadequate solution—was first to make a list of ten important genres, and then to select one masterpiece as a representative of each. The absence of some essential genres—art song, piano sonata, etc.—is a misfortune of which I am all too painfully aware.

So, in chronological order, here we go! But not without one final disclaimer: *Warning! This list represents the opinions of the writer on one specific day, and in no way should be construed as a representation of his opinions on another day.*

Sacred Choral Music—Bach: *St. Matthew Passion*

Bach is "the supreme arbiter and lawgiver of music," and the *St. Matthew Passion* is one of his crowning achievements. Although he never wrote an opera, his *Passion* contains all the ingredients and dramatic spirit inherent in that genre. Every moment is filled with genius and a divine sense of music's expressive powers.

Solo Keyboard—Bach: *The Art of Fugue*

Generations of musicians have been awed by the genius of *The Art of Fugue*, Bach's final work. Its eighteen canons and fugues, all based on the same subject (or one of its variants), transcend all that was known about counterpoint. The final movement, an enormous triple fugue, was left unfinished at the time of his death. Right at the point where it stops, the notes

B-A-C-H appear as a new counter-subject, suggesting Bach's intention to take this already elaborate triple fugue one step further! The experience of hearing the B-A-C-H theme, followed by abrupt silence, is startling. We can only imagine how he might have carried it to the end.

Concerto—Mozart: Concerto for Piano and Orchestra in D Minor, K. 466

He may have rivals in the world of opera, the symphony, and the string quartet, but Mozart is, even today, the undisputed king of the piano concerto. Their variety and sheer number is breathtaking, and I could have picked almost any one of the twenty-five for my list. The D Minor Concerto, K. 466, is perhaps the most dramatic and frequently performed of all. I especially love the simple serenity of the middle movement.

Opera—Mozart: *Don Giovanni*

Don Giovanni may well be the greatest opera ever composed. The second scene is a remarkable example of uninterrupted music that points to the continuous dramas of Wagner and Verdi. (This is the scene alluded to in the movie *Amadeus*, in which Mozart brags to the emperor about how a duet becomes a trio, then quartet, quintet, sextet, septet, octet! "How long do you think I could sustain that for?" Mozart asked. The emperor replied, "Oh, I don't know, six or seven minutes...eight?" Mozart: "Twenty, Sire, twenty minutes of continuous music!").

Symphony—Beethoven: Symphony No. 3 in Eb (*Eroica*)

The *Eroica* is my favorite Beethoven symphony. (It was also *his* favorite). This icon of heroic expression represents a major turning point in music history, almost single-handedly announcing the end of eighteenth-century Classicism. The first movement alone takes the idea of sonata form to gargantuan levels. Even more remarkable is the organic way in which themes grow out of each other with a constant sense of urgency.

Programmatic Symphony—Berlioz: *Fantastic Symphony*

If Beethoven's *Eroica* represents a revolution in musical architecture, Berlioz's *Fantastic Symphony* represents the beginning of modern orchestration. His use of wildly imaginative colors to reflect real characters, images, and emotional states had a profound influence on Wagner, and everybody else for that matter. Above all, the piece celebrates the notion that, in music, *anything* can happen.

Chamber Music—Brahms: Piano Quintet in F minor, *Op. 34A*

Brahms is the undisputed king of nineteenth-century chamber music, and the Piano Quintet in F Minor is the jewel in his crown. It is a perfect work to study for its beauty, expressive power, and thematic unity. It also contains extraordinary counterpoint that looks back to Bach, while bearing Brahms' own personal stamp.

Orchestral song cycle—Mahler: *Song of the Earth*

Song of the Earth is, arguably, Mahler's most moving and best known work. Its six poems, translated into German from Chinese, traverse a massive range of emotions, and Mahler captures the varying moods with all the power of his genius. The long coda of the final song, based on a seven-fold echo of the word "forever" *(ewig),* floats magically. It is some of the most transcendent music ever penned.

Ballet—Stravinsky: ***The Rite of Spring***

The Rite of Spring is one of the most daring creations in music history. Its metric wildness, primitive power, and almost total abandonment of the established rules of harmony and melody caused a genuine revolution. The work is essential for study because it changed the way we think about music.

Orchestral—Bartok: ***Concerto for Orchestra***

Bartok's *Music for Strings, Percussion and Celeste,* and his last three string quartets may be bolder masterpieces, but none have enjoyed the enduring popularity of his last completed work, the *Concerto for Orchestra.* Not only is it popular with audiences, but also performers, all of whom are treated like virtuosos. The orchestration is masterful, and the expressive range is huge; from the ghostly beginning to the playful "Game of Pairs," and finally to the fiery *perpetuum mobile* of the finale.

I. Ten Composers Whose Music Overall Speaks to Me in Especially Meaningful Ways

I am in awe of **Bach.** I've been studying and teaching his music for years, yet I still find it to be an inexplicable wonder. It's not just his counterpoint that impresses me. His melodic gifts rival those of just about anyone else for sheer grace and beauty.

One of the things I love most about **Mozart's** music is best summed up in one of his own letters to his father: "Here and there...are passages which *only connoisseurs* can appreciate...yet so written...that non-connoisseurs cannot fail to enjoy them, though without knowing why." He was referring specifically to his piano concertos, but the statement also rings true for his other music. It has been compared to a watch. There is this incredibly rigorous workmanship, but it is hidden behind a simple, elegant surface.

Of all the composers on this list, it is **Beethoven** whose music most deeply affects me. It has a lot to do with the burning sense of urgency that drives the music right to the very end. No other composer can move my soul with such directness and power.

Brahm's music utilizes such a passionate harmonic language, but it is held in check by a rigorous and objective formal control. The resulting tension is like a caged lion. I am also captivated by the nostalgic quality of some of his slow movements. I love playing his intermezzos at the piano. Opus 118, no. 2 in A Major is one of my favorites.

Mahler's symphonies ended what Haydn and Mozart began. Nobody since has dared to take the symphony any farther, and for good reason. His symphonies contain the full range of human existence. I think I admire most the courage it must have taken him to conceive and carry out such big ideas.

Every composer has had to come to grips with **Stravinsky,** and not just for his rhythmic innovations. There is so much more, including the harmonic boldness in works such as *The Rite of Spring,* the spirituality in works such as *Symphony of Psalms,* and the extraordinary use of color in works such as *Agon.* No other twentieth-century composer's music has changed me more deeply at every level than that of Igor Stravinsky.

I went through a huge **Bartok** phase in my student days, and, although I'm less obsessed with his music now, I still love it for its richness and freshness. I am also inspired by the way in which he managed to combine folk and modern influences to form such a deeply personal and powerful language. His writing for strings is particularly bold, and never fails to arouse my imagination.

Britten's music has a freshness and originality about it, yet without use of any particularly radical musical language. I am not only astonished by his operas, but also by his vocal works, his orchestral works, and his chamber music. One of my personal favorites is his Cello Sonata. Even his earliest works bore the markings of a master with extraordinary lyrical gifts. (I'll never forget how depressed I became when I learned that he composed his *Holiday Diary* as a student).

Although **Copland** was essentially a classically trained composer, he managed to incorporate so much more into his music—folk songs from the Americas, dance rhythms, jazz idioms—and without ever sounding contrived or artificial. Instead, the music is wide-awake, pure, and wholly American.

Bernstein was an underrated composer during his lifetime, partly because his creative accomplishments were overshadowed by his fame as a conductor, pianist, teacher, and musical personality. I think he had his finger on the heartbeat of American music. His music certainly speaks to me, and not just the Broadway musicals. (A bit of trivia: In addition to everything else, Bernstein also did some band arranging for publishers under the pseudonym Lenny Amber).

There are dozens of living composers whose music speaks to me, not the least of whom are my USC colleagues. (Donald Crockett's orchestral work, *Wedge,* Stephen Hartke's Clarinet Concerto, and Morten Lauridsen's choral masterpiece, *Lux Aeterna* are just three of the many stunning achievements of my cohorts). Nevertheless, with only one spot left on the list, I am compelled to cite **John Adams** as a living composer whose music has been particularly significant for me. He has ventured far beyond mere "minimalism" to create a very personal, yet wildly eclectic style that can be jazzy, lyrical, sometimes raucous, and always fun. His early works, such as *Harmonium* and *Harmonielehre,* still resonate with me, and later works, such as *Naive and Sentimental Music* and *Gnarly Buttons,* bear the marks of an imaginative and mature composer who refuses to stop growing.

J. The Future of the Wind Band

I am generally optimistic about the future of wind bands. Some of the leaders in the field are among the most dynamic and adventurous musicians on the planet, and many of them are actively pursuing exciting ways to shape the evolution of the medium. The core repertoire is improving steadily. The music is alive and breathing. I constantly remind my composition students that writing a band piece is as good a way as any to ensure a positive rehearsal/performance experience. No other area of music is more caring about composers and the fragility of a new piece. This collective big heart goes a long way to ensure the staying power of concert bands.

But there are tough challenges facing not only those in the band world, but everyone in the field of concert music. In this country and in most of the civilized world, music is largely defined by popular culture, and anything that lies outside of that realm has become increasingly incomprehensible to the average person. The corporate world, which produces most popular music, also happens to own the television networks, radio stations, magazines, and newspapers that stress popular music. This, combined with the slashing of music education in our public schools, has made it nearly impossible for "serious" music to compete. Nowadays, even among well-educated people, concert music is often considered to be intimidating and distant. Professional orchestras, choruses, and wind ensembles of all sizes and budgets face ever-growing challenges to keep classical music relevant in their communities.

One of the best ways to enhance musical literacy in our society is to insist on strong public school music education programs. The benefits of music-making seem obvious to most of us, but not to the many public policy makers who continue to cut funding for music education. We have to tell them over and over, like a mantra, in simple, direct language: "Music-making is good for the soul, enhances self-esteem, and teaches beauty, discipline, and the importance of teamwork."

If that isn't enough to gain the support of the most skeptical of politicians and administrators, try this: *It has been scientifically proven that music can make you smarter*! A few years ago I had the fascinating experience of serving as a musical advisor for Gordon Shaw, the physicist who discovered "The Mozart Effect." Through a series of highly controlled tests, he and his research team made conclusive discoveries about how music enhances spatial-temporal skills and other brain functions. His findings received worldwide attention and have been made available in his recent book, *Keeping Mozart in Mind*. Like most musicians, I don't need such evidence to convince me of the power of music. Music's beauty alone is enough for me. But if a scientist's proof of its links to intelligence impresses those who control public school funding, then it becomes one more weapon in the fight for the cause.

If it is true that we need to produce a more musically literate public, bands can play a major role in that cause. Because of its close ties to the local community and its legacy of strong appeal on a grassroots level, the band has the unique power to serve as a kind of bridge between those who understand and enjoy concert music and those who don't. But music education alone won't solve everything. There are many other big questions that have to be addressed, and I don't pretend to have all the answers. How should the medium continue to evolve without neglecting that which has made it unique? How can the quality of the music and music-making continue to improve? What can be done to encourage more first-rate conductors, performers, and composers to embrace the medium? Should commissions encourage more diversity of genres—more concertos, vocal music, chamber music, and operas? Finally, and this brings me back to the beginning of the topic, how can we make concert music more approachable and relevant in our society? How can its beauty and power speak to more people? Questions such as these have been asked for a long time, and every generation must revisit them.

K. Other Facets of My Everyday Life

Shari and I met during graduate school at the University of Michigan, and we have been married since 1992. Although she has two music degrees, she is now a classroom teacher at a private elementary school. We have a four-year-old daughter named Hannah (another palindrome!), and a newborn son named Joshua.

Children force you to live in the moment, because they have needs right now, not five minutes from now. The experience of being a father has forced me outside of myself. This was a good thing, because all of the anxieties that were paralyzing my work before having children seemed less important afterward. When I'm not composing or obsessing about it, I try to spend as much time as possible with my family. We enjoy lots of things as a family—games, vegetable gardening, picnics in the mountains, excursions of all kinds, and of course, bedtime stories every night.

I got tired of not being able to speak Italian, so I bought a wonderful Italian course one year ago and have devoted about thirty minutes each day to it. It's a lot of fun. I think I'm making some good progress, but I'm sure I'll be humbled if and when we get over there. I am due for a sabbatical in a couple of years, and my family and I are fantasizing about living in Italy during part of that time.

I love to read fiction, especially in the summer when I have more time. Recent books I've read are pretty wide ranging—older ones like *The Good Earth* by Pearl Buck, to newer ones like *Prodigal Summer* by Barbara Kingsolver. I read a lot of poetry too. I'm always looking for the perfect poem to set to music. Fortunately, this need forces me to read far more poetry than I might otherwise get around to.

I used to play a lot of tennis, but it has taken a back seat since becoming a father. I wish I had more available time for vacations, or all-day recreations like sailing and golf. Maybe someday, but not right now. Between composing, teaching, guest conducting, and taking care of little ones, there just isn't time left for much else. I'd probably be terrible at golf anyway.

L. Comprehensive List of Works for Band

All of Frank Ticheli's works for concert band are published by Manhattan Beach Music.

Short Symphony

(tentative title, in progress). Commissioned by a consortium of twenty-five university wind conductors in honor of the retirement of Florida State University Director of Bands, James Croft. Grade 5; Duration c.15 minutes.

Loch Lomond (2003)

Commissioned by Nigel Durno for the Stewarton Academy Senior Wind Ensemble, East Ayrshire, Scotland, with funds provided by the Scottish Arts Council; Grade 3; Duration 6 minutes.

Simple Gifts: Four Shaker Songs (2003)

Commissioned by the Tapp Middle School Band, Powder Springs, Georgia, Erin Cole, Director; Grade 3; Duration 9 minutes.

Ave Maria (2003)

Arrangement for concert band, based on Schubert's work for voice and piano; Grade 3; Duration 5 minutes.

An American Elegy (2000)

In memory of those who lost their lives at Columbine High School on April 20, 1999. Commissioned by the Columbine Commissioning Fund, a special project sponsored by the Alpha Iota Chapter of Kappa Kappa Psi at the University of Colorado on behalf of the Columbine High School Band; Grade 4; Duration 10 minutes.

Vesuvius (1999)

Commissioned by the Revelli Foundation for the Paynter Project, on behalf of the National Honor Band of Bands of America, H. Robert Reynolds, Director; Grade 4; Duration 9 minutes.

Shenandoah (1999)

Commissioned by the Hill Country Middle School Symphonic Band, Cheryl Floyd and Brad Smith, Directors, in memory of their beloved friend, Jonathan Paul Cosentino; Grade 3; Duration 6 minutes.

Blue Shades (1997). Commissioned by a consortium of thirty American wind bands under the auspices of the Worldwide Concurrent Premieres and Commissioning Fund; Grade 5; Duration 10 minutes.

Sun Dance (1997)

Commissioned by the Austin Independent School District for the Silver Anniversary Celebration of the 25th Annual All-City Band Festival; Grade 4; Duration 6 minutes.

Cajun Folksongs II (1997)

Commissioned by the Indiana Bandmasters Association for the Indiana All-State High School Band, Allan McMurray, Director Grade 4; Duration 11 minutes.

Pacific Fanfare (1995, 2003)

For antiphonal concert band, arranged from the original version for orchestral winds; Grade 5; Duration 6 minutes.

Postcard (1994)

Commissioned by H. Robert Reynolds in memory of his mother, Ethel Virginia Curry, for the University of Michigan Symphony Band; Grade 5; Duration 5 minutes.

Gaian Visions (1994)

Commissioned by the Gamma Phi Chapter of Kappa Kappa Psi for the Stephen F. Austin State University Wind Ensemble, John Whitwell, Director; Grade 6; Duration 11 minutes.

Amazing Grace (1994)

Commissioned by John Whitwell in memory of his father, John Harvey Whitwell, for the Michigan State University Wind Symphony; Grade 3; Duration 5 minutes.

Cajun Folk Songs (1990)

Commissioned by the Murchison Middle School Band, Cheryl Floyd, Director; Grade 3; Duration 7 minutes.

Fortress (1989)

Dedicated to Robert Floyd and the L.V. Berkner High School Band, Richardson, Texas; Grade 3; Duration 5 minutes.

Portrait of a Clown (1989)

For very young musicians; Grade 2; Duration 3 minutes.

Music for Winds and Percussion (1988)

Winner of the Walter Beeler Memorial Composition Prize, from Ithaca College School of Music; Grade 6; Duration 16 minutes.

Concertino for Trombone and Band (1987)

Awarded First Prize at the 11th Annual Symposium for New Band Music in Radford, Virginia. Commissioned by trombonist H. Dennis Smith; Grade 5; Duration 13 minutes.

Works for Orchestra

Blue Shades (2001)

Orchestral version commissioned by the Pacific Symphony Orchestra, Carl St.Clair, Music Director; Duration 10 minutes; Published by Manhattan Beach Music.

On Time's Stream (1995)

Commissioned by the Pacific Symphony Orchestra, Carl St.Clair, Music Director; Duration 17 minutes; Available through the composer.

Radiant Voices, a fantasy for orchestra (1995)

Commissioned by the Pacific Symphony Orchestra, Carl St.Clair, Music Director; Duration 20 minutes; Published by Helicon Music of European American Distributors.

Postcard (1994)

Orchestral version commissioned by the Pacific Symphony Orchestra, Carl St.Clair, Music Director; Duration 5 minutes; Published by Manhattan Beach Music.

Pacific Fanfare, for orchestral winds and percussion (1995)

Composed as a gift to the Pacific Symphony Orchestra for the opening concert of their 10th anniversary season; Duration 6 minutes; Published by Manhattan Beach Music.

Images of a Storm (1983)

Awarded First Prize in the Texas Sesquicentennial Orchestral Composition Competition, for the Austin Symphony Orchestra, Sung Kwak, Music Director; Duration 10 minutes; Available through the composer.

Works for Soloist(s) and Orchestra

Symphony No. 1 (2001)

For orchestra, with tenor solo in last movement. Commissioned by the University of Miami School of Music Abraham Frost Commission Series for the university's 75th anniversary celebration concert given by the University of Miami Symphony Orchestra, Thom Sleeper, Conductor; Poem by the composer; Duration 30 minutes; Available through the composer.

An American Dream (1998)

A symphony of songs for soprano and orchestra. Commissioned by the Pacific Symphony Orchestra, Carl St.Clair, Music Director; Poems by Philip Littell; Duration 38 minutes; Available through the composer.

Playing With Fire (1992)

A concerto for small jazz band and orchestra. Commissioned by Jim Cullum, and composed in collaboration with him for the Jim Cullum Jazz Band and the San Antonio Symphony; Duration 25 minutes; Available through the composer.

Concerto for Trumpet and Orchestra (1990)

Composed for, and dedicated to late great trumpeter, Armando Ghitalla. Funded by a grant from Trinity University for the Winters Chamber Orchestra; Duration 16 minutes; Available through the composer.

Works for Chorus

There Will Be Rest (2000)

For SATB chorus, a cappella. Commissioned by the Pacific Chorale, John Alexander, conductor; Poem by Sara Teasdale; Duration 6 minutes; Published by Hindon (Hinshaw) Music.

Published Chamber and Solo Works

For a listing of non-published chamber works please refer to the composer's website at www.FrankTicheli.com.

Out of the Blue (2000)

For saxophone quartet. Funded by a grant from Chamber Music America, the quartet, *Prism;* Duration 12 minutes; Publisher pending.

Songs of Tagore (1992)

For soprano, pno, alto sx. Composed as a farewell gift for three colleagues at Trinity University; Poems by Rabindranath Tagore; Duration 12 minutes; Published by Encore Music.

Back Burner (1989)

For saxophone quartet. Commissioned by; Duration 8 minutes; Published by Encore Music.

Concertino for Trombone (1987)

Version for solo trombone, 2 pnos., perc. Chamber version created at request of trombonist H. Dennis Smith; Duration 13 minutes; Published by Manhattan Beach Music.

The First Voice (1983)

For solo trumpet. Duration 9 minutes; Published by PP Music.

Acknowledgements

William Baker
Kenneth Bloomquist
Elizabeth Curtis
Linda Gillingham
Jere Hutcheson
Miles Johnson
Jill Mahr
Shari Majumder
H. Owen Reed
Hannah Ticheli
Joshua Ticheli
Denise Wheatley
Marguerite Wilder
John E. Williamson